MW00773162

Gobsmacked!

To Nancy Friedman, Jonathon Green, and
Lynne Murphy, without whose scholarship,
suggestions, and support this book would be
much the worse

Contents

Gobsmacked!

Introduction

I AM AN AMERICAN, New York born, but I started to spend some time in London in the 1990s, teaching study-abroad classes. Being interested in language, and reading a lot of newspapers there—one of the courses I taught was on the British press—I naturally started picking up on the many previously unfamiliar (to me) Britishisms and differences between British and American terminology.

Then a funny thing happened.

Back home in the United States, I noticed writers, journalists, and ordinary people starting to use British terms I had encountered. I'll give two examples that stick in my mind because they're tied to specific news events, and hence are easily dated. In May 2001, Chandra Levy, a congressional intern . . . well, what *did* she do? "Disappeared" was the traditional choice, and it was fine as far as it went. After weeks passed, and Levy did not reappear, the word began to seem a little threadbare. Perhaps that's why, on May 18, Helen Kennedy wrote the following sentence for the next day's *New York Daily News*; I've put the key two words in italics.

"Police don't know exactly when Levy *went missing*, but that was the last E-mail or phone call anyone got from her."

1

Go missing wasn't a venerable expression even in the United Kingdom, having been in wide use only since the 1960s; it was virtually or completely unknown here. I believe that its repeated iterations in U.S. coverage of the Levy case marked the beginning of its American ascendance. (Her story ended very sadly: her remains were found in a Washington, D.C., park in 2002, and a man was tried for and convicted of her murder.) In any case, now, when I tell people of a certain (young) age that Americans didn't always say "go missing," they look at me in disbelief.

A scant two years after the Levy story broke, it became clear that the United States would invade Iraq. Months passed; we did not invade. Then we did. Journalists again faced a question: What should we call that preliminary period? In September 2003, the *New York Times'* Thomas Friedman chose a Britishism to offer a collective answer that now appears inevitable, referring to "how France behaved in the run-up to the Iraq war."

Run-up quickly began to be very widely used. How do I know? I know because of the invaluable application and time-suck Google Books Ngram Viewer, the online tool that can measure the relative frequency with which a word or phrase appears in the vast corpus of books and periodicals digitized by Google Books (including separating out British and American use). Ngram Viewer shows that between 2000 and 2005, American use of *the run-up to* increased by 50 percent.

These two phrases were not—to use a Britishism that's dear to my heart—one-offs. Over the next several years, I started noticing dozens and dozens of other examples. Finally, in 2011, I decided to chronicle this phenomenon in a blog called *Not One-Off Britishisms*, which can be found at notoneoffbritishisms.com. To date, I have written more than nine hundred entries, and the blog has been viewed more than three million times. In this book, I have taken the cream of the crop of the blog and organized, updated, and expanded the entries.

Among the most enthusiastic and, sometimes, gobsmacked readers of *NOOBs* have been British people. This is because they have been absorbed in an alternative narrative since 1781. In that year, John Witherspoon coined the term *Americanisms* and started complaining about the way words concocted by the ex-colonists were polluting the purity of the English language. Far from diminishing over the years, the resentment bordering on outrage has continued apace. Just a few years ago, on the BBC website, the English journalist Matthew Engel bemoaned the corrupting influence of U.S. words on British English and invited readers to weigh in with their picks for the worst of the worst. Within a day, nearly 1,300 people had responded, with nominations including *Can I get a . . . ?*, *24/7*, and *deplane*. (Lane Greene, who writes *The Economist*'s pseudonymous language blog *Johnson*, pointed out that most of the entries weren't Americanisms at all but rather clichés, neologisms, or merely expressions that happened to annoy the complainer.) Subsequently, Engel expanded his screed into a book, *That's the Way It Crumbles: The American Conquest of English*.

So it can come as a shock to Brits to learn that their words and expressions have been worming their way into the American lexicon just as much, it would appear, as the other way around. The westward flow is, to be sure, a more recent phenomenon. Residents of the colonies and then the United States developed their own words and expression from the get-go, but it took until the late nineteenth century for an American to note that the British had been coming up with some new lingo of their own. The noticer was the literary critic Richard Grant White (father of the architect Stanford), and in 1868 he complainingly coined the term *Briticisms* to describe these words and phrases. White didn't especially approve of them. Among the instances he cited was a peculiar British use of *directly*:

> *Directly.*—The radical meaning of this word is, in a right line, and hence, as a right line is the shortest distance between two points, it means at once, immediately. Its synonym in both senses is a good English word, now, unhappily, somewhat obsolete, *straightway* [see chapter 3]—our equivalent of which, *right away*, is laughed at by brother Bull as an Americanism. But John Bull himself uses *directly* in a way which is quite insufferable—to wit, in the sense of when, as soon as. This use of the word is a widespread Briticism, and prevails even among the most cultivated writers. For instance, in the London "Spectator" of May 2, 1867, it is said that "Directly Mr. Disraeli finished speaking, Mr. Lowe rose to oppose," etc. . . . . It is difficult to trace by continuous steps the course of this strange perversion, for which there is neither justification nor palliation.

White also complained about a supposed British insistence on saying *ill* instead of *sick* to describe someone who was under the weather.

> They sneer at us for not joining in the robbery and the imposition. I was present once when a British merchant receiving in his own house a Yankee youth at a little party, said, "Good evening! We haven't seen you for a long while. Have you been *seeck*" (the sneer prolonged the word), "as you say in your country?" "No, thank you," said the other, frankly and promptly, "I've been *hill*, as they say in yours."

> He went on, "For the use of ill—an adverb—as an adjective, thus: an ill man, there is no defence and no excuse, except the contamination of bad example." Like many language peevers

through the ages, he was on shaky ground. In fact, there was
nothing new about adjectival *ill*: "By my troth I am exceeding
ill" is a line from *Much Ado About Nothing*.

Another complaint was *awfully* to mean "very," instead
of its early meaning of "in a manner that inspires awe or terror." White wrote, "The misuse is a Briticism; but it has been
spreading rapidly here during the last few years." And here he
was on the mark. In fact, I put forth this intensifier *awfully* as
the very first NOOB.

Awfully and other early examples are explored in chapter 1 of this book; chapter 2 documents some of the numerous
NOOBs that came out of the British military in World War I
and especially World War II. There are numerous examples
in each chapter, and I could have included more. Yet overall,
in the nineteenth century and through most of the twentieth,
the flow of Britishisms into the United States was more or less
a trickle. In the 1936 edition of his classic *The American Language*, H. L. Mencken remarked, "It is most unusual for an
English neologism to be taken up in this country, and when
it is, it is only by a small class, mainly made up of conscious
Anglomaniacs." When Mencken published a lengthy supplement to the book nine years later, he suggested that the trickle
had become a bit more robust, noting that England was "the
fount of honor and mold of fashion to all Americans of social
aspiration, including the tonier sort of pedagogues, and they
make efforts to imitate English cultural patterns, including the
linguistic." As examples, he discussed American adoption of
swagger, swank, master's bedroom (later shortened to *master
bedroom*), *swim-suit*, and, as an affectionate term for "mother,"
mummy (see chapter 3).

The trickle became a wave in the period of High NOOB-
ishness, which I date from roughly 1990 through the present,

and which the rest of this book concerns itself with. Chapter 3 presents forty of the most popular recent NOOBs, and the succeeding chapters cover, in order, insults and off-color terms (not surprisingly, a rich vein); words from sports, or, as the British say, "sport"; the culinary lexicon; American borrowing from British spelling, grammar, and punctuation; and cases where Americans have either adopted a faux Britishism (like pronouncing *divisive* to rhyme with *missive*) or somehow changed a real Britishism's meaning. Chapter 9 zooms out a bit and looks at some more general and quirky topics, and the final chapter considers what might happen in the future.

Why *did* the big importation start in the early 1990s? As a case study, consider the word *laddish*. That adjective derives from a new spin on a particular meaning of *lad*, defined this way by *The Oxford English Dictionary* (*OED*): "A young man characterized by his enjoyment of social drinking, sport, and other activities considered to be male-oriented, his engagement in casual sexual relationships, and often by attitudes or behaviour regarded as irresponsible, sexist, or boorish." Brits have been tossing around *laddish* since at least around 1986 (again, according to the *OED*), but the word didn't become current in the United States for another fifteen years or so. The rock critic Ann Powers was an early U.S. adopter, writing in the *New York Times* in 1999, "Blink 182 showers its fans with laddish love." Since then *laddish* has appeared in the Lexis-Nexis database of major U.S. newspapers more than 325 times. (The total count is somewhat clouded by the arrival on the sporting scene of Mandy Laddish, a women's soccer player for Notre Dame University, in 2010.)

We have adopted *laddish*, first and foremost, because media and technology have dramatically sped up linguistic cross-pollination among national or regional forms of English. Once, *Upstairs, Downstairs* and David Frost accounted for pretty much all the British people on American television. Now—with *Downton Abbey*, *The Crown*, *Call the Midwife*, John Oliver, James Corden, and both *Doc Martin* and *Doctor Who*—we cannot escape them. And if writers can sit in their homes in Indianapolis or Perth Amboy and have immediate access to *The Guardian*, *The Economist*, BritBox, and BBC, the fresh new words and phrases they find there will surely find their way into their prose. In addition, the chattering classes—a useful Britishism that can be broadly defined to include all manner of blogger and online correspondent—have a persistent desire for ostensibly clever ways to say stuff. They have borrowed from Wall Street, Silicon Valley, teen culture, African American vernacular, sports, and hip-hop, and they increasingly borrow from Britain.

I date the run-up (that's an alternate meaning of *run-up*: "increase") in Britishisms to the early 1990s, and it's surely significant that this was when such journos as Tina Brown, Anna Wintour, Andrew Sullivan, and Christopher Hitchens came to the United States or consolidated their prominence here. Shortly thereafter, the Spice Girls had a hand in popularizing *posh* and *ginger*. That latter word—used by Brits as a noun equivalent to the U.S. *redhead*—became even more pervasive with the Harry Potter books, one of whose main characters, Ron Weasley, is famously a ginger. J. K. Rowling introduced to American eyes quite a few other Britishisms as well, brilliantly cataloged on the Harry Potter Lexicon website, including *barmy*, *berk*, *bin*, *biscuit*, *blimey*, *bloke*, and *bog-standard* (and that is obviously just the Bs).

A long time ago, the *Harvard Lampoon* published a parody of *Life* magazine, which included an article called "Flying Saucers: Threat or Menace?" And so I ask: NOOBs—threat, menace, or boon? In order to answer that question, it's useful to divide NOOBs into categories. The ones I've discussed so far—*go missing, laddish,* and the rest—have caught on because they offer value: first, describing a thing for which there's no precise American equivalent and in the process giving the American language a brisk, thanks-I-needed-that slap in the face.

On the other hand, what about the American chaps who say *chap* and talk of their time *at university* (see chapter 3)? The threat and menace of NOOBs, such as it is, is pretentiousness, and this rears its head most directly in the case of Britishisms that have an exact U.S. equivalent: for example, *advert* (advertisement), *called* (named), *bespoke* (custom-made, chapter 3), *chat show presenter* (talk-show host), *queue* (line, chapter 3), *whilst* (while, chapter 3), and *full stop* (period, chapter 3). There exists in our country a perfectly good word for the smaller dish that is consumed before the main dish, and it's *appetizer. Starters* are for people who wear hunting jackets with Turnbull & Asser ascots, which really isn't appropriate dress at Famous Dave's. (And as for calling dessert *afters,* fuhgeddaboutit.)

A third category comprises terms like *kerfuffle, plonk* (cheap wine), *twee,* and *gobsmacked.* They have the advantage and suffer the fate of all vogue words and catchphrases. At first, they come off as clever and hip, but their expiration date (or as the Brits say, sell-by or expiry date) comes swiftly, after which they're nothing but clichés.

I've included in this book a few of the comments on my original blog posts, because, in contrast to the well-deserved bad rap internet comments often get, *NOOBs* readers are frequently erudite, funny, and informative. Every once in a while, they fill me with wonder and delight. That was the case when I heard from Helen Kennedy, the first journalist, according to my unscientific investigation, to write that Chandra Levy had gone missing. She said reading my mention of her in the *go missing* post had made her day:

> I always knew I would amount to something, and having some small part in the downfall of American English—well, could one be more subversive? No, one could not.
>
> I'm half-American and half-Irish, raised in England and Italy. I am CONSTANTLY having to turn to my colleagues to ask if "advertising" has a Z here, etc. . . . I genuinely had no idea that "gone missing" was not regular Ammurican.

Finding out that the expression was apparently blown to these shores, like some exotic seed, by someone who learned it in the U.K. left me—and there's no other way to express it—gobsmacked.

Terminology, Abbreviations, and Resources

TERMINOLOGY AND ABBREVIATIONS

At the end of each entry about a word or phrase, I tag it with an assessment of its current level of adoption in the United States: *On the radar* (meaning only such *New York Times* writers as Sam Sifton, Dwight Garner, David Brooks, and Maureen Dowd are using it), *Emerging* (other journalists and writers are starting to adopt it), *Taking hold* (real people are using it, including in speaking), *Fully arrived* (it seems to American ears like a completely normal word), or *Outpaced* (it's now used more in America than Britain). There are also a few *Outliers* whose appearances in the United States are, well, one-offs. The tagging starts in chapter 2, as all the words in chapter 1 have long been established in America.

The word *Britishisms* (which I prefer to the old-fashioned *Briticisms*) is in the title of my blog *Not One-Off Britishisms* (abbreviated as NOOBs), and *British* is in the subtitle of this book, but the meaning of "British" is complicated and not universally agreed on. I use it as an adjective referring to the United Kingdom, a country composed of England, Scotland, Wales, and Northern Ireland. In both the blog and the book, I also cover words and phrases that originated in Ireland, Australia, and New Zealand, even though I understand they are not British. To my ears, imports from those countries are part of the same general phenomenon. I often use *American* to refer to people or usages from the United States, in part because *United States* does not yield a good adjective. I wrote this book from a desk in Swarthmore, Pennsylvania, and I sometimes use the word "here" to refer to U.S. practice. The *OED* is *The Oxford English Dictionary* (see below).

PRINCIPAL RESOURCES

The Oxford English Dictionary is a regularly updated proprietary online dictionary that gives not only the definition of words and phrases but, vitally, a history of their use. For example, the *OED* entry for *gobsmacked* defines it as "flabbergasted, astounded; speechless or incoherent with amazement," and shows that the first use the dictionary staff and their far-flung minions have been able to find came in 1935, from a journal called *Bee-Keepers' Record*. It and the successive citations (or "cites") tell a story. The line from *Bee-Keepers' Record* is in Yorkshire dialect: "When he landed back Martha wad be fare gob smacked at the yarns he wad tell 'er about Yorkshire clod-hoppers." The second use is a line of dialogue from a 1956 novel: "I'm so amazed that only the Malderbury dialect can express my condition: I'm 'properly gob-smacked.'" (There is no such place as Malderbury.) The third—from the Labour politician Roy Hattersley in 1980—associates *gobsmacked* with "the patois of the place whence I came" (i.e., Yorkshire). The Hattersley quote is notable as well because of the quotation marks ("inverted commas" in the United Kingdom) around the word. That's often a sign that a word or phrase is unfamiliar or has recently become current. By the time of the next quote, in 1998 from the (American) magazine *Spin*, the word needs no explanation or special punctuation. In a word, it's unremarkable.

Note that the *OED* does not claim that its first citation is the first use of the word. New words frequently enter the spoken—and now, online—language years or decades before they see print. And for the most part, the *OED* only tracks written, published sources. (For recent decades, there are some citations from transcripts of television shows or other spoken sources.)

Green's Dictionary of Slang, a creation of Jonathon Green, is a free online dictionary (https://greensdictofslang.com) modeled on the *OED* but with, as its name suggests, a specific focus. Green's timelines are greatly helpful for my purposes because each citation includes a flag indicating country of origin. For example, *bonkers* is defined as "stupid, insane, eccentric"; the first solid citation is a quote from a British book published in 1958. The first American example is from the *Minneapolis Star* in 1967: "The final tipoff that she [i.e., a cat with dementia] has gone completely bonkers occurred Thursday." There follow citations from Australia and Ireland, as well as the U.K. and the U.S., and the final one is from the *Washington Post* in 2022: "The new Conservative government led by Prime Minister Liz Truss faces almost no constraints. She was expected to be bold. She is turning out to be bonkers."

I would not have been inspired to maintain my blog for over a decade and to write this book without Google Books Ngram Viewer (https://books.google.com/ngrams), described in the introduction, especially its remarkable feature of being able to

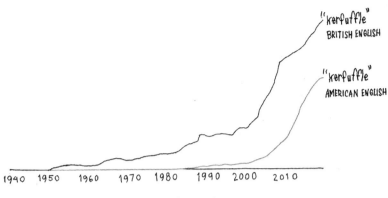

Figure 1

sort out the use of words or phrases from American and British sources.* Like the *OED*, Ngram Viewer is limited to written sources, but with that caveat understood, it is invaluable.

Figure 1 shows Ngram Viewer's depiction of American and British use of *kerfuffle* between 1940 and 2019 (the most recent year for which Google Books has data).

The graph shows a typical progression for a modern NOOB. *Kerfuffle* emerged in Britain in roughly 1950, increased steadily for the rest of the century, and then shot up in the first two decades of the new one. In the United States, meanwhile, the word was an outlier until about 2000, when it began a rapid ascent. This is a typical progression, the very late twentieth century and early twenty-first being the Age of NOOBs.

---

* Google Books doesn't say precisely what it means by "Britain." My sense is that it means the traditional Great Britain—England, Scotland, and Wales. Incidentally if you want to try it yourself, here's how. Go to the site and erase what Google has put in the search bar ("Albert Einstein,Sherlock Holmes,Frankenstein"). Type in the following:
word or phrase:eng_gb_2019,word or phrase:eng_us_2019
Do not use quotation marks, whether you're searching for a word or phrase. The "About Ngram Viewer" link gives instructions on how to refine searches.

A regrettably technical note on the graphs. On the Ngram Viewer site, alongside the y-axis (vertical) are a stack of very small numbers that signify the frequency, expressed as a percentage, of the word in question in the universe of all the words published that year (or, if it's a two-word sequence, what percentage of all the two-word sequences, and so on). In the case of *kerfuffle*, at its high point, in 2019, it represented 0.0000116541 percent of all words published in Britain. The graphs in this book, rendered from Ngram Viewer by Eric Hanson, do not include these numbers, because the numbers by themselves aren't important. More so is the change over time, and a comparison of British and American uses. Also note that each graph must stand on its own—that is, one cannot be overlaid on top of another. The values in the y-axis of each one are very different.

As for the horizontal x-axis, representing time, Ngram Viewer allows you to search for any range of years from 2019 back to, well, as far as you want to, with the understanding that results before 1700 or so will be extremely spotty. In each case, I've chosen what I consider to be the most useful stretch of time. In some cases that's the long term, in others just a decade or two. There's no point in showing a graph that goes all the way back to 1800 for a word coined in the 1990s.

In conjunction with Ngram Viewer, I use Google Books (https://books.google.com). On it, one can search for all the occurrences of a word or phrase in any range of years. And depending on copyright restrictions, the application will often display an image of the page from a book or journal on which the term occurs.

Another invaluable resource is English-Corpora.org (https://www.english-corpora.org), a collection of more than a dozen searchable corpora, or databases, comprising some forty billion words from British and American sources. Several of the corpora allow you to go beyond print to more informal sources like blogs and other online discourse, plus transcripts of films, television shows, and parliamentary utterances.

Because Urban Dictionary (https://www.urbandictionary .com) is user generated and supplies the bare minimum of moderation, you usually have to wade through a lot of muck to find something useful. But, especially for recent slang, it can be helpful, especially because each entry is dated. Thus, I can find that in 2007, a user posted this definition of *can't be asked* (see chapter 8): "Used by some Southern UK speakers in place of can't be arsed because they misheard it, or want to be more polite. 'I can't be asked to tidy my room—I'll do it tomorrow.'"

Also useful for searching informal American use of a word or phrase is, or was, Tweetdeck. Before Twitter became X, the Tweetdeck application allowed you to search all of Twitter for a word or phrase and filter for a certain location. I would generally set it to a two-hundred-kilometer radius from New York City; good stuff came up.

Finally, the *New York Times*.* The newspaper is invaluable (I seem to be wearing that adjective out) for two reasons. First, its vast archives are searchable back to its founding in 1851, and hence offer the most convenient gauge of American use of a word. Second, current-day *Times* contributors are, as a group, the most enthusiastic users of NOOBs. Simply put, if a *Times* writer hasn't used it, it ain't a NOOB.

---

* I promise to try to avoid confusion between this newspaper and the British one, *The Times*. I'll always call the American one the *New York Times* on first reference, and then the *Times*. I'll call the British one *The Times* (of London), and subsequently *The Times*.

CHAPTER ONE

Historical NOOBs

Immediately after Great Britain and the United States went their separate ways, each country began coining words and expressions. It took about a century for the Americans to start adopting Britishisms. Here are a few choice examples from the early years.

"Awfully"

As noted in the introduction, one of the "Briticisms" Richard Grant White complained about when he coined the term in 1868 was *awfully* meaning "very"—as opposed to an earlier meaning of the word: "in a manner that inspires awe or terror," or "badly." ("He dances awfully.") I have to admit that when I read White's complaint I had an awful start, because it seems awfully American. But he was right and I was wrong, and by my reckoning, *awfully* is the very first NOOB.

The early citations in the *OED* (which labels it "colloquial") are all British, starting with an 1820 one from *The Times* (of London), rhetorically wondering whether a defendant has "awfully strong grounds for protesting against the tribunal."

At one point in William Makepeace Thackeray's *Vanity Fair*—
published in 1847–1848 and set in the 1810s—Becky Sharp
thinks, "I suppose he will be awfully proud, and that I shall be
treated most contemptuously." Ngram Viewer also confirms White's impression, showing
much more common use in Britain in the second half of the
nineteenth century (White's era) and America topping Britain
in about 1920. Since then, the use of the adverb in both countries has been, well, awfully similar.

"Brunch"

This portmanteau word apparently originated as university
slang. *The Independent* reported in 1895, "Breakfast is 'brek-
ker' in the Oxford tongue; when a man makes lunch his first
meal of the day it becomes 'brunch.'" Five years later the word
had spread far enough for the *Westminster Gazette* to use it (in
quotation marks, indicating recent coinage) as the punchline
of a comic poem: "Perish Scrambling breakfast, formal lunch! /
Hardened night-birds fondly cherish / All the subtle charms
of 'brunch.'"

Brunch took a while to catch on in the United States.
The first American citation in the *OED* is from 1930; as late
as 1939, the *New York Times* felt the need to put the word in
quotes and define it as "the present-day phenomenon of the
breakfast-luncheon, or 'brunch,' as it is affectionately called."

That was then, this is now. Ngram Viewer shows that right
about the time of the *Times* article, Americans passed Britons in their use of *brunch* and have stayed comfortably ahead
ever since. What's more, around about 2000, Americans stole
the British *boozy* (see chapter 6) and came up with the *boozy
brunch*, meaning that for a set price, you can have all the
mimosas you want.

"Come a cropper"

Gary Martin, on his Phrase Finder website, has a good explanation of the origin of this expression, which has to do with the nether quarters of a horse—the "croup" or "crupper."

> In the 18th century, anyone who took a headlong fall from a horse was said to have fallen "neck and crop"; for example, this extract from the English poet Edward Nairne's *Poems*, 1791:

> > A man on horseback, drunk with gin and flip,
> > Bawling out—Yoix [see chapter 9]—and cracking of
> >   his whip,
> >
> > . . .
> >
> > The startish beast took fright, and flop
> > The mad-brain'd rider tumbled, neck and crop!

"Neck and crop" and "head over heels" probably both derive from the 16th-century term "neck and heels," which had the same meaning. "Come a cropper" is just a colloquial way of describing a "neck and crop" fall. The phrase is first cited in Robert S. Surtees' *Ask Mamma*, 1858: [He] "rode at an impracticable fence, and got a cropper for his pains."

Come a cropper is defined in the 1874 edition of *Hotten's Slang Dictionary* as meaning "to fail badly," and the following year it was used (in quotation marks) in Anthony Trollope's novel *The Way We Live Now*: "He would 'be coming a cropper rather,' were he to marry Melmotte's daughter for her money, and then find that she had got none."

As for American use of the phrase, Ngram Viewer shows it popping up here in the late 1870s—about twenty years later than in Britain—with use increasing for the next hundred years or so, until tailing off after around 1960, when I would imagine it started to sound a bit old-fashioned.

But that hasn't stopped the *New York Times*, which has used the phrase more than ninety times, with all but thirteen of the uses coming since the 1970s. Probably the most interesting example in the newspaper's archives is a quote from then-president Richard Nixon in the White House transcripts released as part of the Watergate investigation in 1973. He's speaking in his typically convoluted manner to his aide John Ehrlichman: "For an inquiry to start with the proposition of [Senators Sam] Ervin and [Howard] Baker, where you don't come a cropper right there at the beginning on whether you can get the three branches. What's your view of the three-branch, John?"

He's speaking about the traditional three branches of American government—congressional, executive, and judicial. But other than that, I have no idea what he's talking about.

"Full of beans"

The expression derives from the idea that horses fed with beans have more energy than those fed with grass or corn, and conveys a sense of high spirits. The *OED*'s alliterative first citation is from an 1843 novel: "'Ounds, 'osses, and men, are in a glorious state of excitement! Full o' beans and benevolence!" In an 1875 letter, Benjamin Disraeli used it in a nonequine context: "The Sultan . . . was full of beans."

All *OED* citations of the phrase are from British sources. In *Green's Dictionary of Slang*, all cites are from Britain or the Commonwealth until this from the American writer Leo Rosten's 1975 novel *Dear Herm*: "Now he is full of beans and vinegar and with a whole new outlook on Life." That seems to me like a euphemistic switch on the roughly equivalent U.S.

phrase "full of piss and vinegar." In any case, I found an earlier U.S. use of *full of beans* in a 1938 *New York Times* article: "Whenever Sage, a cowboy with whom I once punched cows on the San Simon Ranch in Eastern New Mexico, felt particularly full of beans of a cool early morning."

But Americans, as is our wont, gave the expression an additional meaning: a euphemism for full of shit—that is, completely wrong. That sense is listed in *Green's* and in Harold Wentworth and Stuart Flexner's *Dictionary of American Slang*, a 1998 edition of which gives a quote from newspaper columnist Mike Royko: "Maybe Ted Williams was full of beans."

My sense is that Americans use the two meanings in roughly equal proportion.

"Have a go"

The original meaning of *have a go*, says the *OED*, was "to aim a blow or shot at someone or something; to make an attack or onslaught upon someone or something." The first citation is from *Lady's Magazine* in 1792: "I felt such a flow of spirits and courage, that I hid myself behind a tree, determined to have a go at him—the moment he passed me, I fired my pistol."

Fairly quickly it took on a broader sense of "to attack verbally or criticize" and the still broader sense (with which I associate the phrase) of "to make an attempt at something; to have a spell or turn of doing something." An 1863 citation is from Charles Reade's novel *Hard Cash*: "You have stumbled on a passage you can't construe. . . . Here, let me have a go at it."

It and all the other citations for all three senses are from British sources. And the phrase gained wide currency in the U.K. by virtue of the BBC radio show *Have a Go*, which ran from 1946 to 1967. According to ukgameshows.com, "Britain's very first broadcast quiz to give away money prizes, *Have a Go* was a hugely popular 'people show' in which Wilfred Pickles (and his wife, Mabel) travelled around the country, turning up in village halls and asking ordinary folk up on stage to talk about their lives and memories." The site reports that the show introduced the catchphrases "How do, how are yer?"; "Are yer courtin'?"; "What's on the table, Mabel?"; and "Give 'im the money, Barny!" I can only imagine the hilarity that ensued.

I can attest from my own experience that *have a go*, with the meaning of "having a try or a turn," has been fairly widely used in the U.S. for some time. For example, a *New York Times* review of the 1961 film *Voyage to the Bottom of the Sea* has the line, "There's no earthly or oceanic reason why [director Irwin] Allen shouldn't have had a go at such a subject on a frank entertainment level." And in a 2020 *Times* article about the television program *Dispatches from Elsewhere*, the (American) reporter writes of an actor, "He had a go at defining the show."

Give it a go, to my ears, means basically the same thing as *have a go*. Neither the *OED* nor *Green's* has an entry for it, but it shows up in two *OED* citations in a definition for *go* (as "try or attempt"). The second is a recent quote from an English newspaper, but the first, surprisingly, is from the *Boston Daily Globe* in 1892: "There was an air of diffidence about the different drug stores that were opened yesterday, which plainly said, 'We are not sure of this matter, but we'll give it a go and see how it comes out.'"

That would appear to be an outlier both linguistically and geographically. Searching the vast Google Books database, I don't find *give it a go* showing up till 1915 or '16, with the early uses all being from Commonwealth sources, especially Australia and New Zealand. A 1922 article from *Australian Garden and Field* has the line, "I told you I would give it a go for a month or two."

Ngram Viewer shows both *have a go* and *give it a go* rising steadily in the U.S. in the 1990s and 2000s, but still used considerably less commonly than in Britain. I would have thought that U.S. use of both expressions would be higher. But the numbers don't lie.

"On the q.t."

This expression means "in confidence" or "just between us." The earliest use I'm aware of is in a quotation in *Green's Dictionary of Slang* (but originally unearthed by a contributor to the Stack Exchange English Language and Usage bulletin board) from an 1874 English play by Walter Devereux Whitty called *My Husband's Secret*, with the slang and dialect of the servant, Straps, presumably evoking much hilarity at the time:

> STRAPS. I wants a word with you, sir, on the Q.T.
> FITZ. Q.T.; why, what's that?
> STRAPS. Lor, sir, didn't you larn that at Hoxford? Q.T.'s short for quiet, sir.

In both the *OED* and *Green's*, all the subsequent nineteenth-century citations except one use the formulation *on the strict q.t.* and are from British, Irish, or Commonwealth sources. The one exception (in *Green's*) is from a Provo, Utah, newspaper in 1894: "We got this on the dead Q-T—and will ask you readers, please don't give it away." And incidentally, the expression gets some literary pedigree via James Joyce's *Ulysses* (1922): "Sailing under false colours after having boxed the compass on the strict q.t. somewhere."

All sources that I've found say that *q.t.* is short for "quiet," and that's convincing, especially since the phrase *on the quiet*, meaning the same thing, can be found well before any *on the q.t.* examples. However, I was intrigued by an alternate theory offered by a contributor to the Stack Exchange English Language and Usage bulletin board:

"Q.T." is an odd abbreviation for "quiet." Since it is of British origin, I would think it would derive from schoolboys' abbreviations, often derived from Latin. The Latin *taceo* means "not to speak" and has solemn meaning sometimes, referring to "passing over in silence." Thus *quae tacenda*, or q.t., would refer to "things about which one should not speak." Cf. Horace, Epodes, 5.49, where Horace speaks of Canidia and *quid dixit et quid tacuit*—what she said and what she left unsaid.

Whatever the original derivation, *on the strict q.t.* quickly became a catchphrase: a Google Books search for the expression yields about a dozen examples from 1877 to 1880. The phrase had fully arrived in the U.S. in the early 1900s. *Green's* has fourteen citations between 1906 and 1999, and nine of them are American, including this lyric from a song by Merle Travis: "You thought your little romance was on the strict Q.T. / So if you want your freedom P.D.Q., / Divorce me C.O.D."

The song came out in 1946, and indeed the phrase has a midcentury feel. The 1997 film *L.A. Confidential* was set in the early 1950s, and the trademark line of the gossipmonger played by Danny DeVito is, "Off the record, on the Q.T., and very hush-hush."

Nowadays, *on the q.t.* has been replaced by *on the downlow* or *on the DL*—though that phrase also has a very particular meaning of its own. Urban Dictionary's top definition: "an expression for a bisexual black man (who 'thinks' he's straight—hah!), married or with a girlfriend, having sexual relations with another man."

"Smarmy"

Smarmy is a useful word, as anyone who has had to listen to an oleaginous colleague drone on in a department meeting or a Zoom call can attest. Unlike most useful words, its origin can be traced to a particular person—who invented it as a lark.

The *OED*'s principal definition for the word is "ingratiating, obsequious; smug, unctuous," and the first citation is from L. Brock, *Deductions of Col. Gore*, published in 1924: "Don't you be taken in by that smarmy swine."

The other recognized meaning of *smarmy* derives from a verb form (sometimes spelled "smalm" or "smawm"), defined by the *OED* as "smear, bedaub" and first cited by the dictionary in an 1847 work, *A Dictionary of Archaic and Provincial Words*. The *OED* has a secondary definition of the adjective *smarmy* as "smooth and sleek," with the first citation from a 1909 source: "A tall, slight, smarmy-headed man." As that suggests, the "smear" meaning became associated with the stuff one smears on one's hair. A little quality time on Google Books gave me an antedate of the 1909 quote, from a 1903 play by Henry V. Esmond, *When We Were Twenty-One*: "You mustn't ruffle my hair, you know, coz the Soldier-Man's coming to lunch, and—if—everybody's hair isn't smarmy, he loses his appetite."

It makes sense that unctuous-*smarmy*, with its sense of behavioral greasiness, would have emerged from the "hair" sense of the word. After I raised the issue on Twitter, Jonathon Green, of *Green's Dictionary of Slang*, supplied his own ante-date of the 1924 *OED* one, from a 1916 edition of an Austra-lian newspaper, the *Barrier Miner*: "I wonder what his game is. . . . He doesn't look the sort she could make a friend of; too smarmy for my taste."

I kept looking and eventually came upon an even earlier use of modern *smarmy*—one that appears to be the very first. A London journal called *The Academy* ran "Literary Compe-titions" in each issue, much as *New York* magazine and the *Washington Post* have done in later years. Here is the invita-tion to No. 14:

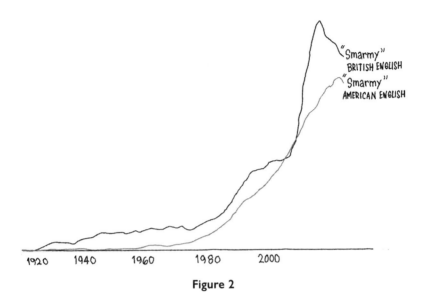

"Smarmy"
BRITISH ENGLISH
"Smarmy"
AMERICAN ENGLISH

1920   1940   1960   1980   2000

Figure 2

Nor necessarily with a view of enriching the language, but certainly in the interests of our readers, we ask this week for new words. Most families have a few pet words, of home-made manufacture, which often are far more expressive and picturesque than anything in Webster's unabridged.

The results were announced in the January 14, 1899, issue. And there, between *screel* ("to feel the sensation produced by hearing a knife edge squeal on a plate") and *scrungle* ("the feeling of hearing a slate pencil squeaked on a slate"), was a definition for *smarmy* supplied by one B.R.L. of Brighton: "Saying treacly things which do not sound genuine." And amazingly, that very meaning was apparently in circulation no later than seventeen years later, in the Australian quote found by Green.

Unlike *screel* and *scrungle*, *smarmy* caught on. Google Ngrams (figure 2) fills out the picture, as well as giving a sense of British and American use.

That is to say, Britain outpaced the U.S. until the decade of the 2000s, after which use increased in both countries, with the U.K. in the lead. That makes sense, given the number of smarmy people who need to be described.

"Smog"

Smog sounds American as American can be, and that was certainly the case in 1970, when Joni Mitchell, in her song "Woodstock," declared, "I have come here to lose the smog."

But it definitely is English in origin. In July 1905, the newspaper *The Globe* helpfully reported its apparent invention: "The other day at a meeting of the Public Health Congress Dr. [H. A.] Des Vœux did a public service in coining a new word for the London fog, which was referred to as 'smog,' a compound of 'smoke' and 'fog.'" The same year the *Journal of the American Medical Association* reported on the development and commented, "London is undoubtedly the proper place for its coinage, for it is said to surpass all other places in the opacity of its smog, but so far as mere darkness is concerned some other British and American cities would afford ample justification for the use of the term."

The U.S. Weather Bureau picked up the word in 1914, causing a wag to comment in the *Kokomo Tribune*, "But why end there? Let's call a mixture of snow and mud 'smud.' A mixture of snow and soot 'snoot,' and a mixture of snow and hail 'snail.' Thus we might have a weather forecast: 'Snail today, turning to snoot tonight; tomorrow, smoggy with smud.'"

But the term was still unfamiliar enough in 1921 for a *New York Times* reviewer of a book by C. W. Saleeby to comment,

America has no counterpart of that strange mixture, thick as pea soup, the color of faded green, sticky and smutty against the human skin and the façade of buildings, with a taste something like stale beer, which serves much of the time as atmosphere in Edinburgh and London. It acts like smoke and looks like fog. Dr. Saleeby has at last found a name for it, a name that is a positive inspiration. It should be in the next edition of all dictionaries. The name is Smog. The adjective is "smoggy."

Things soon changed as American cities (notably Pittsburgh and Los Angeles) developed the problem, and Americans adopted the word. Indeed, Ngram Viewer shows that since the early 1920s, U.S. use of *smog* has surpassed that in Britain by a comfortable margin.

"Ta-ta"

At the moment, my post on *ta-ta* is the third most popular, all time, on the *NOOBs* blog, with 53,761 views. (It trails *European Date Format* [see chapter 9] and *mewling quim* [a quote from an *Avengers* movie].) I'm fairly certain that most of the 53,761 viewers were disappointed. That's because I assume they were looking for information on a slang term for (female) breasts, *ta-tas*, or *tatas*. They didn't find any joy on the blog, because that term is an Americanism which sprang up in the 1980s, apparently inspired by its use in the film *An Officer and a Gentleman*. It has been especially prominent since 2004, when an anti-breast-cancer foundation was founded with the name Save the Ta-tas.

The NOOB *ta-ta* is an affectionate way of saying goodbye. I didn't really think of it as a Britishism till 2013, when the *New York Times*' Sarah Lyall ended eighteen years as a London correspondent for the newspaper and titled her farewell article, "Ta-Ta London. Hello, Awesome." My main association with the term had been a memory of my mother jokingly saying, "Ta-ta, *tatele*"—the latter word being a Yiddish diminutive for "father," for some reason often applied to infants. A Google search also reminded me of a 1993 *Seinfeld* episode where George quits by saying to his boss, Mr. Tuttle, "Ta ta, Tuttle!"

But *ta-ta* is indeed of British origin. The *OED* defines it as a "nursery expression for 'Good-bye'; now also in gen. colloq. use." The earliest citation is from 1823, and a notable one can be found in T. S. Eliot's 1923 *The Waste Land*: "Goonight Bill. Goonight Lou. Goonight May. Goonight. Ta ta. Goonight."

None of the dictionary's examples come from U.S. sources, but it caught on here fairly early, as is illustrated by an 1889 *Times* article titled "'Ta-Ta, Hubbie,' Was Her Farewell":

> It was on July 21, 1888, that Miss Jennie Roessler and Anton Kasa were married by the Rev. Vincent Pisek, at the Protestant Church of the Bohemian Brothers in this city. On Aug. 4, 1888, Kasa saw his wife stepping into a carriage with Alexander Riese. Mrs. Kasa caught sight of him at the same moment. Leaning out of the carriage window she waved her handkerchief and called out, "Ta-ta, hubbie." From his investigations set on foot by this little incident, Kasa found that Riese was an old sweetheart of Mrs. Kasa and that the two had gone to Milwaukee together.

During the 1940s, an initialized version of the expression merged via a character on the BBC radio program *It's That Man Again* (later abbreviated as *ITMA*). According to the *OED*, a "famous saying" of the Cockney charlady Mrs. Mopp (played by Dorothy Summers) "were the letters 'T.T.F.N.'—a contraction of 'Ta-ta for now' with which she made her exit." *TTFN* emerged decades later as an example of teenage online lingo, seemingly on both sides of the Atlantic, peaking sometime in the middle of the decade of the 2000s. I gather that from a comment to a 2012 *Times* review of a play called *Peter and the Starcatcher*: "It tries so hard to be contemporary that it manages to date itself to about five years ago by overusing pop culture references and slang ('TTFN,' 'guuuuuuuurl,' 'as if,' and 'Oh. My. God.' To list just a few) from that time."

A similar-sounding British term, also with nursery origins, but apparently with no connection to *ta-ta*, is *ta*, meaning "thank you." This still hasn't made any inroads in the U.S. I had a brief moment of hope when a Google search found it (along with two other Britishisms) in a line of dialogue in a 2003 William Gibson novel, *All Tomorrow's Parties*: "'Cheers,' Tessa said, 'ta for the lager.'" But when I investigated further, it turned out that Tessa is Australian.

CHAPTER TWO

Military Slang

Soldiers and sailors are smushed together in stress-ful situations and often have to "hurry up and wait," so it's not surprising that they would come up with colorful slang and expressions, some of them printable in family publications. The Brits seem to have a particular knack for these formulations, and not a few have found their way across the Atlantic.

THE GREAT WAR AND EARLIER

"Cushy"

The *OED* tells us that *cushy* derives from words in Persian and Urdu that connote pleasure or convenience, and suggests that the etymologically distinct *cushion* or *cushiony* may also have had an influence. The definition for the most frequently used sense is "of a job, situation, etc.: undemanding, easy; requiring little or no effort; (later) *spec.* involving little effort, but ample or disproportionate rewards."

The specifically military sense predates the Great War; the *OED* has a brilliant 1895 quote from the *Penny Illustrated*

Paper: "He told me that I had got into a 'cushy' (easy) troop." And *Green's Dictionary of Slang* gives a 1912 example of a now familiar formulation: "A lot of them have rare cushy jobs."

The *OED* notes a particular World War I sense of *cushy*: "Of a wound: serious enough to necessitate one's withdrawal from active duty, but not life-threatening or likely to have permanent consequences, such as disability." It provides this 1915 quote: "When you are in the trenches a cushy wound . . . seems the most desirable thing in the world."

This 1918 *New York Times* article uses an interesting noun form in the headline:

"Cushies" for the Front
British Agitation to Make Holders of "Soft Jobs"
Do Guard Duty

Henry W. Benson, a wool merchant who arrived yesterday from London on his way to Sydney, Australia, said that when he left England there was a strong agitation under way to have all the holders of "cushy jobs" sent to the Continent to do guard duty and let the men who have done the fighting and endured the hardships of the war come home.

The first example I've seen of an American using the term is Jonathon Green's citation from Budd Schulberg's 1947 novel *The Harder They Fall*: "My job with Nick was like a jail, a comfortable, cushy jail." The *New York Times* first used the expression *cushy job* in 1964; since then, it's appeared in the paper well over one hundred times.

And so it isn't surprising that Ngram Viewer shows American use picking up in the 1970s, and surpassing British use in the 1990s (figure 3).

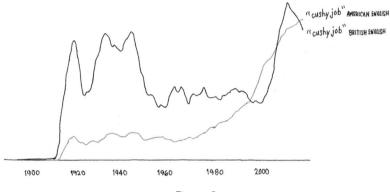

"cushy job" AMERICAN ENGLISH

"cushy job" BRITISH ENGLISH

1900   1920   1940   1960   1980   2000

Figure 3

Adoption | Fully arrived
● ● ● ● ●

"Gadget"

The word was used as early as 1868, according to the *OED*, to refer to a piece of equipment used in glassmaking. Not long after that, nautical and navy slang gave it another meaning. From an 1886 book: "Then the names of all the other things on board a ship! I don't know half of them yet; even the sailors forget at times, and if the exact name of anything they want happens to slip from their memory, they call it a chicken-fixing, or a gadjet, or a gill-guy, or a timmey-noggy, or a wim-wom."

The term had arrived in the U.S.—and adopted a new spelling—by 1917, when the *New York Times* carried an Associated Press dispatch describing a gunner who "called many parts 'gadgets,' and then explained that it was hard to define the word 'gadget,' but that in naval parlance it meant anything for which there was no other name."

Also in World War I, the word adopted a new meaning, the one we associate it with today—in the *OED*'s words, "a

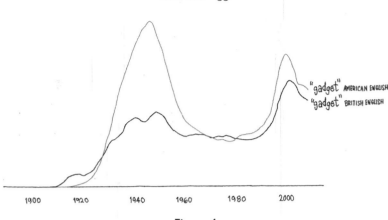

Figure 4

(small) mechanical or electronic device, esp. one regarded as ingenious or novel." At first it was used in a specifically military context. Rudyard Kipling wrote in *The New Army* (1915), "They have installed decent cooking ranges and gas, and the men have already made themselves all sorts of handy little labour-saving gadgets."

The word quickly spread to other realms. Correspondent H. Tapley-Soper wrote to *Notes and Queries* in 1918, "I have . . . frequently heard [*gadget*] applied by motor-cycle friends to the collection of fitments to be seen on motor cycles. 'His handle-bars are smothered in gadgets' refers to such things as speedometers, mirrors, levers, badges, mascots, &c., attached to the steering handles."

And it quickly spread to the United States. A 1919 *Times* article about a transatlantic flight noted, "It was no unusual sight to see [the pilot], tools in hand, busily fitting some 'gadget.'"

Within ten years, Americans were using it more than Britons, according to Ngram Viewer (figure 4).

That spike in the 1930s and 1940s is presumably what caused the *New Yorker*, under the editorship of William

Shawn, to actually ban *gadget* from the magazine's pages, along with a remarkable number of other words. In a remembrance of Shawn published after his death in 1992, *New Yorker* editor Daniel Menaker recalled a sentence he and his colleagues employed to help them remember all of the terms they had to eliminate or find replacements for: "Intrigued by the massive smarts of the balding, feisty, prestigious, workaholic tycoon, Tom Wolfe promptly spat on the quality photo above the urinal and tried to locate his gadget." (They left out *gotten*; see chapter 9.)

Adoption | Outpaced
● ● ● ● ●

"Kit"; "kit out"

The sense of the word that concerns us here originated in the military. Francis Grose's *A Classical Dictionary of the Vulgar Tongue* (1785) says, "The kit is . . . the whole of a soldier's necessaries, the contents of his knapsack." It's seen in the title and first line of the World War I marching song "Pack Up Your Troubles in an Old Kit Bag, and Smile, Smile, Smile." And according to commenters on *Not One-Off Britishisms*, it's still used by soldiers and sailors.

By the nineteenth century, the word had expanded to mean "a collection of personal effects or necessaries, esp. as packed up for travelling" or "the outfit of tools required by a workman, esp. a shoemaker." Two twentieth-century variations have always been common in America: a percussionist's collection of instruments and accessories, called a *drum kit*, and a collection of parts sold for the buyer to assemble, as in a make-your-own-radio kit.

A meaning that hasn't crossed over (except perhaps in the most uber-pretentious soccer circles) is defined by the *OED* as "the special clothing and equipment needed for a particular sport." The first citation, referring to cricket, comes from 1862, and the most recent from *The Sun* in 2019: "The gold-painted statue shows a curtain-haired Becks [David Beckham] in his Man U [Manchester United] kit."

In 1969, a U.S. Army major testified to a House of Representatives committee, "The turret, sir, is a steel piece of kit." And *kit* seems to have crossed over to America via military use of that particular phrase, *piece of kit.*

It took a long time to come into civilian use. American rocker Lenny Kravitz had the line "nice piece of kit" in his 1999 song "Black Velveteen," but the phrase didn't really arrive here for another decade or so. In 2012, sharp-eyed Nancy Friedman sent me a blog post by John Scalzi about the new iPhone, which included this line: "As advertised, it is a very lovely piece of kit." I poked around the web and found a bunch of other uses by techies like Scalzi. Thus Zack Whitaker, on ZDNet: "It doesn't matter where you are in the world: a media on-the-go bag has to have every piece of kit you may or may not need." And Elizabeth Fish, in *PCWorld*: "The Sandia Hand by Sandia National Laboratories is an impressive piece of kit for a troop to own."

The phrase has been fairly commonly used since then in noncomputer contexts, as in a 2017 *New York Times* article about the photographer Stephen Shore, who "was on the road again in 1972, but this time he had a new piece of kit: a Rollei 35-millimeter camera, equipped with a flash (a rarity for him) and stocked with color film."

The verb form, which basically means "equip" and can be either intransitive or transitive (usually followed by "with"), arrived no later than 1919, the date of a line cited by the *OED*: "Now we have been 'kitted up,' as the nautical expression has it." *Kit out* had arrived by 1960, as seen in this quotation from Kingsley Amis: "There are cases on record of writers having to kit out contemporary narratives with aliens and space-ships in order to make a sale."

The first American use I'm aware of came from *New York Times* writer Israel Shenker in 1989: "In Grovewood, a palatial exercise room kitted out with machinery designed to put muscles to the test, I am relieved to see a large TV screen designed to put brain to rest." Shenker was a noted Anglophile and he was writing about a Scottish spa, so it was a bit of a special case with a chameleon quality to it. But Ngram Viewer shows American use starting to climb in the 1980s and skyrocketing in the 2000s.

I wrote about it on the blog in 2016, with these examples from that year:

- "A 23,500-square-foot behemoth at the corner of Sunset and Vine, the store is kitted out to the point of preposterousness with, among other things, a sushi bar, a supermarket, a florist, a warren of frozen-yogurt kiosks and a sidewalk cafe."—*New York Times*
- "The 50-minute film, supposedly unearthed at a yard sale by Ron Howard, is kitted out perfectly as a 1980s relic, with a VHS hiss in the background and even an original theme song written by Kenny Loggins." —*Vanity Fair*, referring to a mock documentary
- "Requests are as varied as the world of books is wide. [Manager Nicky] Dunne has kitted out a hotel, at least one cruise ship and a fleet of private jets."—The *Times* again, on the London antiquarian bookshop Heywood Hill

Adoption | Taking hold
● ● ● ● ●

"Posh"

Admittedly, *posh*—meaning swanky or fancy-shmancy—doesn't sound like it came out of the military. But it did. The earliest citation in the *OED* comes from a 1914 book called *The British Army from Within*: "The cavalryman, far more than the infantryman, makes a point of wearing 'posh' clothing on every possible occasion—'posh' being a term used to designate superior clothing, or articles of attire other than those issued by and strictly conforming to regulations."

And the second cite comes from a letter to the *Daily Mail* two years later: "Your contributor 'O. S. P.,' in his article 'War Words and Phrases,' omits one word in common use among soldiers at the front. It is the word 'posh,' which appears to have more than one meaning. . . . I have heard a good meal described as 'very posh,' and it is also used as a substitute for 'swank' on occasion."

The word quite quickly fell into general use, as in P. G. Wodehouse's *The Inimitable Jeeves* (1923): "Practically every posh family in the country has called him in at one time or another."

As to the etymology of the word, the *OED* says, bluntly, "origin unknown." It goes on to say,

A popular explanation (still frequently repeated) is that the word is [derived from] the initial letters of the phrase *port outward, starboard home*, with reference to the more comfortable (because cooler) and more expensive side for accommodation on ships formerly travelling between Britain and India. It is often suggested that the Peninsular & Oriental Steam Navigation Company stamped tickets for such cabins on this route with the letters *P.O.S.H.*, whence the word. However, no evidence has been found for the existence of such tickets.

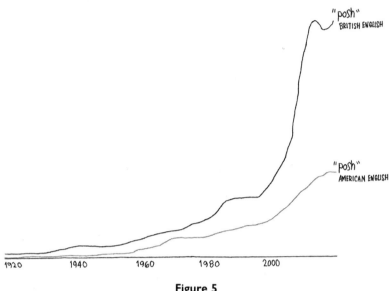

Figure 5

That apocryphal explanation appeared as early as 1932 (in a newspaper article unearthed by the researcher Bonnie Taylor-Blake). It is invoked in a song called "Posh!" in the 1968 movie *Chitty Chitty Bang Bang*. And the canard persists, appearing in multiple books published in the twenty-first century.

Ngram Viewer shows a familiar pattern (figure 5).

I ascribe the sharp American upturn in the 1960s to *Chitty Chitty Bang Bang*, and the even sharper one in the late 1990s and 2000s to the Spice Girls. The group was formed in 1994, but it was two years later that *Melody Maker* magazine bestowed nicknames on the members. Victoria Adams (now Victoria Beckham) actually had an upper-middle-class (what the Brits would call middle-class) upbringing, but she was dubbed Posh Spice because of her bearing, which was, well, posh.

Adoption | Fully arrived

"Scrounge"; "wangle"

These two verbs both mean roughly the same thing, emerged in Britain as World War I slang, and after a few decades got adopted in America.

The *OED* definition for *wangle* is "to accomplish (something) in an irregular way by scheming or contrivance; to bring about or obtain by indirect or insidious means (something not obtainable openly)." There's a 1917 military citation: "He had come in from the North Atlantic Cruiser Patrol, and when in home waters had 'wangled' a few days' leave."

Scrounge is more specifically about getting; the dictionary defines it as "to seek to obtain by irregular means, as by stealth or begging; to hunt about or rummage." The *OED* cites a 1909 book, *Passing English of the Victorian Era: Dictionary of Heterodox English, Slang, and Phrase*, which defines "scrunging" as "('Country Boys'), stealing unripe apples and pears—probably from the noise made in masticating." The word, with an added *o*, gained wide currency and a more general sense during the war. George Goodchild's 1918 book *Behind the Barrage* provides this explanation:

> In the category of "odd jobs" came "scrounging." "Scrounging" is eloquent armyese—it covers pilfering, commandeering, "pinching," and many other familiar terms. You may scrounge for rations, kit, pay, or leave. Signallers are experts at it, and they usually scrounge for wire. Scrounging for wire is legitimized by the War Office, and called by the gentler name "salving."

Ngram Viewer shows British and American use of *wangle* starting to rise in the 1920s, then tailing off in the '40s, possibly because there was a new war about and the term was redolent of the previous one (figure 6). *Scrounge*, however, tells a different story.

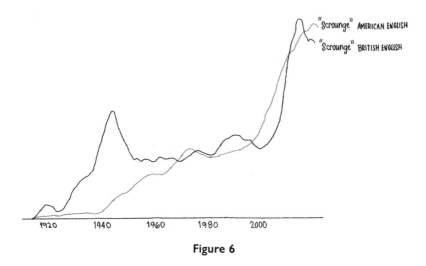

Figure 6

For whatever reason—possibly the consonantal crunch at the beginning—Americans took a shine to the word. It actually occupies a warm spot in my heart because the student center where I used to have lunch with my good friend and late colleague at the University of Delaware, Don Mell, is called, you got it, the Scrounge.

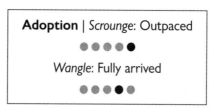

Adoption | *Scrounge*: Outpaced
●●●●●

Wangle: Fully arrived
●●●●●

WORLD WAR II AND AFTER

"Boffin"

A nice word, defined by *Merriam-Webster's* as "a scientific expert; especially: one involved in technological research." *M-W* offers this further note:

It is a relative newcomer to the English language, only appearing toward the end of World War II. Despite its youth, however, the origins of "boffin" are a mystery to us. The term was probably first applied by British Royal Air Force members to the scientists and engineers working closely with radar technology. The term was soon being more broadly applied to scientists involved in technological research. British speakers also use "boffin" colloquially to refer to academics or intellectuals in general, often in a manner that is synonymous with "nerd" or "egghead."

The *OED* offers some illuminating early citations:

1945 *Times* 15 Sept. 5/4 A band of scientific men who performed their wartime wonders at Malvern and apparently called themselves "the boffins."

1948 "[Neville] Shute," *No Highway* iii. 61 "What's a boffin?" "The man from Farnborough. Everybody calls them boffins. Didn't you know?" . . . "Why are they called that?" . . . "Because they behave like boffins, I suppose."

1948 Ld. Tedder in A. P. Rowe, *One Story of Radar* p. vii I was fortunate in having considerable dealings in 1938–40 with the "Boffins" (as the Royal Air Force affectionately dubbed the scientists).

Like *Merriam-Webster*, the *OED* considers the etymology of *boffin* a mystery. The editors sniff, "Numerous conjectures have been made about the origin of the word but all lack foundation"; apparently Charles Dickens's character Mr. Boffin in *Our Mutual Friend* is not considered worthy of mention. However, the boffins over at the American Dialect Society mailing list have applied themselves to the etymology of the word and come up with some solid results. Notably, Garson O'Toole, proprietor of the invaluable Quote Investigator website, found a British newspaper article from 1945 containing this explanation:

> Once upon a time a Puffin, a strange and peculiar bird, was crossed with a Baffin, an obsolete Fleet Air Arm aircraft of equally peculiar habits; and the result, according to Service fantasy, was a "Boffin."
>
> This was a creature of intensive energy, strange appearance and unbelievable inventive capacity, whose eggs, as fast as you pushed them away from you, rolled back again.
>
> That, then, is the origin of the nickname "Boffin," given to the civilian scientists who perfected Radar.

Boffin is still widely used in Britain. Early in the COVID-19 crisis, Prime Minister Boris Johnson gave briefings in which he often appeared with his chief medical officer, Chris Whitty, and chief scientific adviser, Patrick Vallance. The press nicknamed the trio "Boris and the boffins."

But is *boffin* a NOOB? Yes, barely. What success it has had is arguably in large part due to Dan Neil, who, as car columnist for the *Los Angeles Times*, used the word six times between February 2008 and January 2009. ("Chrysler's product boffins created the front-wheel drive K-cars and mini-vans.") The *New York Times* did its part, using *boffin* about a dozen times in the decade of the 2010s (not including quotes from British people), for example:

- "the World Science Festival, the annual jamboree of science, culture and art that mixes boffins and boldface names."
- "Alexander Hoffmann is no white-coated mad scientist, but a 'quant,' a computer boffin."
- "The boffins at the Bureau of Economic Analysis have promised to investigate further and will report back in July."

- "If you can't describe the second law of thermodynamics, you're just as illiterate as any boffin who can't quote Shakespeare" (referring to C. P. Snow's 1959 book *The Two Cultures*).

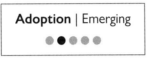

"Bonkers"

This adjective meaning "crazy" or "insane" is now so common in the U.S. that it wouldn't strike many Americans as British, much less British military slang. But that is its origin. The *OED* cites a 1943 glossary of Royal Navy slang that defines it as "light in the head," and in some early examples it's used to mean "drunk." In *A Dictionary of Forces' Slang* (1948), Eric Partridge speculates on its etymology: "Perhaps from *bonk*, a blow or punch on the *bonce* or head." The "crazy" meaning shows up as early as 1945, in a quote from the *Daily Mirror*: "If we do that often enough, we won't lose contact with things and we won't go 'bonkers.'"

Throughout the 1950s, the uses of the word I've turned up are all from British writers:

- From a 1951 novel by Philip Loraine, *A Break in the Circle*: "'You bonkers?' enquired Rocky. 'Maybe.'"
- From John Osborne's play *The Entertainer* (1957): "We're drunks, maniacs, we're crazy, we're bonkers, the whole flaming bunch of us."
- From Kingsley Amis, *Take a Girl like You*, in 1960: "Julian's absolutely bonkers too you know."

The first *New York Times* use was in a 1965 article by the same Israel Shenker we met in the *kit* entry: "In 'Paranoia,' his newest picture, Italy's Marcello Mastroianni goes slowly bonkers sharing bath, bed and Bedouin with three co-stars." The word got pretty popular pretty quickly, Ngram Viewer showing a roughly tenfold increase between 1970 and 2000.

At this point, it's so present in the U.S.—seventy-seven uses in the *Times* in 2021 and a remarkably consistent seventy-eight in 2022—as to reach the point of cliché. In Britain, meanwhile, the word's similarity to *bonk*, a slang synonym for *shag* (see chapter 4), led to many jokes, including this exchange on the TV comedy *Blackadder*:

> PRINCE: You know the kind of girls I like, they've got to be lovers, laughers, dancers . . .
> EDMOND: And bonkers!
> PRINCE: That goes without saying!

Adoption | Fully arrived
● ● ● ● ●

"Dicey"

Reader Tony Mates, from Seattle, wrote in to say, "I am surprised that 'dicey' is not on your list. Though fairly common in the US nowadays, I do recall having to ask my English mother about it back in the 1980s."

"Fairly common" might understate the case. Let's go to Ngram Viewer. It tells a clear story about the word, which the *OED* defines as "risky, dangerous; uncertain, unreliable" (figure 7).

That is, the word originated in Britain, was picked up in the U.S. in the 1970s, started to be used more frequently here in about 1990, and is now so common that Americans (meaning me) had no idea it originated across the pond.

The *OED* describes the word as "Air Force slang" and gives as its first citation Nevil Shute's 1950 novel *A Town like Alice*: "He . . . made a tight, dicey turn round in the gorge with about a

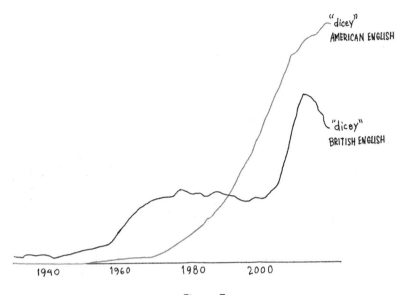

Figure 7

hundred feet to spare." (Shute—born Nevil Shute Norway—was an Englishman with an aeronautics background who moved to Australia late in his life.) Using Google Books, I found what seems to be a use in the British journal *Flight International* from 1945, with telltale quotation marks around the word: "To attack a train under those conditions was 'dicey' and not recommended. But, caught out in the open, a train was a lovely target, and one which couldn't run away, or hide in the jungle."

Green's Dictionary of Slang has an American quote from 1961, and after that, as the graph suggests, it was off to the races. The *New York Times* used it just twelve days ago, as I write ("The Obama administration tackled the dicey politics of immigration in part by removing undocumented workers"), and a total of forty times in 2021.

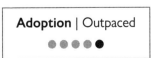

"Go pear-shaped"

This phrase—meaning "go overwhelmingly or dramatically wrong," as in, "After everybody on board developed food poisoning, the cruise went pear-shaped"—has generated a lot of analysis and speculation, most of it apparently wrong. The *OED* identifies it as Royal Air Force (RAF) slang and offers a first citation from 1983: "There were two bangs very close together. The whole aircraft shook and things went 'pear-shaped' very quickly after that. The controls ceased to work, the nose started to go down."

But no small number of people feel strongly that they encountered it earlier than that. Consequently, the 2007 BBC series *Balderdash & Piffle*, which crowd-sourced efforts to antedate *OED* citations, put out an appeal for pre-1983 instances of *go pear-shaped*. No joy (see the next entry).

The claim has also gone around that Margaret Thatcher used the phrase in one of her public appearances with Ronald Reagan in the 1980s, confusing American reporters. Wikipedia published this factoid, but it pretty clearly isn't true, and hence Wikipedia has taken it down.

And finally, one encounters the claim made, in this instance, by a former RAF pilot who posted to English.stackexchange .com: "'Pear Shaped' is a direct euphemism for 'Tits Up,' meaning 'dead' or 'completely broken.'" I haven't seen any evidence for this, from him or anyone else.

What's indisputable is that *go pear-shaped* took off in popularity in Britain in the 1990s.

In 1999, the American journalist Phillip Weiss wrote that a British friend, Eve MacSweeney, had used it in an email, and he asked her what it meant:

> She tells me that "pear-shaped" is the reigning metaphor
> in England now. Things are going pear-shaped. They say

it in the financial district when a stock goes bad. They say it in W11 [the posh London district consisting of Notting Hill and Holland Park] about a marriage. Ms. MacSweeney says the term resonates because English women are frequently referred to as being pear-shaped, the men in England being buttless, but she and I agree that when the phrase gets here—the land of the aging, big-butted male— it will have wider resonance.

Ngram Viewer reveals that the phrase peaked in Britain in 2008 and started a steady decline. However, it has consistently risen in America, surpassing British use in 2015. On the issue of whether the popularity here had anything to do with American male physiognomy, I will keep my own counsel.

Adoption | Taking hold

"No joy"

For some readers, these two words will bring to mind the 1888 American poem "Casey at the Bat," with its closing line, "But there is no joy in Mudville—mighty Casey has struck out."

That is a case of literal "no joy"—an absence of elation—and no doubt the two words have been paired in that way for centuries on both sides of the Atlantic. My subject here is a more ironic use of *joy*, which first popped up among RAF pilots in World War II. The 1943 book *It's a Piece of Cake: or, R.A.F. Slang Made Easy* has this entry: "Joy, satisfaction. Thus, 'Johnnie took the new kite up this morning—had bags of joy,' or 'no joy at all.'" (For *piece of cake*, see the next entry.)

Taking the two examples separately, the first—the positive sense—has, as far as I can tell, been used exclusively in

Britain and Commonwealth countries, as in this quote from a 1971 novel: "'Any joy there?' She looked up. 'There's not much more than I told you last night.'" The negative *no joy* is more common and is the NOOB. It seems to have started here with American pilots who picked it up from their British counterparts. *NOOBs* reader Charles Mayfield commented,

> I was a U.S. Navy pilot in the 1960's and '70's and the terms "Tally ho" and "No joy" were used in response to ground radar operator warnings of other aircraft traffic in one's area. The operator would warn of "traffic in your 2 o'clock position, 15,000 feet, closing" and you would look in the area indicated and respond "Tally Ho" if you spotted the other aircraft or "No joy" if you couldn't see anything.

The first nonaviation American use I've found is from a 1992 episode of *Columbo*: "No joy on the fingerprints?" (A British detective probably would have said, "Any joy on the fingerprints?") But it remained an outlier for some time. What may have stimulated North American use was a Canadian rock band called No Joy, formed in 2009.

By the mid-2010s the phrase was growing in frequency. *Boston Globe* tech columnist Hiawatha Bray (born in Chicago) wrote, "I've asked Facebook for a comment, but no joy so far." And Tom Maxwell (born in Baltimore) said in a *Salon* review of BBC Music's video of the Beach Boys' classic song "God Only Knows," "Elton John, looking pained, covered in computer-generated blue butterflies, singing, 'You'll never need to doubt it.' From the look of things, he should be singing, 'Everything is satisfactual,' but no joy."

Adoption | Emerging

● ● ● ● ●

"Piece of cake"

It started with an email from my eclectic friend Wes Davis. He said he'd been reading *Tinkerbelle*, by, he told me, "Robert Manry, a copy editor for the *Cleveland Plain Dealer* who, in 1965, took a leave of absence from his job and sailed a 13-and-a-half-foot wooden boat across the Atlantic, from Falmouth, Mass., to Falmouth, England." Wes had come upon a passage he thought would interest me. Manry is just starting out and it's a beautiful day, "the wind strong enough to keep us moving along briskly." He observes, "I told myself that if most of the days ahead were as pleasant as this, our trip would be a breeze, or, as the English say, a piece of cake."

Wes sent me the quote because his sense (like mine) was that *a piece of cake* is as American as red velvet cake. So what was with Manry's attribution to the English?

As usual in such matters, I turned first to Ngram Viewer (figure 8).

Thus, at the time Manry was writing, it was still predominantly a British phrase, but that would soon change.

There's a bit of noise in the graph—that is, it tracks not only the figure of speech but literal uses, like "What they served me was a piece of cake." The *OED*'s first citation for the metaphorical phrase is from a 1936 poem by the American Ogden Nash: "Her picture's in the papers now, / And life's a piece of cake." But I feel that's an outlier—likely a fresh metaphor concocted by Nash. I wasn't able to turn up any additional uses until 1942, and all of the ones from then through the early '50s are British.

And specifically British military, and even more specifically the RAF. The first quote in the Google Books database comes from a 1942 *Life* magazine article written by an RAF pilot: "It sounds incredible considering that we were 150 miles from the

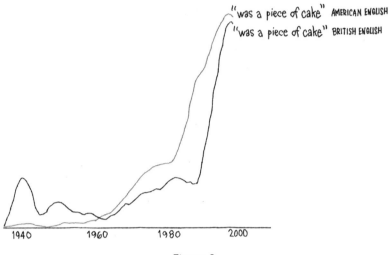

"was a piece of cake" AMERICAN ENGLISH
"was a piece of cake" BRITISH ENGLISH

1940   1960   1980   2000

Figure 8

target but the fires were so great that it was a piece of cake to find the target area." The phrase, so redolent of the plucky fliers, really caught on. The same year, Terrence Rattigan's play *Flare Path* has the line, "Special. Very hush-hush. Not exactly a piece of cake, I believe." By 1943, it had become so well known that Cyril Henry Ward-Jackson titled his book *It's a Piece of Cake: or, R.A.F. Slang Made Easy.*

As the Google chart indicates, American use started to pick up, but often (as with Manry) with attribution to the English. A 1951 article in an American flying magazine had the line, "The radio operator's weather reports show all stations ahead in good shape and as the English say, 'It's a piece of cake.'" Eventually, we took it to heart, and rightly so, since it's a great phrase, nicely complementing *easy as pie* (which refers to a process, rather than a task) while still staying in the realm of baked goods.

There's a coda to the tale. Fans of Roald Dahl may recognize "A Piece of Cake" as the title of one of his short stories, included in his 1946 collection *Over to You: Ten Stories of Flyers and Flying*. That story is actually an extensive reworking of Dahl's first published work, an article in the August 1942 edition of the *Saturday Evening Post* called "Shot Down over Libya." In the piece, labeled a "factual report," Dahl talks about being given the assignment, in 1940, to bomb a group of Italian trucks in the Libyan desert. One of his fellow flyers remarks, "Hell's bells, what a piece of cake!" Another agrees, "What a piece of cake." (This is retroactive evidence of an earlier British use of the expression than given in the *OED*, but it can't be included in the dictionary as such since the publication date is 1942.)

It wasn't a piece of cake for Dahl. As the story describes, he had a rough landing and was badly injured. But the story was far from a "factual report." His plane was not shot down, as the title asserts and the text strongly implies. Dahl's biographer Jeremy Treglown writes, "He stopped twice to refuel, the second time at Fouka, where he was given directions that may have been confused by events. 80 Squadron was not where he expected to find it, and as dusk gathered over the North African desert and his fuel gauge fell, he decided to try to land."

The 1946 reworking was presented as fiction but had a more accurate account of the forced landing. In fact, just about the only thing it has in common with the 1942 version is *a piece of cake*.

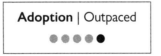

Adoption | Outpaced

"Shambolic"

The definition of the adjective is "chaotic, disorderly, undisciplined"—that is, in a state of shambles. The *OED*'s first citation is from *The Times* of London in 1970, but there's also an odd note: "Reported to be 'in common use' in 1958." Doesn't say who's doing the reporting.

In any case, there are definitely antedates to the 1970 quote, and even to 1958. Here are some I found, moving in reverse chronological order:

- August 3, 1965: "Mr. William Yates: The hon. Member must understand that so long as the country is willing to pour more and more money into this ancient, shambolic building in this area of London, there is no chance of getting that or having any of the facilities that he wants."—Parliamentary debate
- July 25, 1965: "Our social life is shambolic."—*Sunday Times*
- 1958: "He said his club had coined a new word 'Shambolic,' which meant spending more time watching the weather than playing."—*West Sussex Times*
- 1952: "One must admit there were those among us who were somewhat on the shambolic side."—*The Tank* (this citation appears in Wiktionary, which links to a Google Books entry, but I don't 100 percent trust it because Google Books doesn't offer a full view and its dating is often dodgy)

Next is a quote I turned up in the ProQuest database. It's an abstract of a 1946 article from the Blackpool *Tribune* reviewing a book by Roland Gant called *How Like a Wilderness*. It's not clear who wrote the abstract, or when, but it has the feel of being composed at the time—and also suggests *shambolic* originated as military slang. The blurb begins, "The author parachuted into the Calvados country on D-Day in an operation which, in the language of those days, would have been described as 'shambolic.'"

All those examples are British; American use didn't pick up till the end of the twentieth century. *Shambolic* first showed up in the *New York Times* in a 1984 William Safire column taking note of it. Between then and the middle of 2022, the word appeared in the paper 365 times.

A related word is *omnishambles*, meaning "a situation that has been comprehensively mismanaged, or is characterized by a series of blunders and miscalculations"—that is, a complete cock-up. It was invented in 2009 by the writers of the British TV satire *The Thick of It* and had sufficiently penetrated to the country at large in three years for the *OED* to name it Word of the Year for 2012.

Omnishambles is still a bit of an outlier in the U.S., however, having appeared in the ProQuest Recent Newspapers only thirteen times, most of them quotes from British people or discussions of the word itself. An exception is the most recent hit, from *Washington Post* columnist Monica Hesse, who in March 2023 wrote that after her association with Donald Trump, porn star Stormy Daniels's "life became an omnishambles of harassment and threats."

Adoption | *Shambolic*: Emerging

◉ ● ◉ ◉ ◉

Omnishambles: On the radar

● ◉ ◉ ◉ ◉

CHAPTER THREE

Modern NOOBs

THE TOP 40

The selections in this chapter are to some extent based on the most popular entries on my blog. For example, as of this writing my post on ta-ta *has racked up 53,761 views and the one on* go pear-shaped *53,672. But I have also included some terms because they're so popular here or have an interesting backstory, or, like* vet *and* non-starter, *don't seem especially British. But they are.*

"Amongst"

About fifteen years ago, this old-fashioned-sounding replacement for the traditional (and synonymous) *among* started showing up in the writing of my students at the University of Delaware. By the time I retired ten years later, it was by far the preferred form.

Among has always been more frequently used than *amongst* in both the U.S. and Britain, with the longer form being more common there than here. However, according to

Ngram Viewer, the frequency of *amongst* in America more than doubled between 1991 and 2015, even as it was dropping in Britain. As previously noted, Ngram Viewer only charts printed sources; I'm confident that *amongst* would show an even sharper rise if speech were taken into account.

I chose that date range not only because it roughly tracks my teaching career. Between 1991 and '94, Mike Myers played the character Linda Richman on *Saturday Night Live*, and one of her catchphrases was "Talk amongst yourselves." Then, between 1998 and 2015, Jon Stewart hosted *The Daily Show* on Comedy Central, and Stewart was a very heavy *amongst* user. He still is. When he was awarded the Mark Twain Prize in 2022, he said about comedy, "The best amongst us just keep at it." To what extent Stewart inspired the *amongst* boom, or merely reflected it, I cannot say.

Amongst doesn't get much love among usage experts in America. *Garner's Modern English Usage* calls it an archaicism and says it's "pretentious at best"; my 1999 edition of *The New York Times Manual of Style* says, simply, "'Among' (not 'amongst')." The rule seems to be holding up at the paper: *amongst* appears a lot in the *Times*, but as far as I can tell only in quotations from interviews or documents.

If *amongst* is pretentious and archaic, what of *whilst*? (Garner: "It has not lost its odor of affectation.") Ngram Viewer shows that in 1980, it was used about eight times more frequently in Britain than the United States, but between then and 2019, American use more than doubled. It's still far less common than *while* in both Britain and the U.S., but it's definitely out there in America. To wit:

- "Since many of us do our talking whilst driving, might they consider coming up with a mobile phone that only works in the house, while we're not spewing emissions

along with our hot air?"—*Bits* blog, *New York Times,* 2007
- "Whilst scouring my mental vault of classroom distractions this past week, I recalled a favorite past time of my youth. Before Facebook and Minecraft, when Netscape Navigator was the browser of choice among proto-hipsters, Cartoon-Network.com ruled my leisure." —*Daily Princetonian* blog, 2011

I imagine that the appeal of both words is that they sound vaguely fancy, as opposed to British. But I'm not sure. Talk amongst yourselves and get back to me with an answer.

Adoption | *Amongst:* Taking hold

●●●●●

Whilst: Outlier

●●●●●

"At the end of the day"

I love it when the *OED* gets frisky. It definitely does with the above formulation, pegging it as a "hackneyed phrase." The meaning, I probably don't need to point out, isn't literal but figurative: not "when the clock strikes midnight," but "eventually" or "when all is said and done." The first *OED* citation is from 1974: "Eschatological language is useful because it is a convenient way of indicating . . . what at the end of the day we set most store by."

But it was around and about long before that, principally—and fortunately, for the purposes of this book—in Britain.

The *Grammarphobia* blog found it in an 1826 sermon:

Christ's flock is but a *little flock,* comparatively considered. . . . They are but little in respect of their numbers.

Indeed abstractly considered, at the end of the day, they will make an "innumerable company, which no man can number"; but, viewed in comparison of the wicked, they are but few.

At the end of the day is not only hackneyed but also pompous and portentous, and thus it's not surprising that the phrase found especially wide use in Parliament. In 1858, the Liberal member of Commons William Gladstone said, "Coming in at the end of the day, then, Russia supported the union." In 1896, an unidentified speaker said, "And now at the end of the day they had a Government which was brought in by a large majority for the purpose of doing justice."

I got these quotes from the *Hansard* corpus, available at English-corpora.org, which shows the phrase becoming more and more popular in Parliament over the course of the twentieth century. *At the end of the day* was uttered in Parliament 12 times in the decade of the 1900s, 36 times in the 1910s, and all the way up to 3,845 in the 1980s, at which point it began to decline.

The main reason for the decline, it's clear to me, would have been the growing realization that it had become a cliché. Indeed, as early as 1986, *New York Times* language columnist William Safire complained about it as a "vogue term." Fifteen years later, Safire returned to the theme. Prompted by a reader's complaint, he looked at an interview between NBC's Tim Russert and the chairman of the Democratic National Committee, Terry McAuliffe, and found McAuliffe "used the phrase . . . seventeen times in the twelve minutes he spoke on the air: 'At the end of the day we won on the issues'; 'At the end of the day if all the votes were counted'; 'There was no swap at the end of the day.'"

The *at the end of the day* backlash continues. Respondents to a 2004 survey by the Plain English Campaign chose it as the

number one most annoying cliché. ("Second place in the vote
was shared by 'at this moment in time' and the constant use of
'like' as if it were a form of punctuation. 'With all due respect'
came fourth.") And in 2010, a *Pittsburgh Post-Gazette* sports-
writer awarded *at the end of the day* his annual Trite Trophy as
the most egregious cliché of the year.

In contrast to Parliament, in the world at large, the deri-
sion has not slowed the phrase's general momentum. Ngram
Viewer shows it increasing in frequency in both Britain and
the U.S., the latter surpassing the former in 2013 and surging
ahead ever since.

> **Adoption** | Outpaced
> ● ● ● ● ●

"Bespoke"

The adjective *bespoke* refers to goods that are made to order, as
opposed to ready-made or factory-made. It derives from a particular sense of the verb *bespeak*—to order goods in advance.
That meaning is obsolete, but *bespoke* is very much with us.

The first citation in the *OED* (1755) refers to a bespoke
play, but for the next couple of centuries the word was most
commonly used about shoes and other articles of clothing.
I first encountered it in high school when I saw the English
short film *The Bespoke Overcoat*, based on Wolf Mankowitz's
1953 play and originally on Nikolai Gogol's short story "The
Overcoat."

In the 2000s, the word began to take off in the United
States (figure 9), and it became understood that it can apply to
virtually anything. *Bespoke* has appeared more than two hundred times in the *New York Times* in the 2020s. In just the
previous two months (as I write), it has been used to describe

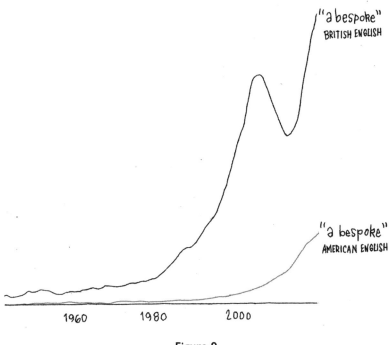

"a bespoke"
BRITISH ENGLISH

"a bespoke"
AMERICAN ENGLISH

1960   1980   2000

Figure 9

wood-burning clay ovens, the "experiences" the developer of
Rockefeller Center is trying to provide to visitors, the Bespoke
Investment Group, the sounds created for the movie *Dune*,
balloon arrangements, and a dance piece that was a "bespoke
response" to another dance piece.

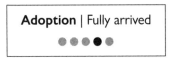

Adoption | Fully arrived

"Bit"

To state the obvious, this is a common term. How common? It
is the 808th most frequently used word in the Corpus of Contemporary American English, just behind *decade* and ahead

of *reduce*. The *OED* considers it to be six separate words—two of them verbs and four nouns. I am concerned here with the noun (the others have to do with the biting of horses, leather flasks, and computer information) that denotes a piece or part of a larger whole, literally or figuratively bitten off. Its entry has within it twenty-five separate senses, most of which are as commonly used in American as British English. (And some more so: as in a "bit part" in a movie, calling twenty-five cents "two bits," and the meaning of *schtick* or well-rehearsed routine, as in this quote from Fred Astaire's autobiography: "We were in Detroit—stranded—and that is where Mother did the pawning-of-the-jewels bit.")

But not a few of the meanings are notably British, and several of these have become NOOBs.

Starting with phrases, the *OED*'s first citation for *doing one's bit*—meaning "to fulfil one's responsibilities or obligations; to make one's contribution to a cause or the like, esp. by serving in the armed forces"—is from George Bernard Shaw in 1889. It gained currency in British Great War propaganda, as in posters with the messages "DO YOUR BIT—SAVE FOOD" and "COME AND DO YOUR BIT—JOIN NOW." The U.S. followed suit with a poster that urged "little AMERICANS" to "do your bit" by eating oatmeal and such and "*save the wheat for our soldiers*."

And in fact, according to Ngram Viewer, we outstripped the Brits in *do your bit* by a healthy margin over the next couple of decades and were roughly equal in the 1950s and early '60s before falling behind again.

Then there are *bits and bats*, *bits and bobs*, and *bits and pieces*, redundant phrases that mean roughly the same thing. The first never made it to America. *Bits and bobs* is an outlier NOOB that shows up either in self-consciously British contexts or in twee formulations such as a *New York Times* Vows column that describes one of the two grooms: "He was always creative and enjoyed making crafts with bits and bobs of paper he had saved, ticket stubs and back-of-the-envelope doodles."

As for *bits and pieces*, it started to rise in Britain in the 1930s and the U.S. in the '40s, had a big American bump in the '60s, doubtless thanks to the Dave Clark Five hit song, and since then has been roughly equally common in both countries.

But for my purposes, the key late twentieth- and early twenty-first-century Britishism is *bit* for what an American would most likely say *part*, often used in the plural and often preceded by an adjective. An example is a humorous 1873 sketch in the *St. Pauls Magazine*, where the narrator describes wandering the halls of Parliament and coming upon a man who's endeavoring to teach the members to "talk better." This fellow poses a question:

> "One of your great debates that fills three or four pages of your *Times* with the smallest of small print and runs over into the supplement—how much do you read of it next morning?"
>
> "Well, I generally glance my eye down the columns, and read the sentences where I see there have been 'laughter' and 'cheers.'"
>
> "Ah, just so, you read only the good bits. Now my plan is to make my pupils say nothing but the good bits. None of them shall speak longer than half an hour, and each sentence shall have a Thought in it."

The juicy bits and *the naughty bits* show up in Britain in the nineteenth century as well, but they really established themselves as phrases in the twentieth. An American would say *the good parts, the juicy parts*, and *the naughty parts*.

Most Americans, that is. One finds the occasional literary sort, like critic Richard Eder of the *New York Times*, writing of a Lina Wertmuller revival in 1976, "Enthusiasm for Miss Wertmuller's later work may arm the spectator with the fortitude to mark out the good bits." The same year, American science fiction novelist Ursula Le Guin wrote of H. P. Lovecraft in the *Times Literary Supplement*, "He imitated the worst bits of Poe quite accurately."

This use of the word picked up steam in the U.S. in the 1990s and 2000s, as in a 1999 quote from *Time* magazine referring to prosecutor Kenneth Starr's report on the alleged misdeeds of President Bill Clinton: "He wants America to believe he'd only included the good bits to help the legislature reach an informed decision." More recently, a *NOOBs* reader reports that the Turbo Tax program, while it's loading, displays the message, "Hold on, we're getting all the technical bits together." (To be really British, it would have said, "Hang on.")

One particular kind of *bits* deserves mention. A 1970 episode of *Monty Python's Flying Circus* had a sketch called "How to Recognise Different Parts of the Body," which included this, well, bit (I quote from the Python Wiki):

A voiceover (John Cleese) points out more parts of the body:

    10. The big toe

    11. More naughty bits (a man standing wearing spotted Bermuda shorts)

    12. The naughty bits of a lady (a lady posing wearing spotted Bermuda bra and shorts)

    13. The naughty bits of a horse (a horse wearing spotted Bermuda shorts)

    14. The naughty bits of an ant

15. The naughty bits of Reginald Maudling (a picture of Reginald Maudling wearing spotted Bermuda shorts)

In his humorous 1988 book *God—the Ultimate Autobiography*, Jeremy Pascall uses the phrase *dangly bits* five times, including in his reference to the creation of Eve: "So much better formed softer, rounder, smoother, with none of those ugly dangly bits." *Dangly bits* caught on as a reference to male genitalia and by 1999, according to *Green's Dictionary of Slang*, had been shortened to just plain *bits*. An example is a quote from Twitter, which I especially like because it uses the word twice: "I was in the Sistine Chapel on Tuesday. My favourite bit was where Michelangelo painted in the Pope's advisor, whom he detested, with a snake eating his bits."

No surprise that at the U.S. vanguard was NOOBs hall-of-famer Dwight Garner of the *New York Times*, who, in a review of basketball star Jerry West's memoir in 2011, wrote, "West seems here like both the Hatfields and McCoys. He shoots himself repeatedly in the head, feet and private bits." The following year, Garner wrote that an author portrayed gay people as "pretty much like straight people, that is, except for what they do with their dangly bits."

Dangly bits and *bits* appeared to be exclusively male provinces. To the rescue came *lady bits*, first spotted in 2005 and growing robustly since then. Google reveals that Lady Bits is currently the name of a soap, a physical therapy practice, a zine, and an Australian cross-dressing salon.

The phrase is still an outlier in the U.S., but I imagine it gained some traction after a 2021 exchange on Drew Barrymore's talk show with Gwyneth Paltrow (an honorary English person, of course). Barrymore tasked her guest with coming up with alternatives to words you can't comfortably say on morning network TV, like "something beginning with *v* that ends in 'ina.'"

"Lady bits?" Paltrow offered.

Adoption | *Doing one's bit*: Fully arrived

● ● ● ● ●

Bits and bobs: On the radar

● ● ● ● ●

Bits and pieces: Fully arrived

● ● ● ● ●

Bits meaning "parts": Taking hold

● ● ● ● ●

Dangly bits: Outlier

● ● ● ● ●

"Brilliant"

The adjective originally meant (literally) brightly shining, then in the mid-nineteenth century developed a figurative sense of very intelligent ("a brilliant mathematician"). Those two senses have always been used in the U.S., but not a third meaning, which the *OED* calls "weakened use: amazing, 'fantastic.' *Colloq.*," and which is used in reference to things and experiences as well as people. The first citation for this is a 1971 academic paper from South Africa, which suggests this sense had been around for some time: "Brilliant is of fairly wide application, e.g., a brilliant board, a brilliant ride, a brilliant pair of baggies."

It swiftly became a part of U.K. vernacular, as in this from Sue Townsend's *The Growing Pains of Adrian Mole* (1984): "I allowed Pandora to visit me in my darkened bedroom. We had a brilliant kissing session." The word presumably got a boost in 2003, when Bono accepted a Golden Globe award for his band U2 and said, over international TV, "This is really, really, fucking brilliant."

In the meantime, two things had happened in Britain. First, the shortened form *brill* arose, as early as 1979, according to a quote from *Melody Maker* in *Green's Dictionary of Slang*. But then it lost some luster and hasn't been used since the 1980s (according to one commenter on *NOOBs*) or the '90s (according to another). The second thing is that the word began to be used ironically, or to describe things that are okay or maybe even good, but not fantastic. A definition of *brilliant* posted to Urban Dictionary in 2009 sums this up:

> A word which in the past meant that something was excep-tionally good, or to express great pleasure: Its strength has been eroded by overuse, and it can now be used to respond to any mildly pleasing news. . . .
>
> In the olden days:
>
> SMITH: "Everyone has the day off tomorrow!"
> JONES: "Brilliant!"
>
> Nowadays:
>
> WAITER: "Are you ready to order?"
> CUSTOMER: "err, yes . . ."
> WAITER: "Brilliant."

As for U.S. use, the "amazing" meaning pops up now and again, the ironic or noncommittal pretty rarely. A music critic wrote in the *New York Times* in 1998, "It was brilliant to pro-gram the Beethoven before the Carter." And in 2011, Phila-delphia Phillies outfielder Raul Ibanez, referring to winter sports activity, said, "I jumped on one of those little sleds and went down a hill. It's brilliant. Whoever came up with that—phenomenal."

Brilliant.

Adoption | On the radar

"Chat up"

This is a transitive verb phrase derived from the now antique transitive *chat*, defined by the *English Dialect Dictionary* (1898) as Londonderry slang for "to flirt with." It spread across Britain and is found in the anonymously authored 1959 book *Streetwalker*: "Big Barbara is chatting a geezer, though the stream of polished professional patter she is directing at him warrants a less terse description." The *up* was added in the 1960s, with the first *OED* citation being this from the *Daily Mail* in 1963: "If you try to chat up a girl and she gives you the heavy fish it means she's ignored your advances."

The phrase is also used, as *Green's Dictionary of Slang* puts it, "fig[uratively], in non-sexual contexts, to seduce with words." *Green's* has an example from a Frank Norman column in *Encounter* in 1958: "If there's one thing I don't look when some bogey chats me up, that's innocent!"

When I wrote about *chat up* on the blog, I described both connotations, and someone commented, "Your definition is totally wrong—at least for the variety of British English I learned, growing up there in the 80s and 90s. 'Chat up' specifically implies a romantic purpose to the conversation." Others averred that it's occasionally (though infrequently) used nonsexually in Britain; but in any case, once Americans picked up the phrase, they for some reason seemed to favor the nonsexual context. And indeed, often we're not even trying to "seduce with words"; we're just shooting the breeze. For example:

- Writing in the *New Yorker* in 1975, Michael Arlen said of the singer Lola Falana, "As a professional talk-show guest, she was supposed to make her appearance, chat up the host, do her number, and generally provide her own small talk—much of which, as is customary, was directed at further chatting-up the host."
- Also in the *New Yorker*, John McPhee wrote in 2003, "At a Union 76 in Ontario, near Riverside, he saw a guy changing a headlamp, chatted him up, and learned that he was independent."
- And more recently, from a 2022 *New York Times* article about marijuana sellers in Washington Square Park: "On a recent sunny March day, customers chatted up vendors while deciding which strain to buy."

From the same root comes *chattering class/es*, which the *OED* says is "freq. derogatory" and defines as "members of the educated metropolitan middle class, esp. those in academic, artistic, or media circles, considered as a social group freely given to the articulate, self-assured expression of (esp. liberal) opinions about society, culture, and current events." The first citation is from 1980, but using Google Books I found this from an 1871 article in *The Spectator* called "The New Indian Danger": "And everything seemed to grow dear at once, to the immense disgust of the chattering classes who bought." It's clearly an outlier, and the phrase didn't arrive in common use till the 1980s.

The first use in the *New York Times* not in reference to Britain came in 1991, when former Reagan speechwriter Peggy Noonan wrote, "I believe I perceive a total perceptual split between the chattering classes . . . and normal humans."

Between then and the end of 2022, the phrase appeared in the paper three hundred times, suggesting it has entered the realm of cliché—at least among the chattering classes.

Adoption | *Chat up*: Taking hold

● ● ● ● ●

Chattering classes: Taking hold

● ● ● ● ●

"Cheeky"

The first version of this word was the noun *cheek*, meaning "impudence, effrontery, audacity." It crops up in the 1820s, and Charles Dickens's 1853 novel *Bleak House* has the line, "On account of his having so much cheek." Various corpora reveal that the noun was used a fair amount in the U.S. in the nineteenth century into the twentieth, including in the title of Max Shulman's 1943 humorous novel *Barefoot Boy with Cheek* (a takeoff on John Greenleaf Whittier's once famous line of poetry "Barefoot boy with cheek of tan").

The adjective *cheeky* popped up in the 1830s and soon established itself as the predominant form. It shows up a bit in U.S. sources, but the concept of and various terms for cheekiness really found a home in Britain. So much so that in 1870, Hugh Stowell Brown took it to task in his *Lectures to Working Men*, contrasting it unfavorably with another word and quality:

> It may be very well at the outset to draw a distinction between "Pluck" and "Cheek." They are not the same thing. "Pluck" is courage, "Cheek" is impudence, hardfaced, unblushing impudence. A "plucky" fellow deserves our admiration, a "cheeky" fellow deserves to be kicked. But

"Cheek" may sometimes be mistaken for "Pluck," or perhaps "Pluck" may take such ways of showing itself as ally it very closely with "Cheek." Now one may be "plucky" without being "cheeky," courageous without being impudent. Many of the men who have most "Pluck" have very little "Cheek," and many of the men who have most "Cheek," when put to the proof, are found to have very little "Pluck."

Brown's efforts proved futile, and *cheeky* continued apace, often if not usually portrayed as a positive quality. (An exception, in Australia, New Zealand, South Africa, and then-Rhodesia, was a racist reference to the supposed impudence of nonwhite people, the equivalent of American *uppity*.) Ngram Viewer shows the word rising steadily in the U.K. in the twentieth century and then sharply declining in the 1990s. That it shot up around this time in the U.S. as well surely has something to do with comedian Mike Myers, who grew up in Canada but whose parents were English, and who also played a part in popularizing *bum* (see chapter 4), *shag* (see chapter 4), and *amongst* (see the entry in this chapter). Myers's *Saturday Night Live* character Simon, a little English boy who for some reason conducted a talk show while taking a bath, would reach for a prop and say, "Don't look at my bum! I caught you sneaking a peek, cheeky monkeys, all of you!" Scotsman Craig Ferguson turned up on American late-night TV sometime later and called his audience "cheeky wee monkeys." And *Cheeky Bastard* was the name of a fictional show-within-a-show featured on a 2005 episode of the animated series *Family Guy*.

(*NOOBs* reader Catherine Rose provided some perspective on the word's evolution in Britain: "*Cheeky* has come to be a positive thing to say about a child—'he's a cheeky monkey' now tends to mean, 'oh isn't he sweet and lively?'—and it tends to be said approvingly about lively little boys rather than girls.

When I was a kid, if my Mum or my teacher called me cheeky it was really serious—I'd 'cheeked' an adult [said something rude or impudent] and there would be hell to pay.")

At this point, *cheeky* is an American commonplace and perhaps cliché. The word appeared 205 times in the *New York Times* in 2022, including in the headlines "Cy Twombly in Los Angeles: Cheeky, Challenging, Classical" and "A Book of Cheeky Obituaries Highlights 'Eccentric Lives,'" and the comment that a movie which reimagines *Romeo and Juliet* "epitomizes a du jour Hollywood adaptation style that's nothing short of agonizing, planting one foot in the source material and the other in a cheeky 21st-century sensibility."

One meaning that has *not* taken hold in the U.S. is defined this way by the *OED*: "Of an item of food, drink, etc., or an activity: mildly irresponsible or illicit; indulgent." The first citation is from a 1989 novel: "Bourke that had his cheeky pint with George Blake in the King's Arms."

This sense was prominent in a 2014–2015 phenomenon involving Nando's, an international chain restaurant that features grilled chicken and fried potatoes (*chips* in Britain). "Having a cheeky Nando's" became the text of a meme, and Americans spectacularly failed to understand what this meant. One problem was this particular meaning of *cheeky*, and another was the British way of using an indefinite article and the name of a restaurant, in this case Nando's, to mean food or a meal from that restaurant. The fun came when British people purported to "'explain' what it means while using as much British slang as humanly possible, for maximum Yank confusion." Here's one example:

> Mate it's hard to explain mate it's just like one day you'll just be wif your mates having a look in jd and you might fancy curry club at the 'Spoons but your lad Calum who's

an absolute ledge and the archbishop of banterbury will be like "brevs lets have a cheeky nandos instead," and you'll think "Top. Let's smash it."

Which is a sentence I'll pull out the next time someone claims that British English and American English have become identical.

And by the way, an English informant tells me that *crafty* has arisen there as a replacement for this *cheeky*, as in "having a crafty pint." No sign of it yet in America.

Adoption | Taking hold

"Clever"

This is the word that gets the most blowback when I write about it on the blog. I think the main reason is that it is and has always been used a lot in America—almost as much as in Britain, in fact. But it means rather different things in the two countries. This has been true for a long time. John Witherspoon, who coined *Americanisms* and was the first to complain about them, observed back in 1781, "Americans generally mean by *clever*, only goodness of disposition, worthiness, integrity, without the least regard to capacity." The meanings had multiplied by 1833, when Captain Thomas Hamilton, touring the U.S., wrote:

> I heard of a gentleman having moved into a *clever* house, of another succeeding to a *clever* amount of money, of a third embarking in a *clever* ship, and making a *clever* voyage with a *clever* cargo; and of the sense attached to the word in these combinations, I could gain nothing like a satisfactory explanation.

In Britain, meanwhile, the word was settling around the sense of "intelligent." Jane Austen wrote in *Emma* (1816), "Emma is spoiled by being the cleverest of her family." That's still the principal meaning across the pond. Children who in America would be deemed "smart" or "bright" or "gifted" are called "clever" in the U.K. (There, the main meaning for *smart* is "stylish or fashionable.") In 2006 Lynne Murphy reported, "The Professional Association of Teachers has voted that bright British school children should [no longer] be labeled clever, but instead should be deemed successful—because among children it's not cool to be clever."

Of course, Britain being Britain, *clever* also has been used ironically, as in the usually disparaging terms *clever boots, clever clogs*, and *clever Dick*, all originating in the mid-nineteenth century and roughly equivalent to *know-it-all*. The *OED* quotes a line from John Braine's novel *Room at the Top* (1957): "'Clever Dick,' she said. 'Think yer knows everythink, doncha?'"

Back to America. By the twentieth century, *clever* had lost its "goodness-of-disposition" sense and was used to indicate a certain *kind* of intelligence. A clever American person doesn't necessarily have a high IQ but can solve a puzzle or a mystery or can trick you into doing something you don't want to. Thus the two relevant definitions and examples from the *Merriam-Webster* online dictionary: "mentally quick and resourceful ('a clever young lawyer'); marked by wit or ingenuity ('a clever solution')."

That brings us up to the age of NOOBs. British *clever* first crossed my radar in 2012, when Republican politician Newt Gingrich used it twice while campaigning for the Republican nomination for president. Complaining about his rival Mitt Romney, Gingrich observed that the media "did exactly what Obama would do this fall, and kept replaying [Romney's quote] 'Oh, I don't really care about the poor.' Which is not a very clever thing for someone who is very wealthy to say." And on another occasion, Gingrich said, "The message we should give Mitt Romney is you know, 'We aren't that stupid and you aren't that clever.'"

That same year, David Sedaris said in a *New York Times* interview, "I was a judge for this year's Scholastic Art and Writing Awards, so until very recently I was reading essays written by clever high school students." Of course, Sedaris had moved to England in 1998, so he presumably had a lot of exposure to the word by then.

A variant that's also a NOOB is *too clever by half*, basically meaning too clever for his, her, or its own good, which appeared by 1829. It became a popular catchphrase in Britain within the next few decades and remained active enough in the late twentieth century for British critic Melvyn Bragg to use a variation in calling the polymath Jonathan Miller "too clever by three quarters."

American use didn't pick up until the 1960s; by 1990 Elizabeth Drew could use it in the *New Yorker* and expect readers to understand: "Some Republican leaders, like their Democratic counterparts, find [Richard] Darman too clever by half." Two years later, both A. M. Rosenthal and Anthony Lewis used "Too Clever by Half" as the headlines for their *New York Times* columns.

To sum up, as Nigel St. Hubbins of Spinal Tap famously said, "There's a fine line between stupid and clever."

Adoption | *Clever* (intelligent): Emerging

● ● ● ● ●

Too clever by half: Fully arrived

● ● ● ● ●

"Dodgy"

Dodge is a venerable noun and verb, dating to the sixteenth century and referring to a trick, cheat, or scheme, or the performance of such a maneuver. *Artful dodge* became a catchphrase in the 1820s and '30s, as in an 1832 sporting article describing a horse who "then tried the 'artful dodge,' which proved alike unsuccessful, although conducted with the greatest courage, skill, and perseverance." Dickens was of course aware of this when he created a character known as the Artful Dodger for his 1838 novel *Oliver Twist*.

Dodgy, the adjective—defined by the *OED* as "full of or addicted to dodges; evasive, tricky, artful"—arrived a little bit after that. The first citation is from 1861 and has a since-discarded spelling: "Beggars divide themselves in several classes:—the humourous, the poetical, the sentimental, the dodgey, and the sneaking." The word came to be applied to inanimate objects that are tricky or dangerous. George Bernard Shaw's *Mrs. Warren's Profession* (1898) has the line, "Take care of your fingers: they're rather dodgy things, those chairs."

An early American use came in 1969. The actor Robert Redford was quoted in *Time* magazine as saying, "When anybody asked me what I wanted to be—whatever that means, anyway—I'd tell them I wanted to be an art director. That seemed to be a pretty dodgy thing to do."

Ngram Viewer shows that the word shot up in popularity in Britain in the 1980s and has never looked back. In 2016, the Associated Press reported, "A lawmaker from Britain's opposition Labour Party was ejected for calling [Prime Minister David Cameron] 'Dodgy Dave' as Parliament questioned him over an offshore company set up by his father."

Dodgy took off in the U.S. in the 2000s, reaching about 25 percent of British use by 2019. That's the last year for which

Ngram Viewer has data, but it would seem the word's ascent has continued since then. It appeared in the *Times* fifty times in 2021 and 2022, starting with Sam Sifton (a NOOB power user) writing that, on account of the pandemic, he missed "cooking in dodgy little weekly rental kitchens." So did we all.

For discussion of a similar word, see *dicey*, chapter 2.

Adoption | Taking hold

"Done and dusted"; "done and done"

In 2015, the astute language observer Jan Freeman tweeted out something the (American) novelist Elinor Lipman had written in a *New York Times* essay. Lipman had broken up with a British man she had been seeing, and, she felt, "I had acquitted myself in relatively menschy fashion. Done and dusted."

That was the first time I'd encountered *done and dusted*, which the *OED* defines as meaning "completely finished or ready." (And by the way, nice adjectival *menschy*.) Its citations are all from British sources, starting with the *British Bee Journal*, which had this line in 1953: "All to be done and dusted before the National Honey Show."

At the time, I labeled the phrase an "outlier," as the only other uses I could find in an American publication were in the *Times* soccer columns of Rob Hughes, a British native. (I was momentarily excited to find a character saying it in a 2001 American-set novel by Lee Child, but then I discovered that Child is English, and his use of the word was an anatopism. For more on anatopisms, see chapter 9.) And even Lipman's use of it wasn't a true NOOB: she replied to Freeman's tweet and revealed that *done and dusted* was a favorite phrase of the erstwhile beau—"'And Bob's your uncle,' he'd add."

But the phrase has gained a bit of purchase in America. Ngram Viewer shows British use shooting up since the 1990s, with a gradual rise in America over the last twenty years. It appears about fifty times in ProQuest's U.S. Major Dailies database between 2000 and 2023. Admittedly, most are quotes from British people, though the first comes from an American golfer who (significantly) had spent time competing in South Africa, South America, and Canada. The database shows American use peaking around 2018 or 2019—which was the time my wife, Gigi, started to use it, for example when she had finished cooking dinner or completed some other task.

But then Gigi started to use a similar-sounding, seemingly tautological phrase in such situations: *done and done.* This initially puzzled me, but when I searched Google News I found lots of examples:

- "I also believe it's a particularly good match for the free-weekend treatment. You get in, you hopefully have a good time, and you get out. Done and done."
  —Destructoid, on a game called *Steep*
- "First, duh, we just replace the iceberg that the *Titanic* crashed into with a giant, ocean-based creature. Bang. Done and done."—Article on *The Ringer* about putting giant animals into classic movies
- "Pink suitcases that could fit everything and still be light—done and done. The opportunity to extend the pastel world is so exciting for us."—Poppy James, of luggage maker Pop+Suki, in *Teen Vogue*

And the *Times* television critic James Poniewozik wrote about Donald Trump's reality-TV-style approach to the issues of the day: "And what does 'ending conflict of interest' look like? A lawyer says the word 'trust' a bunch of times, and there's a big pile of documents. Done and done!"

It turns out that *done and done* is much older than *done and dusted*. Richard Bleiler of the University of Connecticut has discovered a 1712 use, and the website World Wide Words found an appearance in the novel *Castle Rackrent* by Maria Edgeworth, published in 1800:

> "Done," says my master; "I'll lay you a hundred golden guineas to a tester you don't." "Done," says the gauger; and done and done's enough between two gentlemen.

World Wide Words explains that *tester* is "a slang term for sixpence" and *gauger* "an exciseman's assistant who checked the capacity of casks." It goes on to say,

> It seems that the usual convention was that a bet was agreed on the mere word of the two principals if both said "done." They both being gentlemen, or assumed to be such, their word was their bond and there was no question of going back on the agreement once it had been made. Hence "done and done" meant that a binding agreement had been mutually accepted.

The expression seems to have become established, as well as crossed the Atlantic, a half century after Edgeworth's book. From James Fenimore Cooper's *The Crater* (1848): "Done and done between gentlemen, is enough, sir."

But the current use of the expression has a different meaning: "done thoroughly and satisfactorily," as Wiktionary puts it—that is, roughly the same as *done and dusted*. Wiktionary's first citation for it is a short story called "A Natural Notion," by the American writer David Seybold, included in the 1985 book *Seasons of the Hunter: An Anthology*, edited by Seybold and Robert Elman: "Done and done, he said to himself. And he felt pretty good. The anger and hurt that only a few hours before had been sharp and deep had dulled."

My sense is that this second meaning of *done and done* took hold after the turn of the twenty-first century and has really taken off in the last few years, especially in the United States. And my hypothesis is that its popularity sprang from the much newer *done and dusted*!

To sum up: *Done and dusted* is a useful expression, the alliterative double verb giving strong emphasis to the idea of a job completed. But it sounds too, well, *British* for Americans to wholeheartedly take it up. So we Yanks cleverly resurrected a similar-sounding, older phrase and cleverly assigned to it the same meaning as *done and dusted*.

Adoption | *Done and dusted*: Emerging

● ● ● ● ●

Done and done: Taking hold

● ● ● ● ●

"(It's) early days"

The *OED* identifies this expression—which describes an early stage in an event or process, often implying *too* early, or premature—as "chiefly British" and finds a sixteenth-century citation from Sir Thomas More: "She telleth hym then that it is but early dayes, and he shall come tyme ynough." It also shows up in Samuel Richardson's 1740 *Pamela* ("'Tis early Days with Pamela, and she does not yet think of a Husband") and frequently in the late 1700s and early 1800s, usually with the word "yet," meaning "still," at the end.

I should note that Americans have always referred to beginnings as "the early days *of*" something. It's just that they only started saying "*it's* early days" around 1980, as Ngram Viewer confirms. An early *New York Times* use came in 2001, when restaurant critic William Grimes wrote about the staff at a venerable French restaurant after a change in management: "It's early days yet, but I think they realize that Lutèce has turned a corner."

By now, the phrase is common enough to be viewed as a cliché or—as the American tech writer Molly White observed in 2022—an excuse. White wrote that when she points out some of the shortcomings of blockchain currency (which has been around since about 2009), she's often told, "It's early days." However, she continues,

> This raises the question: How long can it possibly be "early days"? How long do we need to wait before someone comes up with an actual application of blockchain technologies that isn't a transparent attempt to retroactively justify a technology that is inefficient in every sense of the word? How much pollution must we justify pumping into our atmosphere while we wait to get out of the "early days" of proof-of-work blockchains? . . . The more you think about it, the more "it's early days!" begins to sound like the desperate protestations of people with too much money sunk into a pyramid scheme, hoping they can bag a few more suckers and get out with their cash before the whole thing comes crashing down.

Possibly creating confusion is the existence of another British expression (which hasn't yet penetrated to the U.S.) with a similar sound and meaning. In the late 1800s, *early door* referred to, in the *OED*'s words, "a door at a theatre which opens for a period of admission ending some time before the performance begins, in order to offer a guaranteed seat or a wider selection of seating, typically for a higher price." In 1901, the *Daily Chronicle* commented, "London playgoers are familiar with the iniquitous 'early-door' system, under which grasping managers trade on the fears of their nervous patrons."

The practice became known as *early doors*, and, according to World Wide Words, G. K Chesterton recorded the phrase as World War I battle cry by Tommies going over the top to attack the enemy. ("If they had only heard those boys in France and Flanders who called out 'Early Doors!' themselves in a theatrical memory, as they went so early in their youth to break down the doors of death.")

By 1979, the term was being used to mean "early on" or "early days"—"frequently," the *OED* notes, "in the context of Association Football" (i.e., soccer). That 1979 quote is from footballer Brian Clough ("Early doors it was vital to me that they like me, too"), but the phrase became strongly linked to commentator Ron Atkinson, a.k.a. Big Ron. In a 1999 interview actor-director Kenneth Branagh took aim at Big Ron:

> He [Branagh] slows down, enunciating the rest of the sentence deliberately and with an infuriated sotto voce contempt: "Which. Sometimes. Drives. Me. Bananas. I think, 'Shut the fuck up.' I mean, you do love him as well, and I was glad that he was there in Barcelona, but sometimes you think, what human vocabulary have you pulled these phrases from? I mean, no footballer has ever uttered them. 'Early doors' or 'He's turboed up there.'"

Adoption | Taking hold

● ● ● ● ●

"Easy peasy"

Of all the entries in the book, *easy peasy* is the one most shrouded in mystery, or at least uncertainty. Start with the fact that most British people's idea of the origin of the phrase—that it came from an advertising slogan for Sqezy [*sic*] dishwashing

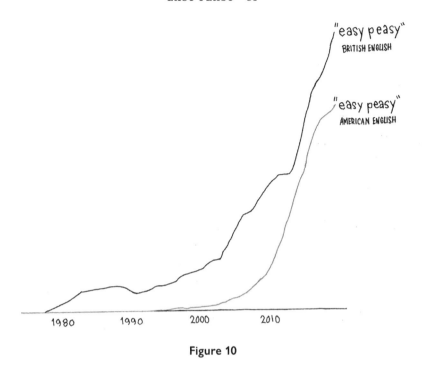

Figure 10

liquid, "Easy Peasy, Lemon Sqezy"—is flat-out wrong. The language historian Barry Popik and Pascal Tréguer, who runs the WordHistories.net blog, have both established that there was never such a slogan. Rather, from 1957 until 1962, the product's tagline was, "It's Easy with Sqezy." Shortly after that, the brand was discontinued. And it wasn't until two decades after that that the first instance of the full phrase was spotted (by Tréguer), in a 1983 article in *The Guardian*: "Chap comes in, sits down, says, 'I want to be a marine biologist.' Easy peezy lemon squeezy."

Another odd thing about the (short version of the) phrase is its nationality. Ngram Viewer confirms it's a NOOB, and that widespread use began in Britain in the late 1970s (figure 10).

Yet two of the three early uses of it cited by the *OED* come from American sources. The first is *very* early and not

American: in a 1923 article about traditional mummers' plays, there is a reference to "the Berkshire Doctor's cure of the 'easy-peasy, palsy, and the gout.'" But then, in the 1940 American film *Long Voyage Home*, the character played by John Wayne says, "Easy-peasy. Take it easy, Drisc!" And a 1953 article in the *Cincinnati Enquirer* noted, "There's a brief air travelogue of highlights of a jet trip from London to Cairo. . . . The flight is such an easy-peasy affair for the air travellers, they seem to be motionless in a fantastic and lovely, sun-drenched cloudland."

My guess would be that in all three cases, the phrase was used not because it was in circulation but because the rhyme came easily to the tongue. The same is true of the other popular variant, "Easy peasy, Japanesey," which Popik has spotted in 1982 (that is, a year earlier than the "Lemon Sqezy/ Squeezy" version). The character played by James Whitmore uses the phrase in the 1994 film *The Shawshank Redemption*, which is set decades earlier and is therefore anachronistic.

Easy peasy was used in the *New York Times* seventy-five times from its first appearance, in 2001, through 2022. That includes a 2012 article about a New York City burglar: "The following morning, he was awakened by police officers in his bedroom. One of them said, 'Easy, peasy, lemon squeezy,' first handcuffing, then dressing" him.

While the phrase is popular in the U.S., it's not common enough to be a target for parody. It is in Britain, where, in Armando Iannucci's 2009 satire *In the Loop*, a U.K. politician says to his American counterpart, "In England we have a saying for a situation such as this, which is that it's difficult difficult lemon difficult."

Adoption | Fully arrived
●●●●●

"Full stop"

The term has two meanings in British English. The first, dating from the seventeenth century, refers to the piece of punctuation Americans call a *period*. The Brits used *period* as well, starting as early as 1582, but seem to have dropped it over the centuries, possibly to emphasize a broader meaning of *period*, which the *OED* describes as "a grammatically complete sentence, *esp.* one made up of a number of clauses formed into a balanced or rhythmical whole." (E.g., "Cicero . . . often postpones to the very last, that Verb or emphatical Word on which the whole Sense of the Period depends."—John Mason, 1749)

Full stop and *period* are both used metaphorically, "indicating," as the *OED* has it, "that the preceding statement is final, absolute, or without qualification: and that is all there is to say about it, that is the sum of it, there is no more to be said." Remarkably, the dictionary's first spottings of both words being used in this way are more or less contemporaneous: *period* showing up in 1914 and *full stop* two years later. ("'But,' argued Petunia, 'I said soldiers' wives are usually nice . . .' 'And I,' said Aunt Jane, 'answered, "yes. Full stop. Mrs. So-and-so is very nice."'"—Mary Wemyss, *Petunia*)

Full stop was the basis of a well-known play on words, pointed out by more than one *NOOBs* reader. It occurred in the book *1066 and All That: A Memorable History of England, Comprising All the Parts You Can Remember, Including 103 Good Things, 5 Bad Kings and 2 Genuine Dates*, a humorous spoof on history that was published in 1930. The last chapter, referring to the aftermath of World War I, reads in its entirety, "America was thus clearly Top Nation, and history came to a." Needless to say, the joke only works if you read the last dot (which is the new, computer-era name for it!) not as "period" but as "full stop."

Americans still do not use punctuational *full stop*, but they do use the phrase as a figure of speech. The first example I've found is from a 1992 *New Yorker* article in which John McPhee quotes the geologist Eldridge Moores: "The Taconic Orogeny is a collision of ophiolitic terrane with the North American continent, full stop." Ten years later, this appeared in *Time* magazine: "Investors haven't lost faith in U.S. stocks. They have lost faith in stocks, full stop." (Pity the investors.)

The utterance achieved cliché status in the mid-2010s. In a 2015 blog post the *Christian Science Monitor* noted examples that occurred over a matter of months:

- "George Washington University political scientist John Sides was asked in May if early polls were relevant to who would take office: 'They are not. Full stop.'"
- "Republican Rick Santorum, queried on Bruce Jenner's decision to become Caitlyn Jenner, responded: 'My job as a human being is to treat everybody with dignity or respect—period, stop, full stop, no qualification to that.'"
- "Iowa pollster J. Ann Selzer discussed Hillary Clinton's supposed political invincibility in the Hawkeye State: 'The reality is, this is a field where nobody has effectively stepped up to challenge Hillary Clinton, full stop.'"

The man who defeated Clinton for the presidential nomination in 2008 was probably the person who really made the expression take off. If you Google "Barack Obama" and "full stop," you get dozens of hits, including this quote from a 2014 press conference where the then-president made what he meant redundantly clear: "Regardless of the circumstances, whatever those circumstances may turn out to be, we still get an American soldier back if he's held in captivity. Period. Full stop."

Adoption | Fully arrived

● ● ● ● ●

"Ginger"

The hair-color sense of the word first appeared on my radar in 2004, when I was in London and read this sentence in the *Daily Telegraph*: "The ginger asthmatic was always going to struggle in Coimbra's oppressive heat." By context clues, I figured out that the reference was to footballer Paul Scholes—and "the ginger asthmatic" still ranks as my favorite all-time example of the class of awkward synonym made famous by H. W. Fowler as "elegant variation." (Coimbra is a city in Portugal.)

Ginger was first used to describe the color of cocks (the fowl) in the 1780s, and of a person's hair, especially men's beards, by 1823. Ginger (the plant) itself isn't red, and the *OED* says that the word initially was used to refer to "reddish-yellow or (light) orange-brown hair." But an 1861 quote reads, "He was called Ginger at school, on account—boys are so rude and severe upon personal peculiarities—on account of his red hair,—for it was red, distinctly red." And the word subsequently became associated with redheads (whose hair isn't truly red, either, of course), as well as the sandy-haired.

Ngram Viewer shows a British uptick in *ginger-haired* in the 1940s (which jibes with the nickname of red-haired drummer Peter "Ginger" Baker, born in 1939) and in the '90s (which jibes with the fame of red-haired Geri Halliwell of the Spice Girls. She was dubbed "Ginger Spice" in 1996).

It's worth noting that somewhere along the way, *ginger* became a term of abuse in the United Kingdom. Wikipedia reports,

> In 2003, a 20-year-old was stabbed in the back for "being ginger." In 2007, a UK woman won an award from a tribunal after being sexually harassed and receiving abuse because of her red hair; in the same year, a family in Newcastle upon

Tyne, was forced to move twice after being targeted for abuse and hate crime on account of their red hair. . . .

In November 2008 social networking website Facebook received criticism after a "Kick a Ginger" group, which aimed to establish a "National Kick a Ginger Day" on 20 November, acquired almost 5,000 members. . . . In December 2009 British supermarket chain Tesco withdrew a Christmas card which had the image of a child with red hair sitting on the lap of Father Christmas, and the words: "Santa loves all kids. Even ginger ones" after customers complained the card was offensive.

For a long time, I thought the Harry Potter books—the first of which was released in the U.S. in 1998—were a factor in American popularity of the word, because of Ron Weasley being referred to as a ginger. But he isn't. Ron is introduced in *Harry Potter and the Sorcerer's Stone* as one of "four boys, all with flaming red hair" and later described as "a redheaded boy." (*Ginger* does appear in the books sparingly, though. According to the Harry Potter Wiki, Ron is called a ginger by "Scabior, Fenrir Greyback, and a drunk man on Tottenham Court Road." And author J. K. Rowling has fun with a Tom Swifty play on words in one of the books, describing Ron as "moving his free hand gingerly up and down his horse's neck." "Gingerly," get it?)

Certainly an influence in America was a 2005 episode of the animated comedy series *South Park* called "Ginger Kids." In it, the character Cartman goes on a tirade against redheads, claiming they have no souls and have a disease called "Gingervitis." In a reversal, he gets turned into a ginger and creates a "Ginger Separatist Movement." Years later, the English ginger singer Ed Sheeran said that the episode legitimized redhead-mocking in the U.S.: "Having red hair in England was always a thing that people took the piss out of you for. But it was never something in America. People never knew what a ginger was in America. That episode of *South Park* fucking ruined my life."

In any case, *ginger* had become common enough in America for the *New York Times* to print this as the opening line of an obituary in 2007: "Marc Torsilieri, who looked like a ginger-bearded lumberjack and played the part in splendid fashion by annually felling the Christmas tree for Rockefeller Center, died on March 12 in Somerville, N.J." Sometime later, Philadelphia Eagles quarterback Carson Wentz became known as "Ginger Jesus" (before he was traded in disgrace).

By 2012, there was already a backlash, as Ken Jennings, the all-time champion *Jeopardy!* contestant, tweeted, "What is going on where we are suddenly calling redheads 'gingers'? People, we won the Revolutionary War, we don't have to put up with this."

Adoption | Taking hold

"Gobsmacked"

The *OED* defines the adjective *gobsmacked* as "flabbergasted, astounded; speechless or incoherent with amazement." The etymology is *gob* = mouth and *smack* = smack—that is, something so surprising that you strike yourself in the mouth when you hear it. The word comes from Yorkshire. The *OED* has a citation from 1935, but in 1980, politician Roy Hattersley, a native of Sheffield, wrote this sentence, which suggests it still hadn't achieved wide currency: "It was his dazzling display of simultaneous social and intellectual sophistication that left me, in the patois of the place whence I came, 'gob-smacked.'"

Neatly, Ngram Viewer shows sharply increasing popularity in Britain starting precisely in 1980—and then the familiar pattern of appearing in the U.S. about twenty years later and ascending sharply here as well. The *New York Times* used the term forty-six times in 2021 and 2022, including in a review of a play about Henry James and Edith Wharton where they are depicted "as giggling, snarking, gobsmacked adolescents."

I learned of a related word via an email from my friend Andrew Feinberg:

> I just came upon the following in a new book called *The Escape Artists: How Obama's Team Fumbled the Recovery*, by Noam Scheiber. On page 41 Scheiber writes: "Simply put, [Lawrence] Summers believed that a $1.2 trillion proposal, to say nothing of $1.8 trillion, would be dead on arrival in Congress because of the political resistance to such gob-stopping sums."
>
> Have you ever come across *gob-stopping*?

Well, no—and neither, I discovered, had the *OED*. It does, however, have an entry for *gobstopper*, to wit: "a large, hard, freq. spherical sweet for sucking." Fans of Roald Dahl may recall the "Everlasting Gobstopper" featured in *Charlie and the Chocolate Factory* and the subsequent film *Willie Wonka and the Chocolate Factory.*

Is Scheiber alone in making a sweet into an adjective having nothing to do with sweets? Well, no again. The word has been used a total of three times by *The Times* (of London), most recently in this restaurant review by A. A. Gill in October 2011: "If you ask me, and I suppose you are, to recommend just one gobstopping, heart-racing dinner in all of London, it would be Hedone."

Moving to the *New York Times*, it appears exactly twice, first in a 2007 quote from the blogger Sara Robinson: "Reading [Steven] Gilley on NYC was like reading Molly Ivins on Texas. You could only sit back, mute, at the gobstopping wonder of it all."

Gobstopping and phrases like *a gobstopper of a* show up occasionally in various internet outposts, generally meaning something along the lines of "astounding" or "amazing." (If you have tender sensibilities, I suggest you do not read the entries at Urban Dictionary, which are very different.)

My best guess is that *gobstopping* happened because *gobsmacked* doesn't easily convert to an adjective meaning "that which causes one to be or feel gobsmacked." But behold, *gobstopper* already existed, as did the suffix *-stopping*, in such words as *heart-stopping* and *show-stopping*. Hence, *gobstopping*.

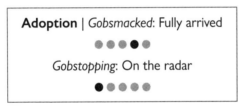

"Go missing"

This verb phrase, which means "to disappear or to vanish" and can refer to an object or a person, is my go-to example when I explain the concept of NOOBs. I take the *OED*'s first citation, from the *New York Herald* in 1845, to be an outlier. The next one is from a Sydney newspaper in 1896 ("There is no other oversea trade . . . where such a large proportion of ships have gone missing"), and all subsequent ones are from British sources. Ngram Viewer shows that "went missing"—the more common past tense—started to get much more common there in the 1980s, and even more so in the 2000s, with America lagging about twenty years behind (figure 11).

In her blog *Separated by a Common Language*, linguist Lynne Murphy cites a researcher who called the phrase a "pet hate" of the BBC and who reported on the way it was dealt

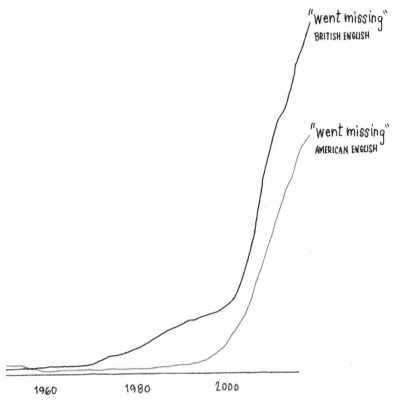

"went missing"
BRITISH ENGLISH

"went missing"
AMERICAN ENGLISH

1960   1980   2000

Figure 11

with in successive style guides issued by the organization. It's four classic stages: unawareness, passive aggression, active aggression, and acceptance (with admirable humor):

Prior to 1992: no mention.

1992: "'Gone missing' was originally Army slang. It now has wider use, and has become journalese."

2000: "People do not 'go missing.' They are missing or have been missing since."

2003: "Go missing is inelegant and unpopular with many people, but its use is widespread. There are no easy synonyms. Disappear and vanish do not convince and they suggest dematerialisation, which is rare."

The introduction to this book sets out my hypothesis that American embrace of the term was related to a news event that took place in 2001. The Ngram Viewer graphs certainly suggests that it got popular right about then. Whether or not my theory is true, it's undeniable that *go missing* has taken such a hold here that when I start my go-to explanation, at least half the people I give it to—and a big majority of those under forty—don't believe that the phrase hasn't always been as American as apple pie.

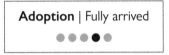

Adoption | Fully arrived

"Gutted"; "gutting"

In 2009, Lynne Murphy published on her blog an email she had gotten from a reader:

> Last year I took to reading the online version of a newspaper in Scotland; I can't remember which one now but I was in the midst of a fascination with the Orkneys so it was probably in that vicinity. In the headline about a break-in and theft at a home, the newspaper said the residents were "gutted." Well! That seemed quite callous to me, to put a word that harsh in the headline. I assumed, you see, that the residents had been killed and eviscerated. So I wrote a note to the editor saying I thought it was pretty bad form.
>
> Imagine my surprise to receive an email from a reader of the newspaper letting me know that the newspaper editor had published my email with a laughing note about the differences in American vs British English! Because, as you know, *gutted* in British English means some variation of "highly distressed."

Indeed. The *OED* reports this sense of the word originated as prison slang and defines it as "bitterly disappointed; devastated, shattered; utterly fed up." Interestingly, the first two citations in *Green's Dictionary of Slang* are from American sources, including this from the poet Charles Bukowski in 1974: "There are very few people I can bear to stay in a room with for more than 5 minutes without feeling gutted." But I'd say that Bukowski and the other American user were (independently) coming up with a metaphor for an emptied-out feeling, not using a term that was in currency at the time. In any case, Ngram Viewer shows this sense of the word shooting up in Britain in the 1990s, with American use following, well behind.

In Britain, the word early on became a sporting cliché. The *OED* cites a line from the magazine *Arena* in 1988: "Think of the sportsman's comment on defeat, 'I feel gutted, Brian [Moore], well gutted.'"

A related adjective, not listed in the *OED* or *Green's*, is *gutting*, defined in a 2007 Urban Dictionary post as "a word used to describe a negative emotional state or experience: 'My partner of two years just broke up with me, gutting mate, absolutely gutting.'" The *mate* suggests British origin, and it's also (over)used in sporting contexts over there, as in a quote from the Liverpool Women's football manager in 2022: "To lose 2–1 at Manchester City was gutting really, because I think we deserved a point at least, and I was gutted for the girls as well."

My unscientific feeling is that American *gutted* shot up on November 9, 2016, because that was how many people felt following the presidential election. To pick just one example, on that day, the writer Ben Greenman tweeted, "I know many people in the press feel gutted, but we need a clear-eyed, unintimidated press more than ever."

The word became popular enough over the next four years that it had, ironically, come full circle. Maggie Haberman of the *New York Times* tweeted in January 2021,

> A lot has happened in the last week, including [soon to be ex-president Trump] losing his Twitter feed, impeachment coming to the fore and the PGA [the Professional Golf Association] withdrawing from Trump National [golf course]. He's "gutted" by the PGA move, a person close to the White House says.

Adoption | Taking hold

"Keen on/to"

The adjective *keen* has a long pedigree, dating back to Old English, where it had two separate strands of meanings: one referring to positive human qualities, including strength and wisdom, and the other referring to sharpness, originally literally, as in knives, and then figuratively for people. Eventually it acquired the sense of eagerness or interest ("When he first begins the new work he is seldom very keen and hearty."—Adam Smith), and by 1771 the modern idiom *keen to* emerged, as in this quote reported by the *OED*: "Still keen to listen and to pry."

Meanwhile, *keen on*, followed by a noun or gerund, and meaning "strongly interested in," including romantically, appears about a century later and is found in this line in a 1936 Rosamond Lehmann novel: "She's attractive, intelligent, amusing—and obviously pretty keen on me, my dear."

I think I first became aware of the expression when I saw the 2002 film *About a Boy*. The Hugh Grant character, Will, is developing feelings for a woman, as Will's young mate, Marcus, explains to the woman's son, Ali:

MARCUS: Oh, don't worry, I think your mum is keen
  on him.
ALI: [*Shouting*] She's not keen on *him*! She's only keen
  on *me*.

(The screenplay was written by Americans Chris Weitz, Paul Weitz, and Peter Hedges, but this exchange is taken quite closely from the original Nick Hornby novel.)

One of the reasons the exchange works so well, I reckon, is that *keen on* already had a somewhat old-fashioned feel in Britain at the time. Ngram Viewer shows it having been overtaken in about 1960 by *keen to*, which grew significantly in popularity in the succeeding decades.

Ngram Viewer also shows American use of both picking up in the 2000s. An early use was in *Time* magazine in 2001: "Scientists are keen to explore cloning as a potential source of embryonic stem cells, which could be used to treat diseases such as Alzheimer's or Parkinson's." Ten years later, the "on" expression was familiar enough for the *New York Times* to print the punning headline "If You're Keen on Quinoa."

The headline had the additional virtue of reminding people like me just how the grain is supposed to be pronounced ("keen-wah").

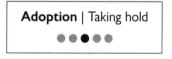

Adoption | Taking hold

"Kerfuffle"

The word, meaning "disorder, flurry, agitation," started as a Scottish word, *cafuffle* or *curfuffle*, which arose as early as 1813. Three years later, this line appeared in Sir Walter Scott's novel *The Antiquary*: "Troth, and my lord maun be turned feel outright, an he puts himsel into sic a curfuffle for ony thing ye could bring him, Edie." The *OED* cites a 1953 line from a London magazine: "The word cafuffle is still in general use in her part of Scotland . . . as a noun meaning a state of confusion."

But by that time, the *k* spelling had already taken root. The *OED* quotes a 1946 book by the New Zealand novelist Frank Sargeson: "I bet it ended up in a good old kafuffle." Google Books turns up a use a year earlier from Dermot McKay's translation of *Both Are My Cousins*, by Ronald Fangen, a Norwegian novelist. It's a line of dialogue followed by an intriguing parenthetical comment: "'I'm in a bit of a kerfuffle.' (There was the word!)"

British use of *kerfuffle* rose gradually from the 1950s till about 2000. As you can see in the Ngram Viewer graph in the "Terminology, Abbreviations, and Resources" chapter, the word then took off like a rocket in both the U.K. and the U.S.

The *New York Times* offers a helpful gauge of U.S. use. The word showed up in the paper a handful of times in the late 1980s and early '90s in British contexts, and in a wholly American one for the first time in 1995, when columnist Maureen Dowd wrote that a tasteless monologue at a presidential event threw "the capital into a kerfuffle." Then it appeared seven additional times in the '90s, including two more by the much-read Dowd, who clearly fancied the word and helped to popularize it.

And popular it is. *Kerfuffle* was used twenty-four times in the *Times* in 2021 and twenty-seven times in 2022, which suggests that it not only deserves its "fully arrived" designation but probably deserves a rest.

Adoption | Fully arrived

"Lose the plot"

A couple of years ago, when a friend wrote in a Facebook post that a certain political figure had "lost the plot," my NOOB-dar came on. I wasn't familiar with the phrase, but it had the definite feel of a Britishism, and sure enough, it is.

The *OED* defines *lose the plot* as "to lose one's ability to understand or cope with events; to lose one's touch; to go off the rails." There is a dubious seventeenth-century citation, with the next not coming till a 1984 quote from *The Times* about a fashion show: "Arabella Pollen showed sharp linens, lost the plot in a sarong skirt and brought out curvaceous racing silk and a show-stopping bow-legged Willie Carson."

That's interesting because the first few uses of the phrase in the Google Books database, from the early 1990s, all emanate from Australia, and a 1994 article in the *American Scholar* refers to it as "a piece of Australian slang." In addition, several Australian *NOOBs* readers reported having heard the phrase there before 1984—but in the absence of documentary evidence, the case is still open.

In Nick Hornby's 1995 novel *High Fidelity*, the narrator says, "I lost the plot for a while then. I lost the subplot, the script, the soundtrack, the intermission, my popcorn, the credits, and the exit sign." And that was about the time the phrase really started establishing itself in Britain, as Ngram Viewer shows (figure 12).

The first American use I'm aware of, contributed by a *NOOBs* reader, is from a 1995 song by a Rhode Island band called Belly: "Now I've lost the plot / I'm not the hero I could be / But not the dog I was." The following year, conservation activist Ike Sugg testified before Congress that the Humane Society of the United States had "completely lost the plot." The phrase first shows up in the *New York Times* in 1998, in another fashion article: "From the parade of Mao worker jackets with frog closures and

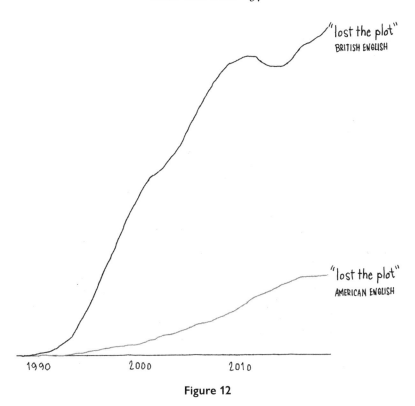

"lost the plot"
BRITISH ENGLISH

"lost the plot"
AMERICAN ENGLISH

1990   2000   2010

Figure 12

cheongsam dresses at Ferragamo to the indiscriminate layering of tulle and other sheer fabrics over trousers and skirts at Anna Molinari, many designers in Milan had a story's worth of ideas, but they had lost the plot."

LexisNexis reports nearly 1,800 uses in American news sources between 2000 and 2022, one of the most recent by Showbiz Cheat Sheet music writer Matt Trzcinski: "During her early career, Taylor Swift tried to seem wise beyond her years. Now, Swift says she lost the plot, paradoxically making her sound more mature than she ever has."

Adoption | Taking hold
● ● ● ● ●

"Mum"

British *mum* is the equivalent of American *mom* and has been around, according to the *OED*, since at least the seventeenth century. The dictionary intriguingly notes that in Britain the term has sometimes been used "to denote a particular type of working-class mother, who retains a dominating influence on the lives of her children, even when they are adults." The dictionary cites a line from a 1957 sociology book: "Where Mum plays so large a part in the lives of her descendants, she should be honoured for what she does." (Incidentally, the expression *mum's the word*, meaning "keep your mouth shut," has an unrelated etymology and has been roughly equally common in Britain and the U.S. for centuries.)

A bit later came *mummy*, which is similar to American *mommy*. The *OED* tactfully notes, "Use by adults is sometimes indicative of a particular social or regional background." I take that to mean upper class, based on my observation that in the Netflix series *The Crown*, all of Queen Elizabeth's children address her that way. The word had crossed the Atlantic by 1945, when H. L. Mencken bemoaned, "Fashionable American mothers teach their children to call them *Mummy*," a term that he described as the "most hideous and irrational of Briticisms."

My sense is that this custom died down, except for in New England, where, according to *The Dictionary of American Regional English*, both *mum* and *mummy* were still found as recently as the early 1990s. A reader commented on *NOOBs*,

> I grew up and lived on the south shore of Boston . . . and I've always said *mum* and *mummy*. All of my friends said it, too. Never did I think of it as a Britishism 'till later, but even then I've felt it was a New England thing that stuck

around along with a few other terms like *rubbish* instead of *garbage.*

Until recently, American *mum* could only intermittently be spotted outside New England. In a 1999 *New York Times* review of Liza Minnelli's one-woman show, Vincent Canby noted, "Some of the patter is awkward, but she is great about both her mum and dad." In 2011, the *Monsters and Critics* blog reported, "Actress Barbra Streisand is set to play Seth Rogen's mum in new movie *My Mother's Curse*." (The film was eventually titled *Guilt Trip.*)

There has recently been a flurry of homegrown uses. Deadline Hollywood wrote that actor Pete Davidson was to star in a series called *Bupkis*, "alongside Edie Falco as his mum." A reader wrote to the *Boston Globe's* advice columnist about a boyfriend who "told me he wanted to get married to me, so I told my family. He told me he'd have his mum call to have the initial discussions with my mum, but that didn't happen."

And a *House of the Dragon* recap on CNET reported, "We see Aegon Targaryen masturbating outside of his chamber windows—the thrills of royalty—but he's interrupted by his mum."

I hate it when that happens.

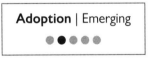

Adoption | Emerging

"Non-starter"

This term for a person or idea with no chance of proceeding, much less succeeding, originated no later than 1839 (the *OED* reports) to describe a horse that hasn't or isn't running in a particular race. The metaphorical use developed (again, according to the dictionary) by 1911. The dictionary's first example of it being used to refer to something other than a human or animal is from 1942: "That's one reason why non-intervention is such a non-starter." But, using Google Books, I found a 1923 play called *Advertising April* in which a character says, "The divorce is a non-starter."

According to Rob Kyff's book *Mark My Words*,

> The popularity of the term in Britain grew gradually during the 1950s and then got a jump-start during the 1960s from *University Challenge*, a TV quiz show in which teams from British colleges competed. The show's original emcee, the delightfully named Bamber Gascoigne, began each round by announcing, "Starter, for 10 [points]," and would occasionally describe a subsequent question as a non-starter.

The term arrived in America in 1960 or so, according to Google Books, and since then has gradually gotten more common. Its first appearance in the *New York Times* came in a 1974 record review: "How such a non-starter got on RCA's Red Seal label is best left to the imagination." In the 1980s and '90s it was widely used by American politicos and journos attempting to put down their opponents' ideas. Since then it has appeared in the paper more than three hundred times, almost all of them as metaphor. One of the more recent was from a writer who had suffered a traumatic brain injury and discovered that "running was, literally, a non-starter."

Adoption | Fully arrived

●●●●●

"No worries"

Another expression that started Down Under. It's adaptable: like the comparable American *no problem*, it can be a response

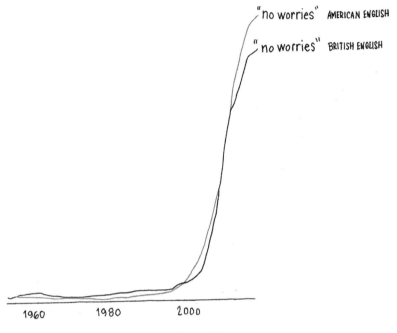

"no worries" AMERICAN ENGLISH

"no worries" BRITISH ENGLISH

1960   1980   2000

Figure 13

to an expression of thanks or apology, or merely an hakuna-matata-esque expression that all is copacetic. The *OED*'s first citations are from the mid-1960s, and it quickly took off in Oz. By the late 1970s, *no worries* (a *mate* is often added) was called Australia's national motto. Eventually it spawned a bawdy Spoonerism, "No wucking furries."

Ngram Viewer suggests it gained popularity at roughly the same time in Britain and the United States, presumably spurred by the popularity of the 1986 film *Crocodile Dundee* (where it's uttered six times) and the Australian TV series *Neighbours* and *The Crocodile Hunter* (figure 13).

It's gotten so popular—in the U.S. at least—that it's spawned a backlash. In 2022, Lake Superior State University put *no worries*—along with *asking for a friend, circle back, wait, what?* and *at the end of the day* (see the entry in this chapter)—on its annual tongue-in-cheek list of banished words.

> **Adoption** | Fully arrived
> ● ● ● ● ●

"One-off"

I have a soft spot for this one—a noun meaning "a one-of-a-kind happening," or an adjective meaning "one-of-a-kind"—as I used it in the title of my blog. The adjective came first, as a manufacturing term meaning "unique" or "not to be repeated," the first *OED* cite being from 1934: "A splendid one-off pattern can be swept up in very little time." The noun followed in 1947, and the *OED*'s first figurative use (with telltale quotation marks) from the *Architectural Review* in 1952: "Hills built the first part of Cheshunt as a 'one off' job, with no guarantees of further business, though of course it was intended to be the first of a line."

Ngram Viewer shows the increasing popularity of the term from the 1950s on (figure 14).

Given the increasing U.S. use in the 1990s and 2000s, it makes sense that *New York Times* language columnist William Safire would have addressed the term in 2007. He offered contemporaneous examples:

> In the splendiferous arts pages of *The New York Sun*, the critic James Gardner hailed a blue landscape depicting a Greek town by Gregory Kondos as "a seemingly effortless one-off act of visual tact."
>
> "When an obscure Russian company comes to town for a one-off performance of a classical ballet," wrote Gia Kourlas of *The Times*, "you never know what to expect."

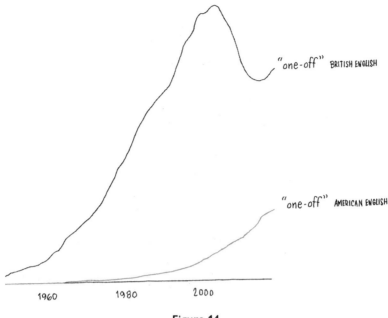

Figure 14

But it was still unfamiliar enough that Safire had to supply a definition. That's not the case anymore, as American *one-off* has become pretty much the opposite of a one-off.

Adoption | Taking hold

"On holiday"

I was talking to an employee of my local health club, a normal-looking bearded guy in his thirties, and I mentioned I was going to be away from home for a few weeks.

"Are you going on holiday?" he asked.

In the pre-NOOBs age, he would have said "on vacation."

On holiday—meaning willingly spending a period of time away from work or school, often in a remote location, usually with relaxation or enjoyment in mind—arose as an expression in the nineteenth century, as in this 1858 quote from the *Stirling Observer*: "This unfortunate man, who was . . . away on holiday at the time, lived for a very short time." *On vacation* started in North America at around the same time, and it became the accepted term here.

Fast-forward a century or so and American *on holiday* began to make its move, Ngram Viewer showing it roughly tripling in use between 2000 and 2019 (though still remaining less than half as common as *on vacation*).

Some American examples, in chronological order:

- "Often it seems that the whole world is on holiday as you drive in heavy traffic."—*Cherokee County Herald*, 1998
- "Apparently Art Conn has been on holiday while the rest of the cast, Jeff Wellington and Susan DeJesus, were rehearsing."—*Leaf Chronicle* (Clarksville, MS), 2011
- "When his parents go on holiday, one of said friends convinces him to take a 'what the [expletive]' approach to life and hire a sex worker for the night."—*New York Times* capsule summary of the film *Risky Business*, 2020

Adoption | Taking hold

"On offer"

The phrase means "available for sale" or, more generally, "available." The first *OED* citation is from the (London) *Daily News* in 1881: "Old wheat scarce and dear. Very little barley on offer." But using Google Books, I came up with an example more than fifty years older, from a September 1826 issue of *Cobbett's Political Register*: "There are few Beans on offer, which are eagerly bought up."

The phrase didn't cross the Atlantic for another century or more, Ngram Viewer showing U.S. use starting a slow ascent in the 1980s. A relatively early use came in the *New York Times* in 1990: "Tens of thousands of Apple Macintosh users visited the Macworld trade exposition here earlier this month, examining the hardware and software on offer." It arrived in the *New Yorker* through British writers—Kenneth Tynan in 1977 and Salman Rushdie in 1992—and was first used there by an American one, Hendrik Hertzberg (using the magazine's famous editorial "we"), in 1994: "We know, for example, that there are people who picked up their first copy of *The New Yorker* on account of a story or a 'casual'—on account of something by O'Hara or Cheever or Salinger or Perelman or Munro or Updike—and only later, and gradually, became aware that other kinds of writing were on offer in these pages too."

But it's all over the place now. The ProQuest Recent Papers database shows 299 uses in 2022, one of the more recent being Joe Queenan rhetorically asking in the *Wall Street Journal*, "Why is Pizza Hut's Detroit Style Pizza only on offer a few weeks a year?"

As sometimes happens, just as American use was taking hold, the meaning of the expression was changing—or at least expanding—in Britain. A reader commented on my *on offer* blog post, "In the U.K. I've only heard this to mean something is marked down in price." That derives from the British sense of an "offer" being what Americans call a "sale": a promoted price reduction. So *on offer* equates to *on sale*—and this sense has definitely not yet arrived on these shores.

Adoption | Taking hold
● ● ● ● ●

"On the day"

Not long after I started spending time in London, I began to pick up on the frequent use of this phrase. I know quite well that Americans use those words, in that order, but not quite in the same context as in the U.K. I searched the phrase on Google News, and the first page of hits all came from British or Commonwealth sources. Here they are:

- "These games are often fifty-fifty at best and even the well credentialled teams are vulnerable to a bit of bad luck on the day."—Australian sports site The Roar
- "Amongst the star performers on the day were young centre duo Jack Roberts and George Catchpole." —*Bourne (England) Local*
- "Umpiring is a real team environment, just as playing is. We prepare to perform well, and all that matters is making sure you get it right on the day."—The Roar, again
- "'Potentially, it's a very useful tool but it's complementary to the main pollsters. It would be feasible to do it on the day [of an election],' he said."—*The Guardian*

That last one is interesting, because the bracketed insertion represents (to my mind) precisely the American version. That is, we are more explicit, saying "on the day of [fill in the event]," or "when the day finally arrived," or "on the day itself." I imagine *The Guardian* added "of an election" either as a gesture to its increasing number of American online readers or because an American happened to edit the story.

When I blogged about the expression, one reader recalled that in the film *Shaun of the Dead*, Nick Frost's character refuses to practice walking like a zombie and says he'll do it "on the day." And another reader, Paul Dormer, commented, "In theatre, the phrase 'It'll be alright on the night' means, 'We'll iron out our mistakes.'" Paul also noted that *It'll Be Alright on the Night* is the name of a bloopers show that has been running on British television since 1977.

The first example I could find of an American using the phrase was in 2015, when Vickie Barker, in an NPR report on a London Muslim center, said, "But on the day, the center was packed with visitors sipping tea, nibbling pizza and cake, and eagerly listening to community members like Zahra Khimji describe a typical week there." I subsequently learned that, at the time of the report, Ms. Barker had lived in London for more than twenty years.

Two years later, Bruce Arians—then the coach of the U.S. national soccer/football team—was quoted as saying (after an important loss), "This game in my view was perfectly positioned for the US team and we failed on the day." And three years after that, Jim Curtin, the manager of the Philadelphia Union, referring to the team's close defeat in an important game, said, "Our players played with an intensity that I think made the fans proud on the night."

Time will tell if the expression will ever expand in the U.S. beyond soccer coaches.

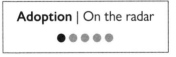

Adoption | On the radar

"Over the top"

This phrase is so common in the U.S. that off the top of my head, I would not have pegged it as a NOOB. But it is. The *OED* labels it "chiefly British" and defines it as "to an excessive or exaggerated degree; beyond reasonable or acceptable limits; too far."

The *OED* also notes another, earlier meaning of *over the top*, stemming from World War I trench warfare: to literally climb over the top of a trench or parapet and go into battle. This took off in America, generating (as listed in the Library of Congress) no fewer than six popular songs called "Over the Top," plus one jauntily titled "'Over the Top' Goes Sammy."

The phrase seems to have taken on a positive figurative meaning, akin to *going all out*, as seen in this item from a 1918 issue of *The Rotarian*:

> The New Philadelphia (Ohio) Rotary Club went completely over the top when it entertained the City Administration at dinner. President Walter G. Nickels presided and the guests were given some idea of the wholesome pep which is a part of every true Rotarian. The cooperative spirit was very apparent and before the evening was over each guest was filled with enthusiasm and had something encouraging to say for Rotary.

The *OED*'s first citation for the phrase with the "excessive" meaning is in a 1935 letter by the American writer Lincoln Steffens: "I had come to regard the New Capitalism as an experiment till, in 1929, the whole thing went over the top and slid down to an utter collapse." But I take that as an outlier—a fresh metaphor on Steffens's part, not his use of a phrase that was in currency. The first definite example I'm aware of comes from a 1965 novel called *The Concrete Kimono* (cited in *Green's Dictionary of Slang*): "I seem to recall your 'over the top' waistcoats." The quotation marks suggest unfamiliarity and recency.

By 1982, the phrase was popular enough in Britain to spawn an acronym. From *The Sloane Ranger Handbook*: "OTT *adj.* Over the top—outrageous. Usually 'absolutely' or 'totally OTT.'"

Ngram Viewer suggests the phrase rose slowly but surely in the U.S. starting in the 1990s and reached roughly half of British use by 2019. Its popularity has certainly continued since then. ProQuest Recent Newspapers shows the phrases *an over the top, is over the top, was over the top,* and *an over-the-top* being used sixty-nine times in 2022, including "Republicans can think [Representative Liz] Cheney is over the top in her focus on January 6" (*Wall Street Journal*) and "Van Gogh was an over-the-top art fan" (*Washington Post*). Who knew?

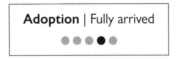

Adoption | Fully arrived

"A proper"

Proper in this sense does not connote "characterized by propriety" (as in *proper behavior*) but rather fits some subsidiary *OED* definitions of *proper*: "senses denoting the accurate or strict use of the word or concept qualified, or the fulfilment of criteria understood or implied by it." Historically, *proper* indicated an excellent example of the thing but more recently has been used to mean "authentic or genuine" (as in Ann Thwaite's 1984 biography of Edmund Gosse: "He had worked with magnifying slides but he had never had a proper microscope"), or "thorough or complete" (as in *Routledge's Every Boy's Annual,* 1871: "There will be a proper blow-up about this").

A 1926 music-hall song called "What I Want Is a Proper Cup o' Coffee" has this tongue-twisting stanza in its chorus:

What I want is a proper cup o' coffee,
Made in a proper copper coffee pot.

I may be off my dot,
But I want a cup o' coffee from a proper copper pot.

A blog reader commented, "'Proper job' is an expression used frequently in Cornwall, to the point of sounding self-consciously Cornish. A lavish meal might be described as a 'proper job.' The St. Austell brewery in Cornwall makes a beer called Proper Job, and the last time I tried it, it was."

Nearly all of the *OED* citations are British, and I can't help thinking there is indeed something very British about thinking about or referring to this quality. Americans don't generally care about whether a particular thing satisfies all the attributes of its category, only whether it does what it's supposed to or is a good buy.

Or, rather, they didn't used to care; over the past couple of decades, that seems to have changed. An early U.S. example came from Marian Burros in the *New York Times* in 2002: "Our distant ancestors probably did not have a proper breakfast when they woke up in their caves, so they gorged whenever they made a kill." Nine years later, *TV Guide* wrote, "Now that Anderson Cooper has come out of the closet about his admiration for Nicole 'Snooki' Polizzi, it's only fitting that they go out on a proper date."

By this point, *a proper* is a proper Americanism. Searching the *Times* database, I found approximately one example a day, including, most recently,

- "There are no particularly moving insights, and it falls short of a proper character study."—Movie review
- "Biking between trail towns has its appeal, but there's something to be said for a trail that feels like a proper wilderness ride."

- "For the first 25 seconds of his 2005 audition reel for 'The Next Food Network Star,' Mr. Fieri presented himself as a proper snob."

Adoption | Taking hold

"Queue"

A queue, meaning a line of people waiting for something, originated as a not one-off Frenchism. The original French meaning of the word was "tail," and it was adapted by the English in the eighteenth century to mean "a long plait of hair"—that is, a pigtail. The French initiated the "line of people" meaning in the 1790s, and the first uses noted by the *OED* either italicized it as a foreign word or used it in a Gallic context, as in this quote from Thomas Carlyle's *The French Revolution* (1837): "That talent . . . of spontaneously standing in queue, distinguishes . . . the French People."

It's an interesting quote because, of course, we now think of the *British* as having a talent for standing spontaneously in queue—seen recently and dramatically in "the Queue" of September 2022, in which people waited for up to twenty-four hours in order to pass by the body of Queen Elizabeth. A blog reader commented, "The only place where people do not queue, in Britain, is the pub. My dad reckoned that was because beer was never rationed during the war." And another reader recalled,

This piece of drivel went round my school playground and ended up in my head: "A lady went to the toilet but saw loads of people standing outside. She said, 'I C A Q A Q I C

I 8 2 Q B 4 I P.'" ("I see a queue, a queue I see. I 'ate [hate] to queue before I pee.")

In the last half of the nineteenth century, *queue*-as-line was used in both Britain and the United States. An example of the latter came from New York representative James Brooks, speaking in Congress in 1864: "Last Monday week I saw a long queue ranged around the New York custom-house waiting turns to buy gold certificates at 65, while gold was selling at 75." And it's worth noting that *line* was used in Britain, as in this 1711 quote from Joseph Addison: "The Officers planting themselves in a Line on the left Hand of each Column."

But in the twentieth century, the British took *queue* up in earnest (figure 15).

And soon a verb form arrived: *queue up* by 1920, and the *up*-less form, *to queue*, some thirty years later.

As the graph shows, American use started ticking up in the 1960s. In January 1960, William Zinsser wrote in the *New York Times* about the 1939–1940 New York World's Fair, "Only on very rainy days was the queue [for the Futurama exhibit] a short one, but few tourists begrudged the hour they spent waiting." *Queue* appeared in the *Times* 5,443 times between then and 2022, including in a clever 2005 headline about a very popular exhibit at the Museum of Modern Art: "The Shock of the Queue."

Some of the increase in use on both sides of the Atlantic has to do with the use of *queue* in computer terminology and, more recently, inspired by Netflix, as a term for a sequence of movies or songs one plans to get to. ("What's in your queue?") Even more recently, some people have referred to a DJ "queueing up a record," instead of the traditional term, *cueing it up.*

Getting back to waiting in a queue, you can understand the word's popularity in America, given the ambiguity-inducing

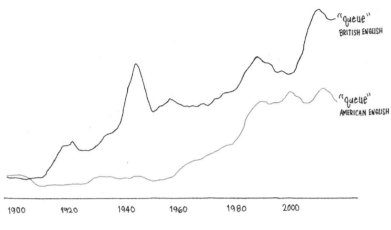

Figure 15

multiple meanings of *line, line up,* and *in line.* (New Yorkers' term for the last is *on line.*) The only downside of *queue*
is that it's hard to spell. The gerund form actually has two
orthographic versions, *queuing* and *queueing* (one of the few
English words containing five consecutive vowels), the former
overtaking the latter in popularity in Britain in around 1990.
In any case, I knew a milestone had been passed about ten
years ago when I was at my local grocery store and noticed
that a sign indicating the "line" for checkout had been replaced
by one indicating the "queue."

Another milestone came in 2016, when President Barack
Obama spoke against the U.K. leaving the European Union.
That would portend badly for any U.S.-U.K. trade deals, he
said: "I think it's fair to say maybe some point down the line,
but it's not going to happen any time soon because our focus
is on negotiating with the E.U. The U.K. is going to be at the
back of the queue."

Leaving aside the policy aspect, British commentators
jumped on the president's use of *queue,* some suggesting he
had been "fed" it by Prime Minister David Cameron. However,

writing in the *Washington Post*, Adam Taylor pointed out that Obama had uttered *queue* numerous times in the past, and was kind enough to cite *NOOBs* on the president's use of the terms *full stop* (see the entry in this chapter), *run to ground*, and *take a decision*.

Adoption | Taking hold

● ● ● ● ●

"Reckon"

In the mid-twentieth century, the American linguist Albert Marckwardt coined the term *colonial lag*, referring to the idea that in America—or at least pockets of America—some old words and pronunciations have been preserved more robustly than in Britain. Subsequent research and analysis are pretty much agreed that the idea doesn't hold true on a broad basis, but there are definitely some instances in which it seems to. For example, the verb form *gotten* instead of *got* (see chapter 9) and the words *faucet* and *closet*; the expression *I guess* (used by Geoffrey Chaucer!) meaning "I suppose" fell out of favor in Britain but kept on keeping on in the U.S.

A somewhat more complicated example is a synonym for *guess*, *reckon*. In America, until recently, the word was a Southern and western regionalism. It brings to my mind the TV comedy *The Beverly Hillbillies*, and in fact it was used five times in the 1962 premiere episode, including in this exchange:

> JED: Granny! Them pigs o' yours got into the corn.
> GRANNY: Did they drink much?
> JED: I reckon they did. This here little fella was kickin'
> blue blazes out of the mule.

Reckon conforms with the colonial lag idea. It dates to the sixteenth century, according to the *OED*, and two centuries later was used by Jonathan Swift ("I reckon the Queen will go to Windsor in 3 or 4 weeks") and Samuel Richardson ("I shall have a good deal of trouble, I reckon, . . . to be decent on the expected occasion"). But shortly afterward, it somehow fell out of circulation in Britain.

But not America. In *The American Language*, H. L. Mencken quotes a Scottish observer, Colonel Thomas Hamilton, who wrote in 1833 that Americans "assume unlimited liberty in the use of *expect, reckon, guess* and *calculate*, and perpetuate other conversational anomalies with remorseless impunity." John Russell Bartlett, in his 1848 *Dictionary of Americanisms*, intriguingly notes in his entry for the word that *reckon* is "provincial in England in the same sense." Hamilton, in his remarks on the Yorkshire dialect, says, "'I reckon' comes out on every occasion, as perhaps aliens would expect from this country of 'ready reckoners.'" (The term *ready reckoner* dates from the 1700s and refers, the *OED* says, to "a book or table listing for ready reference the results of standard numerical calculations." And an old saying has it that "a Yorkshireman is a Scotsman with all the generosity squeezed out of him.")

The Ngram Viewer graph for *I reckon* (figure 16) tells an interesting story.

In the nineteenth century, American use grew just as Hamilton and Bartlett were taking note of the word. Then, in the twentieth century, use dropped off in both countries; to the extent it was a spoken regionalism, it would not have shown up much in the published books Ngram Viewer tracks.

But then came the twenty-first century, when, for some reason (possibly a fashionable use of an old-fashioned word?), *I reckon* spiked, more dramatically in Britain but notably in the U.S. as well. Now, it's in the air. *New York Times*

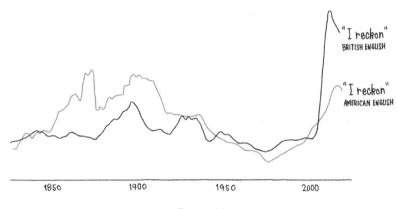

"I reckon"
BRITISH ENGLISH

"I reckon"
AMERICAN ENGLISH

1850 1900 1950 2000

Figure 16

food editor Sam Sifton recently used it in citing another NOOB-loving colleague: "Now, it's only a little bit about food but Dwight Garner got me to order Robert Menasse's satirical novel *The Capital*, and I reckon you ought to do the same."

As did David Frum, writing in *The Atlantic* at the time of the 2020 U.S. presidential election:

> With only a week remaining before Election Day, [Senator Mitch] McConnell crammed through the confirmation of a sixth conservative justice to the U.S. Supreme Court. The people who tally such things reckon that Amy Coney Barrett is the first justice since 1869 to receive not a single vote from the minority party in the Senate.

And in 2022 it was felt to be familiar enough to be used in a headline for a *Times* opinion column by linguist John McWhorter: "I Think It's Fine to Say 'I Feel Like.' I Reckon Others Do, Too."

Adoption | Emerging

"Run-up"

This compound noun has a long history in Britain. It emerged in the nineteenth century in dog racing, to mean the section of the chase up to the first turn. Next, it referred to a preliminary run taken by an athlete before a long jump or—most common in recent years—a cricket bowler's throw. The figurative use—"a period of time or series of occurrences leading up to some significant event"—arrived no later than 1961, when *The Times* referred to "the run-up to the next general election."

As noted in the introduction, the term became popular in the U.S. in the early 2000s because it filled a need: journalists and politicians had to describe the period of several months before the United States invaded Iraq in 2003, and the American dialect had no such term. Ngram Viewer shows a doubling of frequency in the U.S. between 2000 and 2006. Note that another meaning of the term is traditionally more common in the U.S. and accounts for some of the uses charted by Ngram Viewer: a rapid rise in price or some other measure. Thus the *Times* notes that the pandemic years saw "a run up on home prices at a pace never seen before in U.S. history."

In America, from 2003 till about 2010, the "period of time" *run-up* was most commonly used to refer to the months before the Iraq invasion. But then it started to spread to other contexts, the *Times* writing in 2011, "The Packers' report is more than a novelty in the run-up to their playing the Pittsburgh Steelers in the Super Bowl on Feb. 6." ProQuest Recent Newspapers shows 1,757 American uses between 2000 and 2022, including references to the Olympics, Christmas, the Capitol riots, and (back to the future) the Russian invasion of Ukraine.

Adoption | Fully arrived

"Spot-on"

A classic example of an early NOOB that caught on because it's better than all the American equivalents. *Perfect, exactly right, right on the money, flawless*: they're all weak, vague, or worn out.

The *OED* has some early twentieth-century examples, all British, in more or less technical senses, like this one from 1936: "We . . . have three variables, namely, the oscillator inductance, the parallel trimming condenser, and the series padding condenser, and three frequencies which are to be 'spot on.'" In the 1950s, it began to be used as a more general adjective ("the performance was spot-on") or interjection, as in this from Alan Sillitoe's 1958 novel *Saturday Night and Sunday Morning*, quoted in *Green's Dictionary of Slang*: "Arthur screwed his sandwich paper into a ball and threw it across the gangway into somebody's work-box. 'Spot-on,' he cried."

The first American use I've been able to find was in the opening of a *New York Times* 1985 restaurant review: "'Oh, it's a mixed bag.' This was the reply I got when I telephoned Eton's, the luxurious new restaurant in Englewood Cliffs, to ask what kind of food we would find there. As it turns out, the gentleman on the telephone was spot on."

A lot of the early uses were in food contexts, as in this quote from *Los Angeles Magazine* in May 2000: "For the lemony, pan-seared garlic chicken with baby spinach and a mashed potato gratin ($21), he suggests the '97 Edmeades zinfandel, which is a spot-on pairing." But three years after that, when it was featured on HBO's *The Wire*, the term still wasn't widespread. The late language commentator Geoffrey Nunberg, speaking on NPR's *Fresh Air*, described its use in the series:

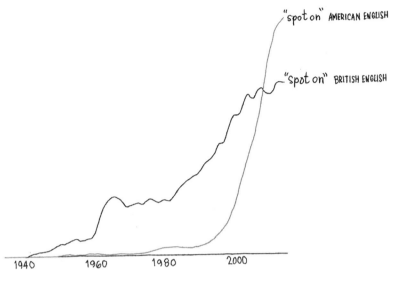

"spot on" AMERICAN ENGLISH

"spot on" BRITISH ENGLISH

1940   1960   1980   2000

Figure 17

Detective Jimmy McNulty is posing as an English business-man in order to bust a Baltimore brothel. He speaks in a comically bad English accent, the inside joke being that McNulty was actually played by the English actor Dominic West. Before he goes in, his boss Lt. Daniels and Assistant DA Rhonda Pearlman are prepping him for his role and giving him the signal to have them come in to make the arrests:

> LT. DANIELS: It'll be your call when we come through the doors. You want us in, you say . . . [turns to Pearlman] what was it?
> PEARLMAN: "Spot on." It means "exactly." And remember, they have to bring up the money and the sex first, then an overt attempt . . . to engage.
> MCNULTY (in an exaggerated English accent): Spot on!

Well, things have changed a lot in two decades, as Ngram Viewer shows (figure 17).

In other words, as of 2012 or 2013, U.S. use topped British use.

Adoption | Outpaced

"Straightaway"

The *OED* cites a use of this term, meaning "immediately," as early as 1662; the subsequent citations, all British, suggest that roughly in 1900, the predominant written form changed from two words (*straight away*) to one (*straightaway*). Thus the *Daily Mail* in 1923: "It was so evident that Evander had been badly hurt that he was straightaway withdrawn." To be sure, the two-word version still exists and has its passionate adherents, as a lively discussion in the *NOOBs* comments section demonstrated.

Most NOOBs become NOOBs in part because they have no precise American equivalent and therefore provide valuable nuance. But *straightaway* means exactly the same as the common American *right away* or *immediately*. So in this case—as in *on holiday* (*on vacation*) and *queue* (*line*)—Americans presumably use the variant because they want to sound British—or they've heard others say it and they like the ring of it.

An early U.S. example appeared in the *New York Times* in 1995: "And as if for extra emphasis, [tennis player Monica Seles] broke Huber straight away in the opening game of the second." Within a couple of decades, it was common, as in a 2012 quote from *Slate*: "I knew straightaway what had gone wrong—caps lock was depressed by accident—but instead of simply taking my lumps and re-entering my password, I vented: 'Is there anything on the computer keyboard more annoying than the caps lock key?'"

According to Ngram Viewer, U.S. use of *straight away* rose steadily in the 2000s and 2010s—though still reaching only about a fifth of how often it's written in Britain. (I searched for the two-word meaning to avoid contamination by the noun *straightaway*, labeled "chiefly U.S." by the *OED* and defined as "a straight course in rowing or sailing. Also, a straight section of a road or racecourse, etc.")

Adoption | Taking hold

"Suss out"

Here's a case where only part of the British usage has crossed the Atlantic. It's interesting to look at the development of the word, as charted by the *OED*. It first shows up in the 1930s as a noun, *sus*, referring to an individual picked up by the police on suspicion of having committed a crime, or the suspicion itself. A 1963 source refers to "men who are, in the prison idiom, 'done for sus,' that is to say, prosecuted as 'suspected persons or reputed thieves loitering with intent to commit a felony.'" (The offense, wisely, was taken off the books by 1981).

In the 1950s, the word (sometimes spelled *suss*) became an adjective, meaning "suspicious," and also a verb, with three separate meanings:

- To suspect someone. ("He turned to Hodge and said, 'Who's sussed for this job?'"—Duncan Webb, *Crime Is My Business*, 1953)
- To imagine, fancy, or surmise something. ("I sussed that all the dodgy bookshops would soon be skint." —*Punch*, 1960)
- And finally, by 1966, the most common usage today: to investigate or figure out something, and generally

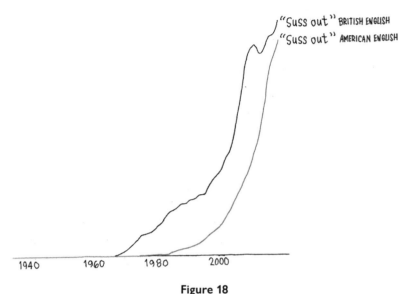

"Suss out" BRITISH ENGLISH
"Suss out" AMERICAN ENGLISH

1940   1960   1980   2000

Figure 18

followed by the word *out*. ("It took me about half a day to suss out the industry and realise how easy it would be to move in."—*Daily Mirror*, 1977)

Only the last form has come to America—with a vengeance. Ngram Viewer tells the story (figure 18).

The phrase shows up in a *New Yorker* article by Hilton Als (about André Leon Talley) in 1994: "Talley begins telephoning in the morning, often as early as six o'clock, to suss out what might be 'the next thing.'" And in the *New York Times* in 2000, just as it was beginning its general ascent, in a review of a Susan Sontag novel: "Although [the narrator] can't speak to the revelers, with a little effort she is able to suss out who they are and what era they belong to."

Adoption | Fully arrived

"Twee"

For a definition of this word, I can do no better than the most popular entry at Urban Dictionary:

> Something that is sweet, almost to the point of being sickeningly so. As a derogatory descriptive, it means something that is affectedly dainty or quaint, or is way too sentimental. In American English it often refers to a type of simple sweet pop music, but in British English it is used much more widely for things that are nauseatingly cute or precious. It comes from the way the word sweet sounds when said in baby talk.
>
> "Belle and Sebastian are the Beatles of twee."

The definition is correct in saying that the word originated as an approximation of the way a young child might say *sweet*, which itself is kind of twee. The *OED*'s first citation is from 1905, but the word fairly quickly adopted, as the dictionary puts it, an exclusively "depreciatory use"—as in the Urban Dictionary definition. Still, for a long time, it was a rather uncommon word even in Britain. In 1963, in volume 3 of his ten(!)-volume autobiography, *My Life and Times*, Compton Mackenzie felt compelled to explain, "'It isn't very twee, is it?' George commented. 'Twee' was the jargon of the moment for something or somebody that was small and jolly." Not sure when George's comment was uttered.

The musical subgenre "twee pop," arriving in the early 2000s, had as its hallmarks, according to AllMusic, "boy-girl harmonies, lovelorn lyrics, infectious melodies, and simple, unaffected performances." Its popularity was a large part of British use of *twee* rising gradually till 2012, according to Ngram Viewer, at which point it took off—increasing eightfold through 2019.

The word turned up in America in the 1980s. The first use I could find in the *New York Times* was in 1982, when a dance critic wrote of a British choreographer, "Americans may find [Ronald] Hynd all too twee (look that one up in your Anglo-American dictionary)."

No small number of recent uses in both countries have been in reference to Belle and Sebastian, the Scottish band mentioned by the Urban Dictionary definer and the exemplars of twee pop. In fact a Google search of "Belle and Sebastian" and "twee" yields 110,000 hits. The word is still far less common in the U.S. than in the U.K., but it's also still a cliché here. *Twee* appeared in the *Times* thirty-nine times in 2021 and 2022, which is about thirty-seven times too many.

> **Adoption** | Fully arrived
>
> ● ● ● ● ●

"University"

Here's the basic deal. In the U.S., institutes of higher education are called "college" (Swarthmore College) unless they have graduate as well as undergraduate programs, in which case they're called "university" (Penn State University). In the U.K. and other Commonwealth countries, the institutions are called "universities" (University of Melbourne), and "college" refers either to a unit within the university (Balliol College, Oxford) or . . . well, it's complicated. Here's how a *NOOBs* reader named Ben Anderson explained it: "A college (in the most common usage) is a higher education establishment that follows on after secondary school that does not offer degrees; they instead offer A-Levels, Certification and NVQ [National Vocational Qualification]."

There are two NOOBs at play. The first relates to what undergraduates are called: in the U.S., they're "college students";

in the U.K., they're "university students." But behold, a Yale sophomore was quoted in the *New York Times* in 2011 as saying, "I think that we as university students should get some sort of deal. I hope the library grants full access to the website."

The second difference has to do with how one's attendance at a college or university is referred to. Traditionally, an American would say "when I was in college" or (less commonly) "at college"—whether they went to a "college" or a "university." By contrast, the British say "at university" or (less commonly) "in university," and sometimes even "at uni." But then there was this sentence (written by an American) in a 2012 *New Yorker* profile of the director Robert Wilson, who attended the University of Texas: "While at university, where he enrolled in business administration to please his father, he took a job as a kitchen aide at the Austin State Hospital for the Mentally Handicapped."

I initially took both the 2011 and 2012 examples for outliers, but more kept popping up. And as the decade of the 2020s dawned, the frequency increased. The following tweets all emanated from a two-hundred-kilometer radius of New York City, in a couple of days in 2020. (See the "Terminology, Abbreviations, and Resources" chapter for an explanation of the Tweetdeck geotagging function.)

- "I finished a quarter early at university."
- "@AndrewYang hey! Thank you so much for your podcast this week. Can relate to your guest on feeling a bit out of my element and out of place at university."
- "Took C to a classical concert at university once and little Z kicked so much in her belly we had to leave."
- "OK, you guys need to adopt me, a poor orphan since my parents died while I was at University."

And in 2021, I encountered for the first time a third variation on this NOOB. In an NPR report about Hollins University in Virginia, the (American) chair of the board of trustees was quoted as saying, "People have a choice about where they go to university."

My first reaction was, "This is not something Americans say." But who knows what the future holds? For now, I'm classifying *university*-for-*college* as "on the radar," but check with me again in five years' time.

Adoption | On the radar

● ● ● ● ●

"Vet" (verb)

The etymology of this word is pretty straightforward. *Veterinarian*, for someone who medically treats animals, dates to the seventeenth century. By 1862, there had appeared a shortened form, *vet*. Some thirty years later, the noun had become a verb, meaning to treat or medically evaluate an animal, as in this 1891 quote: "Beau is shaky in his fore legs. I shall have him vetted before the races." A mere seven years later, the word had developed its current-day meaning—"to screen, assess or evaluate a person"—as seen in this *OED* citation: "The married people in this regiment . . . never entertain, or ask you to put your legs under their mahogany; but we will make a new departure. You will be having them round to 'vet' you." And within a couple of decades it had broadened to refer to the scrutiny of a thing, especially a document. In a 1933 book on slang, Eric Partridge wrote, "*To vet* a book is to revise it, whether for the author or for his publisher."

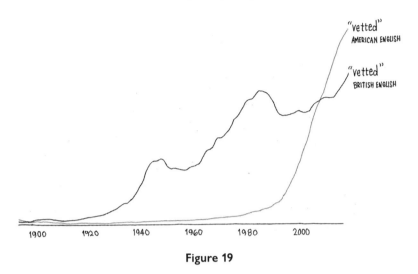

"vetted"
AMERICAN ENGLISH

"vetted"
BRITISH ENGLISH

1900   1920   1940   1960   1980   2000

Figure 19

As Ngram Viewer shows, the word remained a Britishism until the 1980s, when American use started picking up
(figure 19).

New York Times language columnist William Safire
looked at the word in 1980; interestingly, the only examples
he gave were of the older use, vetting documents, as in a
Newsweek quote about a Ronald Reagan speech: "His edited
version was routinely retyped without further vetting." Safire
returned to *vet* in 1993, and this time the emphasis was the
earlier established meaning—and the most common one
now—vetting humans who have applied for or are being
considered for positions.

At the time, the most prominent vettee in the news was a
judge named Kimba Wood, whom Bill Clinton had nominated
for attorney general but who (it turned out) had once hired an
undocumented alien as a nanny. She ultimately withdrew her
name from consideration but asserted that she had broken no
laws and had been forthcoming and truthful in the process,

stating, "My household-help files were received by the White House 'vetters.'" A *Times* editorial opined that her chances were destroyed by "clumsy vetting."

The Ngram Viewer chart suggests that the Wood affair started an exponential American growth in *vet*, which has not let up. And I infer that the word's popularity in the U.S. led to a more modest uptick in the U.K., starting in the 1990s and not letting up there either.

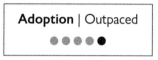

Adoption | Outpaced

"Whinge"

This word has the same root as *whine*, which makes sense since it means the same thing as that verb. The *OED* describes it as originating in Scottish and northern dialect and impressively has citations circa 1150. More than seven hundred years later, James Joyce used it in *Ulysses* (1920): "You crossed her last wish in death and yet you sulk with me because I don't whinge like some hired mute from Lalouette's." The word gained some currency as part of an antipodean catchphrase *The Times* referenced in 1984: "'What sort of people do Australians hate most?' 'The whingeing Pom . . . Poms that come over and do nothing but whinge.'" (In Australia, *Poms* is a derogatory term for the English.)

Ngram Viewer shows that British use didn't really pick up till the 1980s, with American use rising more slowly. It was unfamiliar enough in the U.S. in 1996 that Walter Goodman, writing in the *Times*, felt he had to define it: "Money alone won't do it [produce happiness]. Listen to the poor rich lottery winners whingeing away. (The word *whinge*, as used in my poker game, is a whine from a winner.)" Fifteen years later, that wasn't necessary, as witnessed in this line from an *Entertainment Weekly* recap of an episode of *The Big Bang Theory*: "And as much as I adore Sheldon's persnickety nature, watching him devolve into a whingeing man-child, bitching about his mother not making him fried chicken or pecan pie, kept what had the potential to be a top-flight episode from ever taking off."

I can understand the word's appeal, since that *g* makes *whinge* more forceful and contemptuous than *whine*. In any case, it or the gerund form (sometimes spelled *whinging*) was used nine times in the *Times* between 2020 and 2022, including in a line from columnist Maureen Dowd before the 2020 presidential election: "In a rare moment of self-awareness, Trump whinged to [Fox News's Sean] Hannity about Biden: 'The man can't speak and he's going to be your president 'cause some people don't love me, maybe.'" Definitely.

Adoption | Emerging

"Worrying"

The syndicated columnist The Word Guy (TWG) wrote not long ago,

> A network-news correspondent recently described a medical issue that has led doctors and researchers to a "worrying conclusion." Now, I've never seen a conclusion worry. I'm wondering whether it knits its brow, rubs its head, and grits its teeth. More and more people are using "worrying" not to mean "fretting" ("a worrying mom") but "causing fretting" ("a worrying event").

I have the same impression as TWG that *worrying* is on the rise as an adjective, meaning roughly the same as the traditional *troubling* or *worrisome*. And indeed, in a Google News search of U.S. sources, three of the first six instances of the word use it to mean "fretting" and these three to mean "troubling":

- "Electronic Arts Stock: Worrying Trends . . ."—Seeking Alpha
- "Worrying Claims Emerge Surrounding Diontae Johnson's contract."—GiveMeSport
- "Tarik Skubal Gets Worrying Injury Blow . . ."—ClutchPoints

TWG asserts that this *worrying* is a new thing, and it is—but only in America. The *OED* has spotted it in Frederick Reynolds's 1826 *Life & Times* ("Your whole conduct is literally worrying and annoying in the extreme") and twice in Dickens, including this from *The Pickwick Papers* (1837): "There are few things more worrying than sitting up for somebody, especially if that somebody be at a party."

And it's not even that much of a novelty in the U.S., according to Ngram Viewer, where a search for "very worrying" shows a steady rise starting in about 1980—though as of 2019 it was only about a third as common as in the U.K.

As for TWG's objections to adjectival *worrying*, they're specious. If he thought about it for a minute, he would realize that he had indeed seen a conclusion worry—for example, "The researcher's conclusion worried his collaborators." Indeed, it is customary, when a person, situation, or thing emotionally *verbs* someone, to describe that person, situation, or thing as *verbing*. Think of *perplexing, frightening, amusing*, and a word he presumably prefers to *worrying—troubling*. In short, chill.

A word that has a similar meaning and raises similar, well, concerns, is *concerning*. The preposition meaning "having to do with," as in John Locke's book *An Essay concerning Human Understanding*, is traditional, but there's also an adjective meaning "causing concern." The adjective sounded to me both new and British; I was half-right on the first and mostly wrong on the second. The first *OED* entry is from Samuel Richardson's *Pamela* (1740): "I cannot bear any thing that is the least concerning to you." But the next isn't until 1890, and an Ngram Viewer search for "very concerning" shows the phrase very little used in both the U.S. and the U.K. until about 1980. At that point use sharply increased over the next forty years: by about 2,000 percent in Britain and nearly *3,000* percent in America—for example, in this recent quote from a Texas Transportation Department official: "It's extremely concerning that drivers still choose to give their attention to things other than the road when they're behind the wheel."

So there's no reason to shun adjectival *concerning* if you're concerned about logic or in the unlikely event that you want to avoid NOOBs. However, I would still advise steering clear of it, because it has become such a worrying cliché.

Adoption | Taking hold

CHAPTER FOUR

Insults and the Naughty Bits

I have to admit that the Brits are better at this kind of thing than the Yanks. And I'm thankful that some of the choicer epithets have made their way over here.

"Bell-end"

The American author Catherynne Valente wrote on Facebook: "Y'all can't stop being hateful and I'm tired of getting notifications that someone else is being [an] absolute bell-end about their fellow man on NextDoor." (NextDoor is a regional communication platform, and apparently, in Valente's town, people had been making virulent anti-immigrant comments there.)

Bell-end (it's variously printed as hyphenated, two words, and one word) is categorized by the *OED* as "British coarse slang." Two definitions are offered, the first being "the glans of the penis"; the earliest citation is the 1961 edition of Eric Partridge's *Dictionary of Slang and Unconventional English*, where it's listed along with the comparable terms *blunt end* and *red end*. The second definition is "a foolish or contempt-ible man or boy." It shows up in 1992, and the most recent citation is from 2008 in *The Guardian*: "Clearly, no one's ever taken them aside and said, 'Er, you sound like a bit of a bell-end here. Perhaps you ought to sit down and be quiet.'" (Bell End is also a village in the English county of Worcestershire.)

Green's Dictionary of Slang notes a derivative noun form, seen in this 2017 quote, also from *The Guardian*: "Arrogant bellendery seems to be common feature amongst the Alumni of Fettes College."

When I posted about *bell-end* on the blog, Nick L. Tipper commented,

> In U.K. football grounds a stand of seating will tend to be named after a local dignitary, sponsor, hero from the club's history, or geographical feature. Such stands, if behind the goal, may be called "ends." Thus Aston Villa FC has the Holte End; Liverpool the Kop End, etc.
>
> In 2003, according to a *Guardian* report, Manches-ter City Football Club sought their fans' opinion of what a new stand should be called. A large majority wanted it to be called after former star-player Colin Bell but there was talk of the poll having been nobbled by fans of other teams wanting Manchester City to be humiliated by hav-ing a stand referred to—at least colloquially—as "The Bell End" (even though it is to the side of the pitch).
>
> There is now a Colin Bell Stand at the Man City ground.

None of the citations in *Green's* or the *OED* are from the U.S., and indeed, I have not been able to find it used by anyone here other than Valente. And speaking of Valente, her website bio notes, "She graduated from high school at age 15, going on to UC San Diego and Edinburgh University, receiving her B.A. in Classics with an emphasis in Ancient Greek Linguistics."

I gather that along with the BA she picked up some salty language.

Adoption | On the radar

"Bloody"

The *OED*'s relevant definition: "As an intensifier, modifying an adjective or adverb: absolutely, completely, utterly. More recently also as a mere filler, with little or no intensifying force (although generally implying some element of dislike, frustration, etc., on the part of the speaker)." The dictionary dates this use of the word from the seventeenth century, with one of the first citations being this stage direction from John Dryden in 1683: "The Doughty Bullies enter Bloody Drunk."

The place where it really caught on was Australia. Jonathon Green notes,

> In his book *Travels in New South Wales* (1847) Alexander Marjoribanks noted the prevalence of the word, claiming that he had heard a bullock-driver use it 27 times in 15 minutes, a rate of speech, he then calculated, that over a 50-year period would produce some 18,200,000 repetitions of the "disgusting word." The Sydney *Bulletin* called it "the Australian adjective" in its edition of 18 August 1894, explaining that "it is more used, and used more exclusively by Australians, than by any other allegedly civilized nation."

In Britain, *bloody* retained a taboo status for a considerable time; "for many speakers," according to the *OED*, it "constituted the strongest expletive available." That's reflected in the large number of euphemisms for it—including *bleeding*, *blooming*, *sanguinary*, and *blerry*. When George Bernard

Shaw's play *Pygmalion* premiered in 1914, it created a sensation because of the line "Walk! Not bloody likely." The *New York Times* reported that at the premiere, the "utterance of the banned word . . . was waited for with trembling, heard shutteringly, and presumably, when the shock subsided, interest dwindled." The scandal gave rise to the humorous euphemistic adjective *Pygmalion*, still in use in 1967, when it appeared in the novel *Rendezvous in Rio*: "'Are you thinking of joining in?' 'Not Pygmalion likely,' Bland returned brusquely."

However, by no later than the mid-1950s, *bloody* had apparently lost its sting. In writing the book for the musical version of *Pygmalion*, *My Fair Lady*, Alan Jay Lerner didn't even bother to use Shaw's "Not bloody likely." Instead, Liza Doolittle shocks with another word when she says, addressing a horse, "Move yer bloomin' arse!" (For *arse*, see the next entry.)

As for *bloody*'s status as a NOOB, it's been in use here for a long time, seemingly initially as a Southern regionalism. *Green's* has a quote from the 1834 novel *The Kentuckian in New-York*: "I reckon I did take a hand or so aginst the bloody Injins." More widespread use apparently stemmed from American soldiers' association with British counterparts in World War I. Thus *bloody* is used in dialogue five times in John Dos Passos's 1921 novel *Three Soldiers*, including, "D'ye remember, Andy, we was both of us brushin' cigarette butts at that bloody trainin' camp when we first met up with each other?" One difference in U.S. use was noted by H. L. Mencken in *The American Language*: "The word is entirely without improper significance in America."

In the 1950s, the word was popular among the Beats. Neal Cassady wrote in 1951, "I got to work now on script so I can pay Uncle Sam his bloody tax," and Jack Kerouac six years later in *On the Road*: "I was in such a bloody hurry to get to the gang in Denver."

These days, the intensifier shows up now and again in U.S. sources. In a 2011 *New York Times* blog post, the author anthropomorphized a spring flower, then self-consciously noted the unusualness of the word in an American paper: "'Relax,' the tulips tell us. 'Soon you'll be complaining how bloody hot it is.' (If the tulips sound very European, there's a good reason for that.)" Ten years later, a reviewer for the same paper said of Catherine Ryan Howard's novel *56 Days*, "It's a thriller, a bloody good one," without need of explanation or apology.

An English friend notes, "Americans use it too much in England, to English people, and sound silly."

Adoption | Taking hold

● ● ● ● ●

"Bottom"; "bum"; "arse"

Of the first two words for the posterior or buttocks set down above, *bum* is the older, with *Green's Dictionary of Slang* offering a 1354 citation. And here's a surprisingly modern-sounding line from Shakespeare's *Measure for Measure*: "Your bum is the greatest thing about you."

As for *bottom*, a more genteel euphemism, the *OED* dates it to about 1800 and has this quote from Thomas Carlyle's *The French Revolution* (1837): "Patriot women take their hazel wands, and fustigate . . . broad bottoms of priests." (Fustigate = to cudgel or beat with a stick.)

Ngram Viewer shows both to be NOOBs, with *bottom* more widely used on both sides of the Atlantic (figure 20).

The rise of U.S. *bottom* in the 1990s (including a couple of years when it even surpassed British use) corresponds with my memory of it being used in addressing or referring to young children, two of which I had at the time. Even earlier than

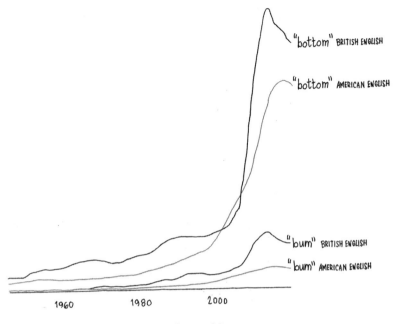

Figure 20

that, in 1971, a pediatrician wrote in the *New York Times*, referring to the spread of pinworm, "Man thoughtfully scratches his bottom and carries the microscopic eggs on his unwashed hands into his mouth, either directly or by means of cigarettes or food." The term was used more generally and widely by 2003, when a *New Yorker* reviewer of a Martha Graham dance performance wrote, "I saw that Gary Galbraith, when he played the Minotaur, was provided with a pair of shorts that covered his bottom." More recently, for reasons that are beyond my pay grade to explain, the word is often used in an erotic or lascivious context.

As for *bum*, U.S. use was surely influenced in the early 1990s by Mike Myers's "Simon" character on *Saturday Night Live*, the little English boy who for some reason hosted a TV show from his bathtub. Simon would periodically rise from the tub to retrieve his "drawrings," then admonish viewers, "Were you looking at my bum? Were you? Bum lookers! Cheeky monkeys, all of you."

Within a decade or so, it wasn't hard to find quotes like this 2009 one, from *Time*: "Runway falls don't get any more straightforward than this: blame the shoes—again. The beauty of this clip, however, is the drunken-looking wobbly-ness of her recovery. The model in question falls on her bum, but looks like she might have bumped her head and seen some little birdies."

That leaves *arse*—the more common, and vulgar, British synonym. It has a precise American equivalent—*ass*. A complicating factor is that usually in Britain, the *r* in *arse* isn't pronounced, so it sounds kind of like "ahss." I don't believe I've ever heard any Americans venturing to use it, with the *r* or without.

As for Americans *writing* the word, it's been around for a long time as a sort of literary novelty item. In a 1921 letter, Ezra Pound wrote, referring to William Carlos Williams, "Possibly lamentable that the two halves of what might have made a fairly decent poet shd be sequestered and divided by the fuckin buttocks of the arse-wide atlantic ocean." Donald Barthelme's first novel, *Snow White*, contained a chapter titled "The Failure of Snow White's Arse." A 1971 letter by the Anglophile S. J. Perelman noted that some *New Yorker* contributors "tend to have a ramrod up their arse, acting as though they invented the paper." (I would say that *paper*, to refer to a magazine, is a Britishism as well.)

Moving up to the present, *arse* has become a bit of a vogue term in the U.S. A 2010 comment on a *New York Times* blog post by someone who signed him- or herself "AmericanYankee" says, "The last thing I want is for bin Laden and his sycophantic arse kissing illiterate supporters to think they are somehow special." A few years after that, blogging his displeasure about the *Times* on the *Esquire* website, Charles Pierce commented, "This is all my arse."

Searching Tweetdeck for uses of the word from accounts located within two hundred kilometers of New York City turned up a multitude of examples, including no fewer than six posted in the previous three hours. One was from @robjobdwyer, who says he's based in New York: "There's a difference between having a point and going about it in a totally arse backward and obnoxious manner."

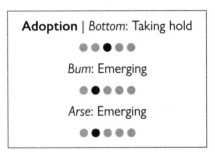

Adoption | *Bottom:* Taking hold

Bum: Emerging

Arse: Emerging

"Codswallop"

Sometimes, writing the *NOOBs* blog is like shooting fish in a barrel. Specifically, cod. For example, one day I was reading Facebook and alighted on a post from the writer Tom Carson in which he said, "Because I just couldn't face another day of yelling at my TV set, I watched *The Man Who Fell to Earth* for the first time in 40 years instead. Yes, it still looks gorgeous—and man, is it ever a preening load of echt-1970s codswallop."

So, *codswallop*. First step, go to Ngram Viewer to confirm British origin adoption. Check—though I was surprised to see the use of the word start in Britain just before 1960, where I would have thought it was Shakespearean. Second, at same source, confirm American adoption sometime later.

Check: U.S. use has gradually risen since the 1970s, though it's still only about a third as common as in the U.K.

On to the next step, the *OED*, which has two definitions. The first is: "*British slang (depreciative*, chiefly *London*). An overly talkative woman, a gossip. Also in more general use, as a mildly depreciative term for a person. Now *rare*." The first citation is from the English newspaper *News of the World* in 1928: "What is a 'cod's wallop'? According to a learned counsel . . . the term is an East-end [of London] colloquialism for 'a woman who cannot keep her mouth shut.'" Then there's a quote from a 2005 interview with the English comedy writer Alan Simpson, who was from Brixton, south of London: "In the thirties, . . . I was about seven or eight and my uncle . . . used to use it as a proper noun, he used to call me codswallop."

Simpson's quote is important, because in other sources he is credited with inventing the word. And the *OED* credits the TV show *Hancock's Half Hour*, written by Simpson and Ray Galton, with the first use of the other (now prevalent) definition, "nonsense, rubbish, drivel." In an episode that aired in 1959, the character played by Sid James said, "Don't give me that old codswallop." And it took off from there.

Incidentally, when I posted about the word on the blog, someone commented,

> The folk etymology that you'll hear most often is that it supposedly comes from early pop bottles, which were invented by Hiram Codd in the 1870s. The idea is that the guzz inside was known as "Codd's wallop." This is almost certainly not true, especially since there's no record of the form "Codd's wallop" anywhere.

As for American use, in the *New York Times* in 2018, Kara Swisher called the idea that Twitter and other platforms are rigged against Donald Trump "codswallop." She continued,

"You can look that fine word up on Google if you want to know what it means, by the way."

Today, she probably wouldn't need that addendum. But her point stands.

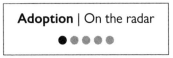

Adoption | On the radar

"Crap" (adjective)

The subtle difference here is between American *crappy* and British *crap*. They appear to be pretty much the same thing, and it's a mystery why one country favored one form of the adjective and the other, the other. For Americans unfamiliar with the British version, the first solid hit in *Green's* is from a 1966 book called *Adolescent Boys of East London*: "Anyway it was a crap school I went to." In 1982, the novel *London Embassy*, by Paul Theroux (a Massachusetts native but longtime British resident), has the line of dialogue, "They're very modern laid-back people with a house full of crap art and heads full of crap opinions."

In 2012, an English acquaintance of mine, then living in Massachusetts, experienced a big snowstorm and posted on Facebook, "Onto our third basket of firewood since noon. I think this is evidence that crap wood is crappier than non-crap wood. Before I ordered the crap wood I read that this was the case, and lo, it is true."

By that time, the British form had made its way to America. Writing in *Slate* in 2009, Timothy Noah referred to a hypothetical health insurance policy as "a crap plan," and two years later, this appeared on the Movie City News website: "I mean, I've seen a lot of mediocre films, even at major fests, but let's assume for the sake of argument that most people who set out to make an indie film are not aiming to make a crap movie."

I should note that *shit* is used as an adjective in Britain in much the same way. The first citation in the *OED* is from John Lennon talking about jazz, quoted in Hunter Davies's *The Beatles* (1968): "I think it is shit music, even more stupid than rock and roll, followed by students in Marks and Spencer pullovers. Jazz never gets anywhere, never does anything, it's always the same and all they do is drink pints of beer."

The question arises, is *crap* the same as *crappy*? In a 2011 essay, "In Praise of Crap Technology," the American science writer Thomas Hayden extolled the virtues of his $19.99 Coby MP3 player, bottom-of-the-line Samsung cell phone, 1995 mountain bike, and other devices that aren't fancy but work. He says of the Coby,

> It's worth next to nothing so I'm virtually assured never to lose it—unlike apparently every iPhone prototype ever— and I don't cringe at all when my toddler flings it across the room. And because the next Coby is sure to be just as mediocre, I'll never need to upgrade—I've stepped off the escalators of feature creep and planned obsolescence, and all the expense and toxic e-waste that come with them. Crap technology, it turns out, is green technology.

I became aware of the essay when I heard Hayden on the public radio program *Marketplace*. In the interview, he asserted that there is indeed a difference between the two forms of the word: "Crap technology is basically stuff that doesn't have cachet, you know? It's not slick, it's not cool, but it works. Crappy technology, on the other hand, is stuff that simply doesn't work. That's the sweet spot of crap technology: no cachet but all the functionality you'll need."

Adoption | Emerging

"Fecking"; "fookin'"

As noted in the introduction, this book is (occasionally) about not only Britishisms but Australianisms and Irishisms as well. *Feck* is an instance of the latter. It emerged in the nineteenth century as a verb meaning "steal." From Joyce's *Portrait of the Artist as a Young Man* (1916): "They had fecked cash out of the rector's room." Some decades later, clever Irish people took advantage of how similar *feck* is to another word and began to use it as a Hibernian alternative. This line appears in *The Bogman* (1952), by the Irish writer Walter Macken: "The whole feckin world I'd give to be with her on the banks of the Ree." Since then, various forms—including *feck off*, *fecker*, and *feck it*—have been seen in the work of other writers, mostly Irish, in reproducing dialogue in novels, plays, and films.

A frequent user is the playwright and filmmaker Martin McDonagh, whose parents were Irish but who was born and raised in London. I was initially excited to see the Corpus of Contemporary American English (part of English-Corpora .org) list fifty-one uses of *fecking* between 1995 and 1999, but it turned out forty-four of them were from McDonagh's play *The Cripple of Inishmaan*, which was published in the American journal the *Paris Review*. Example: "Oh thank Christ the fecker's over. A pile of fecking shite." (The other seven *fecking*s in the corpus came from Irish contexts as well. For *shite*, see the entry later in this chapter.)

There has been a sprinkling of American use over the years, for example in the title of a 2014 blog post by Charles Pierce of *Esquire*: "Not in My Fecking Backyard." (It had to do with a controversy in Ireland.) I've noticed an uptick recently, which I peg to McDonagh's popular 2022 film *The Banshees of Inisherin*. The word is used endlessly in it, including in costar Kerry Condon's mic-drop line "You're all feckin' boring!"

In an interview, Condon contended, "It's not a swear word. You can say it until the cows come home. My mother doesn't swear ever. But she says 'feckin' all the time." Stan Carey, who is both Irish and a scholar of language, bears her out, noting that in the 1990s TV comedy *Father Ted*, Father Jack shouts "Feck off!" regularly enough to make it a catchphrase. "*Feck* is family-friendly," Carey wrote on his blog, "even according to advertising standards authorities. . . . As expletives go, it has a playful, unserious feel. People who are genuinely furious—as opposed to merely annoyed—or who want to be properly abusive, tend not to use *feck*: it just isn't forceful enough."

Fooking—commonly rendered as *fookin'*—is an example of what is known as eye dialect, spelling a word the way it's pronounced, in this case from the north of England. Someone offered this definition on Urban Dictionary in 2003: "The result of someone with a Mancunian accent trying to say the word 'fucking.'" An oft-repeated quote from singer Louis Tomlinson, from West Yorkshire, is "I hate fookin' avocadoes." And Adrian Chiles's book *We Don't Know What We're Doing*, about supporters of West Bromwich Albion football, has the line, "He can't see a fookin' thing . . . and he's got to drive we home." (Note also the regionalism of "we" as the object of a verb.)

As for American use, it's sparse but growing. Journalist Charles Pierce, again, has a favorite epithet on Twitter: "Fookin' eejit" (idiot). I searched Twitter for tweets containing *fookin* and emanating in a two-hundred-kilometer radius of New York City and turned up a couple dozen hits over the course of a week, including this from an account from East Hampton, New York: "For fook sake man! Im eating my fookin lunch here!!"

> **Adoption** | On the radar
> ●●●●●

"Knickers in a twist"

My investigation of this phrase started when faithful reader Hal Hall sent a link to a CNET article and wondered whether the last three words of the opening sentence were a Britishism: "Verizon Wireless's new family share plan has gotten lots of knickers in knots. But is the new plan really as bad as some people fear it is for consumers?"

The answer (to Hal's question, not the CNET writer's) is yes, though it's less popular than a similar, less alliterative phrase, usually expressed in imperative form: "Don't get your knickers in a twist." Both expressions are derived from the British sense of knickers as girls' or women's underwear. The first example of either that I'm aware of is a line of dialogue from a 1965 book by Wilbur Smith, a native of Rhodesia, now Zimbabwe: "Okay, okay, don't get your knickers in a knot, bucko."

The *OED*'s first citation for the "twist" version is from 1971: "Britain's Foreign Office mandarins have had their knickers in a twist for the past fortnight." Variations quickly arose. In 1973, a contributor to *The Listener* observed that on *The Basil Brush Show*, "the theme of underwear attracts repeated variations, received by the children with undiminished relish: 'Don't get your knickers in a knot / combs in a commotion / undies in an uproar / tights in a tangle."

Colorful as it is, the phrase not surprisingly got picked up in the U.S.; the earliest sighting in the *New York Times* by an American came in a quote from the fashion editor Joe Dolce. Two years later, the paper's TV critic, Bruce Weber, wrote of a Sunday news show, "I rather like all those quasi-pundits with their collective knickers in a twist getting exercised at one another as they exercise freedom of speech." The "knot" version first appeared in a 2003 quote from gossip columnist Cindy Adams: "These celebrities get their knickers in a knot if you write that they were loud somewhere. Please!"

One problem is that most Americans probably have never developed a clear sense of what "knickers" are. And therefore there are homegrown variants, the most popular being the one Sam Shepard apparently invented and put in the mouth of Mae West in his 1971 play *Mad Dog Blues*: "Don't get yer panties in a bunch. It's just the call a' the wild."

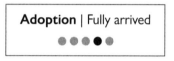

"Knob"

The day after the January 6, 2021, U.S. Capitol insurrection, a *New York Times* reporter tweeted the news that a publisher had canceled plans for a book by Senator Josh Hawley, who had offered visible support to the insurrectionists. A writer named Hillary Kelly retweeted it, with her comment: "Cue all the knobs who will claim that this is censorship."

Knob, according to the *OED*, has two groups of meanings. The first, used in both Britain and America, refers to "a rounded lump or protuberance, and related senses." This is now commonly used in cooking contexts, especially to refer to a knob of butter.

The second set of meanings, mainly British, refers to a penis, literally and figuratively. The first literal citation is from 1922. Fifty-one years later, Martin Amis used it in his novel *The Rachel Papers*: "My knob was knee-high to a grasshopper, the size of a toothpick."

Someone posted on *NOOBs* an admittedly "awful" joke that punned on the two meanings: "Waiter, waiter, do you have a knob of butter?" "No, it's just the way I walk."

Moving right along, the first figurative citation, denoting "an annoying, unpleasant, or idiotic person (esp. a man or boy)," is from way back in 1920. All the examples in the *OED* are from British, Irish, or Canadian writers, an example of the last being Douglas Coupland in his 1991 novel *Generation X*: "I'd made all these plans to meet before, but he kept breaking them, the knob."

In looking for American uses, other than Kelly's, my best luck was the Tweetdeck geotagging tool. There was a good bounty, surely because so many knobs had been acting knobbish in this country. This one came from the Adirondack Mountains of New York: "Yes our system of government is a constitutional republic. But our election process is still democratic. You knob."

Another one, from Rhode Island, suggested new avenues for research: "Trump and his #gop knob polishers are getting away with sedition and treason."

Incidentally, *knob* does not appear to be related to *nob*, a noun meaning a person of wealth or social distinction. Unlike *knob*, *nob* has not penetrated into the U.S. The only non-British *OED* citations—both of which use the adjectival form *nobby*—are the American Anglophiles Cole Porter ("Nowadays it's rather nobby / To regard one's private hobby / As the object of one's tenderest affections") and S. J. Perelman ("A serried row of floodlit edifices . . . trumpeted to the newcomer that he was in the nobbiest winter playground ever devised").

Adoption | On the radar

● ⦿ ⦿ ⦿ ⦿

"Pillock"; "wazzock"; "numpty"; "shitgibbon"

An ad that aired during the 2016 Super Bowl showed Dame Helen Mirren sitting before a hamburger, being served a Budweiser (not bloody likely), and counseling, in strong language, against driving drunk. Anyone who does so, she averred, is a "shortsighted, utterly useless, oxygen-wasting human form of pollution." She concludes, "Don't be a pillock." (By the way, Dame Helen said "drunk driving" but the British phrase—not seen or heard in the U.S. as yet—is "drink-driving.")

My guess is that somewhere north of 99 percent of the people who saw the spot in America had no idea what a pillock is—though they could clearly tell by context clues that it wasn't a good thing. I certainly wasn't familiar with the term and went straight to the *OED*, whose first definition is, "Orig. *Sc[ottish]*. The penis. Now *Eng. Regional* (*north.*) and *rare*." The copywriter for the Mirren commercial was clearly going for definition no. 2, which is, "Chiefly *Brit. Colloq.* (mildly *derogatory*). A stupid person; a fool, an idiot." The first *OED* citation for the figurative use is from 1967, the most recent from a rugby magazine in 2004: "Those mindless pillocks in New Zealand who slated England for the way they played in Wellington in June."

Another meaning, unmentioned by the *OED*, is suggested in Angus McClaren's 2007 book *Impotence: A Cultural History*. In the early modern period, he writes, an impotent man was scorned as a "malkin, pillock, fumbler, fribble, bungler, bobtail, domine-do-little, weak-doing man, Goodman Do-Little, and John Cannot."

Pillock may have rung a faint bell in the minds of English majors. It is likely a shortening of another word for "penis" that turns up in *King Lear*. Edgar, in his guise as the mad beggar Poor Tom, pipes up at one point with a line from a perverse ditty: "Pillicock sat on Pillicock hill. La, la, la, la!" (Use your imagination for the meaning of "Pillicock hill.")

The Mirren advert seems to have sparked a small uptick in U.S. uses of the word. It appeared in a 2020 *New York Times* blog and, memorably, in a 2022 article by Devorah Blachor noting one advantage of the new Mastodon social network over Twitter (as it was then called) under Elon Musk: "All the servers are interlinked, and there's not even one ego-bloated pillock amplifying Nazis or getting publicly owned by Doja Cat." And speaking of Twitter, now X, the word is used now and again by Americans there, including this in 2021 (not sure who the New York–based tweeter is talking about): "I'll take your word for it as I live in the USA & have no idea who he is except you seem to be implying he's a pillock."

Clearly, the British have a knack for insults. Another pungent one is *wazzock*, which came on the American radar in 2012, when the *Daily Telegraph* hurled it at Republican presidential candidate Mitt Romney. *New Yorker* contributor John Cassidy fondly described the epithet as "a term of abuse that I hadn't heard since my childhood in Leeds, West Yorkshire." History kind of repeated itself four years later, after a petition advocating banning the next Republican nominee, Donald Trump, from setting foot in the United Kingdom attracted some six hundred thousand signatures. The House of Commons actually considered the question. They ended up not taking a vote, but in the course of debate, MP Victoria Atkins said Trump was a wazzock.

Surprisingly, this word seems never to have meant "penis"; the OED labels it "unknown origin" and defines it as "a stupid or annoying person." As Cassidy suggests, it comes from the north of England and probably sprang up around the time of his childhood, in the 1970s. It seems to be used a bit less in the U.S. than *pillock*, one exception being Marty Kelley, writing in *Wonkette* in 2021. He addressed Tucker Carlson as "you pampered millionaire Fox News wazzock."

It would appear that Trump has inspired an insult renaissance in the U.K., as well as spillover in the United States. Another term that has been applied to him is *numpty*.

The *OED* describes it as originating in Scotland and gives this possible etymology: "Origin uncertain; perhaps an alteration of numps n. or numbskull n., with ending perhaps remodelled after humpty-dumpty n." The first citation is from 1985 ("'They are a pair of turkeys,' he said. 'Numpties, the both of them.'"—P. Firth, *The Great Pervader*), and more recent ones show a migration to England. One *NOOBs* reader reported that it was the only nonprofane insult regularly used by Jamie McDonald in Armando Iannucci's satiric comedy *The Thick of It*, and another reader said, "My favourite description for the relatively new Scottish Parliament is 'the Numptorium.'"

Neither the *OED* nor *Green's Dictionary of Slang* shows U.S. use, but the term did appear in the *New York Times* in 2009, when Dallas-born novelist Bill Cotter said,

> In the mid-'80s, Boston's Kenmore Square, where part of [his novel *Fever Chart*] is set, was home to three-card-monte men, ordinary punks, beer-devastated Red Sox bleacher-seat numpties, the Guardian Angel menace, and the only music venue worth visiting in that fourth-rate city, the Rat, a black basement often populated with bloody-nosed hardcore girls swinging tiny fists of stone.

More recently, it has been seen on Twitter and X, inevitably regarding the most frequent subject of all these insults, the former U.S. president. Here are some tweets posted in the course of a day, all within two hundred kilometers of New York City and tagging Trump:

- "Numpty you are a joke."
- "You're a real numpty."
- "Numpty you realize how you are becoming more of a laughing stock than you were prior to G7."

And now we come to *shitgibbon*. (When I started my writing career, I could not have predicted that one day I would compose that sentence.) Unsurprisingly, it's not in the *OED*, but *Green's Dictionary of Slang* defines it as "a general insult, usu. characterizing Donald Trump." Some sleuthing by the indefatigable Ben Zimmer found what appears to be not only the first use but the invention of the word, in a line written by British music journalist David Quantick. He told Zimmer that "spunk-faced shitgibbon" was "a phrase I used in a 1988 column in *New Musical Express* and have put in most of my writing since." Quantick can also claim responsibility for introducing the term to the United States, as he wrote an episode of HBO's *Veep* in 2012 where the character Senator Andrew Doyle calls a rival a "gold-plated fucking shitgibbon."

The Trump connection came in 2016, when he falsely claimed that Scotland had voted for Brexit, and someone posted on Twitter, "Scotland voted to stay & plan on a second referendum, you tiny fingered, Cheeto-faced, ferret wearing shitgibbon."

Among the Americans to pick it up was a Democratic state legislator from my home region, the suburbs of Philadelphia, who tweeted, "Hey @realDonaldTrump I oppose civil asset forfeiture too! Why don't you try to destroy my career you fascist, loofa-faced, shitgibbon!"

Adoption | On the radar

"Piss off!"; "taking the piss"; "pissed"

To start, I should sort out the transatlantic variations in the adjective *pissed*. In Britain, it began to be used to mean "drunk" in the early twentieth century. And this use has continued to the present day, with no NOOB-y action, other probably than the occasional pretentious Brooklynite. Meanwhile, *pissed off*, meaning "angry," started as American World War II slang and was adopted in Britain by the 1990s. Americans also use the shortened form *pissed*—but Britons, because of the obvious potential for confusion, do not.

Piss off is a transitive verb phrase in the U.S.—"Never piss off your boss"—but also a British rude imperative meaning "go away." *Green's Dictionary of Slang* has an example from *This Gutter Life*, by Julian Franklyn (1934): "A knot of cheap prostitutes standing before the Pavilion Theatre was dispersed by the showily-dressed bullies who lived on them. 'Go on! Go on! P**s off! Don't stand there chewin' the rag! Hustle, you bloody bitches, will you?'"

Its arrival in America was surely encouraged by the 1993 film *Mrs. Doubtfire*, in which the voiceover actor played by Robin Williams quits his job and (in a Porky Pig voice) tells his boss to piss off. It also shows up in a line from a 2018 episode of *Orange Is the New Black*: "And you're an old cunt who needs to piss off."

Now to *taking the piss*. It means "to tease, not gently," or "to put one on, josh, have someone on." The first citation in *Green's* is from a 1946 World War II memoir: "In the Brigade of Guards . . . we have a language of our own, referring to this harmless, if at times extremely irritating, practice of 'blackguarding,' or 'taking the piss out of' one's fellows." There's also an intransitive version of the expression: "Are you taking the piss?" Subsequently, there sprang up the posh or mock-posh version *extracting the urine* and the bowdlerized equivalent *take the mickey* (sometimes claimed, without evidence, to be rhyming slang for "take the Mickey Bliss").

It took a while for the phrase to travel west. In 1995, Bill Bryson, a U.S. transplant in England, wrote (referring to Americans), "Wit, and particularly the dry, ironic, taking-the-piss sort of wit, was completely beyond them. (Do you know that there isn't even an equivalent in American speech for 'taking the piss'?) Yet here in Britain it is such a fundamental part of daily life that you scarcely notice it."

It was still unfamiliar in 2013 when one of the hosts of *CBS This Morning* had an exchange with Keira Knightley; the leading actors of a movie she was in had been featured on the cover of *Time* magazine:

> KNIGHTLEY: Yes, I love that it's got Benedict Cumber-batch right there and I will enjoy taking the piss out of him for that *Time* cover.
>
> NORAH O'DONNELL: Taking the piss out of him?
>
> KNIGHTLEY: Yes.
>
> O'DONNELL: Not a phrase we use here but I love it. It sounds so good. . . . What does taking the piss out of someone mean?
>
> KNIGHTLEY: I didn't know how you say it here. Well, teasing.
>
> O'DONNELL: I should take the piss out of Charlie Rose every once in a while.

But the expression was soon to make its move. In 2015, the author and television presenter Anthony Bourdain said about his daughter in an interview, "She takes the piss out of me a lot. I'll say, 'Honey, will you clean up that stuff on the floor?' and she responds, 'Why don't you ask your fans!'"

The *New York Times* would surely have used it sooner if not for its rather harsh policy about off-color language. But it was onboard by 2020, when *take the piss* or *taking the piss* appeared four times in the newspaper, including in a quote from minor celebrity Clay Aiken about his time on the TV show *Celebrity Apprentice* with Donald Trump Jr.: "He was perfectly fine to take the piss out of himself, but sometimes he'd make a joke about his dad—and then you could tell he was really nervous his dad wouldn't like it. His self-esteem was in the gutter."

Adoption | *Piss off!*: On the radar

● ● ● ● ●

Taking the piss: Emerging

● ● ● ● ●

"Poo"

No one can say this book is not willing to tackle the profound issues of the day. I submit to you a headline from *Smithsonian* magazine: "The Most Exclusive Coffee in the World Is Harvested from Elephant Poo." Seeing it solidified my sense that British *poo* was taking over from the traditional American *poop* in the fecal euphemism department.

The question turns out to be a somewhat complicated one, as these questions tend to be. The *OED* has separate entries for *poo* and *poop*, with separate etymologies. *Poo* derives from an onomatopoeic interjection dating from the 1600s, when it was more commonly spelled "puh" or "pooh," or, as Henry Fielding rendered it in this quote from *Tom Jones*, "'Pugh,' says she, 'you have pinked a Man in a Duel, that's all.'"

It's not precisely clear to me why A. A. Milne called his anthropomorphic bear Winnie the Pooh. Milne writes, cryptically, "His arms were so stiff from holding on to the string of the balloon all that time that they stayed up straight in the air for more than a week, and whenever a fly came and settled on his nose he had to blow it off. And I think—but I am not sure—that that is why he was always called Pooh."

The word's association with excrement comes later. *Green's Dictionary of Slang* has examples from Australia and New Zealand of it being used in a nursery context in the 1950s and '60s—for example, "I did poo, Mummy." Around the same time, the expression *in the pooh* shows up in Australia as a euphemism for *in the shit*—that is, in trouble.

And it shows up in the U.S. as well, at least according to Harold Wentworth and Stuart Berg Flexner's 1960 *Dictionary of American Slang*, which defines *poo* as "feces." The first British example I have is from *The Guardian* in 1981 (via the *OED*): "That doggy's doing a poo." A memorable instance comes in *Harry Potter and the Order of the Phoenix* (2003), in which a sparkler is seen "resolutely spelling out the word 'POO.'"

Poop has a whole different backstory. The *OED* cites a definition from an early eighteenth-century dictionary: "to break Wind backwards softly." By the 1920s, *poop* had acquired, in the United States, solidity.

Complicating manners are at least three additional meanings of *poop*. One, derived from the term for the rear of a boat, refers to the rear of a person or animal. The second is an American slang term, originating in the military, for inside information. (Ezra Pound wrote in a 1940 letter, either intentionally or unintentionally punning, "This federation poop is just the same old . . . secret committee of shit.") The third, which probably isn't relevant, is *pooped*, an Americanism meaning "exhausted" or "worn out."

In any case, Ngram Viewer makes it clear that, at least when it comes to canines, *poop* is the more common American term and *poo* the British one, with the alternative making headway on both sides of the Atlantic (figure 21).

In terms of American adoption of *poo*, a key event seems to be a 1997 episode of the animated TV satire *South Park*.

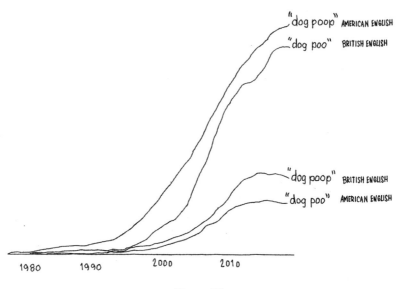

Figure 21

"Mr. Hankey, the Christmas Poo." According to Wikipedia, "The episode follows Kyle as he feels excluded from the town's Christmas celebrations due to being Jewish, finding solace in Mr. Hankey, a sentient piece of feces."

Further research is clearly needed. For the time being, my sense is that my fellow Americans are rather conflicted on the matter, sometimes, as in a *Huffington Post* piece, trying to have it both ways:

> Poop. Is there anything it can't do? On Wednesday, The Denver Zoo introduced what is believed to be the world's first poo-powered motorized tuk tuk showcasing The Denver Zoo's very own patent-pending gasification technology.

Make up your mind, HuffPo!

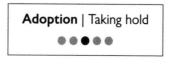

"Shag"

Shag is both a transitive and intransitive verb: you can shag someone (as in Mike Myers's film *Austin Powers: The Spy Who Shagged Me*), or merely shag, full stop. It's also a noun, memorably used by Myers in full Powers mode: "Fancy a shag?"

Interestingly, the first citation in the *OED* is from Thomas Jefferson in 1770: "He had shagged his mother and begotten himself on her body." Since then, it has been primarily used in Britain, with some under-the-radar or backwoods American use. In 1953, American folklorist Gershon Legman published this portion of a limerick: "Simple shagging / Without any wagging / Is only for screwing canoeing." Six years later, Alfred Zugsmith wrote in *The Beat Generation*, "They're too chicken themselves to willingly shag with anybody but their husbands."

The Powers films opened the floodgates to American use of the various forms of the word. There is no shortage of examples, including in a 2018 *New York Times* review of a book by an Obama White House aide that "shatters the genre of the Washington memoir. Nowhere in George F. Kennan's *Memoirs* does he recount how many times he drunkenly shagged someone named Jennifer." Florida novelist Carl Hiaasen has a line, also political, in his 2002 book *Squeeze Me*: "She's shagging one of her Secret Service guys."

As common as the British meaning has become in America, the word is still capable of creating confusion. In 2010, a writer for *The Guardian* quoted a passage from "Main Currents of American Thought," a 1939 short story by Irwin Shaw: "Across the street, on the public athletics field, four boys were shagging flies." The *Guardian* journo went on:

> My confused yet amused eyes tripped and staggered over
> the sentence, but made no sense of it, retraced their steps
> several times, then sat on the kerb [U.S.: "curb"] of the

full-stop [see chapter 3], under the shade of the quotation mark, and scratched their chin in bemusement. Boys shagging flies? Not only is that physically impossible, but why on earth would a celebrated American writer, working in a more decorous pre-Monty Python and Little Britain age, stoop to such crudity? It had to be something else.

Some sleuthing around and further research—the *OED*, Google and a couple of American friends—cracked the mystery. Rather than implying that a group of young lads were attempting intercourse with insects, the sentence was actually about baseball and catching fly balls.

And yes, in long-standing American usage, *flies* are baseballs hit high in the air, usually with a fungo bat (look it up), and *shagging* is catching them in a practice session. And at golf practice ranges, the entry-level job is shagging balls, or collecting them from the ground.

Along these lines, I have a confession to make. In 2002, I was touring Scotland and stopped in at a friendly-looking pub for a pint. Intrigued by one of the taps, I told the barman, "I'll have a sheep's hagger." The titters that came from him and the folks at the bar clued me that I had made a misstep. Looking at the name again, and the logo of a sheep with a come-hither look, I realized that the correct pronunciation was "sheep-shagger."

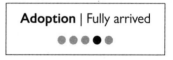

Adoption | Fully arrived

"Shite"; "gobshite"

To state the (probably) obvious, *shite* means "shit" and rhymes with "fight." It can be substituted for every meaning of the four-letter version, from the "taking a" evacuative to the one-syllable interjection to the "full of" metaphorical. Of Irish origin, it was a favorite of James Joyce, who wrote in *A Portrait of the Artist as a Young Man* (1916), "They moved in slow circles, . . . their long swishing tails besmeared with stale shite."

Ernest Hemingway, interestingly, was partial to the metaphorical use, and it's amusing to imagine that he might have picked up the word from Joyce when they crossed paths in Paris in the 1920s. In a 1928 letter Hemingway wrote, "Bloody near 2550 words. Probably shite too." And in another letter the following year, "You must have thought me a shite not to write."

I have the sense that through the twentieth century, the Irish held on to the literal meaning. As late as 2022, there was this bit of dialogue in the film *The Banshees of Inisherin*:

> COLM: The other night, two hours you spent talking to me about the things you found in your little donkey's shite that day.
>
> PÁDRAIC: It was me pony's shite, which shows how much you were listening.

Meanwhile, the figurative sense was picked up by British as well as American people who wanted to sound colorful. The midcentury English literary buddies Kingsley Amis, Philip Larkin, and Robert Conquest were fond of it. In a 1941 letter, Larkin wrote, "What is truth? Balls. What is love? Shite." And Conquest penned this limerick:

> There was a young fellow called Shit,
> A name he disliked quite a bit,
> So he changed it to Shite,
> A step in the right
> Direction, one has to admit.

In common with *fecking* (see the entry in this chapter), *shite* is less offensive than its Anglo-Saxon four-letter variant.

As someone posted to Urban Dictionary, it can be "the best way to say 'shit' without getting told off, as you can simply say that you were trying out being Irish for the day."

Hemingway would be happy to see that his fellow Americans have taken up the word, a bit. In an early mainstream use, Jack Shafer wrote in *Slate* in 2004 that former *New York Times* editor Howell Raines "all but comes out and writes that his predecessor, Joseph Lelyveld, produced shite." More recently, Emma Barty wrote in *Cosmopolitan*, "Despite 2021 being kind of a shite year overall, it was actually a fairly good year for movies."

As for *gobshite*, it is a general term of abuse that, the *OED* notes, is "chiefly Irish English" and (thanks!) "derogatory." Hugh Leonard's 1973 play *Da* has the line, "Hey God, there's an old gobshite at the tradesmen's entrance." Stan Carey has noted that the word is "insulting, yes, but like many Hiberno-English pejoratives it's also occasionally used with some affection (as for example when someone you're fond of is too generous or compliant, or is simply talking rubbish)."

According to a comment by Phil Jones on the *NOOBs* blog, even years ago, the word was not *exclusively* Irish. Jones wrote,

> It is also a Liverpool expression and dates back decades. My father used to use it when irate. My mother who was more genteel would wince if she heard him use it which she seldom did as it was not considered a word to be used in mixed company. It has nothing to do with loquaciousness or talking nonsense. A gobshite is a expectorated lump of saliva. To call someone a gobshite is to equate them to such a lump. I have never heard it used affectionately. I have met several.

Interestingly, there was an earlier American meaning: an enlisted seaman in the navy. In 1910, the publication *Our Navy* counseled, "The use of the slang words 'gob' and 'gobshite' and 'jackshite' is to be deplored." Whether or not it was because of this admonition, the word fell out of favor in the U.S. But it popped up in the twenty-first century. In 2013, Nancy Friedman emailed me asking, "Is Charles Pierce the only U.S. journalist who uses 'gobshite'?" She provided a link to an *Esquire* blog post by Pierce titled "What Are the Gobshites Saying These Days?"

Nancy was not the only one to notice this. I found a 2012 quote from a "political observer" named Charlie Cooke, who wrote, "Pierce's hyperbole transcends mere disagreement, as does his dismissal of all those who dissent as 'gobshites.'"

Pierce himself was alerted to my discussion of his use of the term, and he responded, "I do not dismiss all who 'dissent' as gobshites. Here at the blog, the term is strictly reserved for the people on the Sunday [political talk shows]. Other people with whom I disagree are omadhauns, gossoons and, occasionally, thooleramawns. I hope that clears things up."

But otherwise, there aren't many American sightings. The Gobshites are a New England rock band, and the combative atheist biologist P. Z. Myers has taken a fancy to the word, referring to one opponent as "a clueless gobshite" and telling another, "You are a silly, ignorant, gobshite, tone trolling, vacuous, dumbfuck."

So, to answer Nancy Friedman's original question: basically, yes.

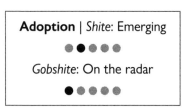

Adoption | *Shite*: Emerging

● ● ● ● ●

Gobshite: On the radar

● ● ● ● ●

"Wanker"

In 2006, Lynne Murphy presented her very first Words of the Year on her *Separated by a Common Language* blog. For the most notable "Import from British English to American English," she chose *wanker*. It comes from the verb *wank*, meaning "to masturbate." The "-er" noun form dates from the 1970s and can be either literally a frequent or habitual masturbator or figuratively a detestable person.

The transition from one to another is explained in a bit of dialogue from Kingsley Amis's 1978 novel *Jake's Thing*:

"Damon, what's a wanker?" . . .

"These days a waster, a shirker, someone who's fixed himself a soft job or an exalted position by means of an undeserved reputation on which he now coasts."

"Oh. Nothing to do with tossing off then?"

"Well, connected with it, yes, but more metaphorical than literal."

At that point, both forms were considered rather crude, but by 1997, in his book *The King's English*, Amis could write that commentators about language could be divided into "berks and wankers." "Berks" are fools (the term originated in rhyming slang for "Berkeley hunt"), while

wankers are prissy, fussy, priggish, prim and of what they would probably misrepresent as a higher social class than one's own. They speak in an over-precise way with much pedantic insistence on letters not generally sounded, especially Hs. Left to them the language would die of purity, like medieval Latin.

That same year, British prime minister Tony Blair, in an unguarded moment, referred to some leftist journalists who had given him a hard time as "unreconstructed wankers."

The word had reached America by 1994, when a dictionary of campus slang defined it as a "loser, uncool person." Seven years later, linguist John Algeo spotted a graffito in a men's room at the University of Georgia: "The MLA [Modern Language Association] Where wankers philosophize about wanking."

Lynne Murphy noted in announcing her selection in 2006,

"Wanker" has been sneaking into American popular culture under the radar for some years (e.g. Peggy Bundy's maiden name on television's *Married with Children* [1987] was Wanker, which was certainly meant as a joke that could make it past the censors' noses—though it would have more trouble doing so on British television). But it came into its own in AmE this year, especially, it seems, in political blogging, where many variants on the term are found, including: "wankiest" (in *American Prospect*), "wankerism" (quoted on Firedoglake), "wank-fest" (in a letter to Salon.com), "wankery" (on Brendan Calling from the Underground).

In 2011, after news came out that Navy Seals had found stashes of pornography in Osama bin Laden's compound, the *New York Post* ran this inspired headline: "Osama bin Wankin'."

In "The Girl Code," a *Simpsons* episode that aired in January 2016, Lisa creates an avatar with a British accent (voiced by Stephen Merchant) who ultimately comes to life and delivers some hard truths, including, "Your species is on the precipice of turning into complete and utter wankers." The use of the word on network TV didn't raise any American eyebrows, but it retained a whiff of naughtiness in the U.K., where a website that provides transcripts of *Simpsons* episodes rendered it "w*nk*rs."

Adoption | Taking hold

CHAPTER FIVE

Sport(s)

Sports are rife with NOOBs, including . . . wait for it . . . soccer.

Not One-Off Footballisms

After the blog had been going for about a year, Jack Bell, who at the time covered soccer for the *New York Times*, emailed me to ask if he could write a guest post. I replied absolutely, as why would I not? Tongue planted in cheek, Jack bemoaned the Britishization of soccer terminology on U.S. broadcasts, "where every chip is 'cheeky,' every player on the wing is 'nippy,' every field is a 'pitch,' every pair of cleats are 'boots,' every uniform a 'kit' and every big play is 'massive, just massive.'"

He lamented that (the American) Major League Soccer "has for some reason allowed a handful of teams to append the letters F.C. to their club names. That stands for Football Club. That's fine if you're in Burnley or Bristol (England, that is), but it's patently absurd in the U.S. . . . F.C. Dallas? Seattle Sounders F.C. Laughable."

He warmed to his theme:

Fox Soccer's nightly report and on comes a story about something called a "tapping up" scandal. Sorry, but WTF? Again, I had never, ever heard the British term for a bribery scandal. Ever. I also broke for the dictionary when another announcer used the word "scupper" to describe something gone wrong. So what's a scupper? It's a nautical term for the spaces on deck that allow water to flow back into the sea. Get it? Man overboard.

The trend apparently spread from the broadcast booth to *supporters* (see the entry later in this chapter), both watching at home and at the ground (stadium). In 2013, the BBC ran an article quoting American soccer blogger Chris Harris on a contentious split "between U.S. soccer fans insisting on using American terms to describe the game compared to Americans who insist on using British language to talk about the game, so they're more accepted by hardcore soccer fans and ex-pats. So when Americans use terms like 'match,' 'nil-nil,' 'kit' and other terms, many U.S. fans will tag those Americans with the 'Euro snob' label."

The following year, NPR host Robert Siegel took special aim at the word *nil* and its

creeping penetration of American English thanks to the World Cup. Nil is a contracted scrap of Latin that survives in a few common bits of American English. We might say the chances of something happening are next to nil. Headline writers always in need of very short words sometimes use nil. But if I said, in the top of the third inning, the Nationals led the Cubs one-nil and then Chicago scored an equalizer the late Harry Carey and Phil Rizzuto [both baseball announcers] would both shout, "Holy cow!" in their graves.

Also in 2014, another *Times* writer, Sarah Lyall, wrote about American fans who talk "about the pitch (field) and the kit (jerseys) and the supporters (themselves) and who, when compelled to use the word soccer, were putting it in invisible quotation marks."

As *soccer* is of British origin (see the entry later in this chapter), perhaps there should be quotation marks around the invisible quotation marks.

"On the back foot"; "wrong-foot"

My blog post on *on the back foot* provoked no small amount of controversy, stemming, in the main, from whether you think of the phrase as deriving from boxing or cricket. The *OED* defines the boxing sense as "in a defensive position or stance; (hence *figurative*) at a disadvantage; on the defensive."

The figurative sense had migrated over to the U.S. at least by the 2010s, when there were these examples, among many:

- "In Oakland, starter Travis Blackley tossed six solid innings while his offense scratched out enough runs to seize their fifth straight win and put the Rangers (93–68) on the back foot."—*Chicago Tribune*
- "Activist investors generally prefer to be on the attack. So it's odd to see them on the back foot, fighting to preserve an important arrow in their quiver."—*New York Times*, mixing its metaphors splendidly

In describing cricket *back foot*, I am handicapped by the fact that I have roughly zero understanding of the rules of the sport. That said, it appears that there are two versions of the phrase. As *NOOBs* commenter David Goodman succinctly put it, "There is a difference in cricket between playing 'off' the back foot, which can result in a stylish, premeditated attacking shot, and being forced 'onto' the back foot, which implies a hurried retreat into a defensive pose. Being 'on the back foot' implies the latter."

As for the transitive verb *wrong-foot*, it originated as (and still is) a tennis expression. If your opponent is running or moving, say to their right, to "wrong-foot" them is to hit the ball to their left, also known as "behind" them. The *OED's* first citation is from the *Daily Telegraph* in 1928, and it uses an odd-sounding gerund form: "His ground strokes had not the same speed and polish as Austin's, nor could he steer all his volleys into the same wrong-footing area."

The first *OED* citation in a more standard verb form doesn't come till a 1959 book on rugby: "You could pick up the ball as though to go one side, and then, having picked up the ball, swing to the other side. . . . It will wrong-foot the attackers, thereby giving you more time for your kick."

However, using Google Books, I found a tennis example from 1935: "He then lost his service after reaching 40–15—two match points—owing to really good defensive play by Henkel who 'wrong-footed' him and caused him to fall by 40–30."

The source is *American Lawn Tennis*, a periodical that, to state the obvious, was American. The quotation marks around "wrong-footed" suggest that the phrase was a relatively new borrowing from British tennis discourse. I am an avid tennis player, and my sense is that the term has long been used by people from all countries, yet it retains a British feel. In fact, when I say something like, "You properly wrong-footed me!" I always do so in a mock-British accent, aspirating the *t* in "footed" instead of using the flapping American "foodded."

Ngram Viewer shows the phrase emerging in the 1960s, rising steeply in Britain and more gradually in the U.S., and as of 2019 being used about three times more often there than here.

I have no doubt that the uptick in both Britain and the U.S. is due to nonsporting, metaphorical uses of the term. The *OED* defines this as "to disconcert by an unexpected move; to catch unprepared." Its first example is from a 1957 book: "'Let me tell you . . . that the Government has made enquiries and we are not at all satisfied with the accuracy of your report.' Kingsley was wrong-footed."

Neither this nor any of the other citations are from American sources, but it has become a popular NOOB, to the point of cliché. The first eight uses of the term in the *New York Times* were published between 1964 and 1977, and all concerned tennis. (There were also two references in music reviews to "wrong-footed rhythms," but I consider that unrelated.) Then a 1982 article had this line: "The Japanese are now busy making many of their cars bigger, not smaller, and could catch Detroit wrong-footed once again if fuel economy becomes less important to consumers."

The trickle has become a flood. The *Times* used the phrase thirty-one times between 2019 and 2022, and only three (none in 2022) had to do with sports. The most recent as I write: "The [financial] markets are efficient enough that it's hard to be better than average for long, and when trends change sharply as they did this year, nearly everyone is wrong-footed."

Adoption | Taking hold
● ● ● ● ●

"Own goal"

The *OED* has two definitions for this phrase. The first is "a goal scored against the scorer's own team, usually unintentionally." The dictionary cites a use of the term in *The Times* (of London) in 1922, but the next one isn't till the *Sunday Pictorial*'s use in 1947, the quotation marks around the phrase suggesting it hadn't yet entered public parlance: "an amazing 'own goal' by Wilf Mannion." The *OED* has a 1998 quote from the *Miami Herald* in reference to hockey, and I would judge that in recent years the term has been commonly used by Americans discussing that sport and soccer.

The second definition is, "*fig[urative]*. (orig. and chiefly *Brit.*). An act that unintentionally harms one's own interests." The first citation is from *The Economist* in 1975: "The doyen of the Tribune group . . . scored an own goal on Wednesday night. . . . His speech at a packed Tribune rally was a gross tactical miscalculation."

This was still unfamiliar in the U.S. in 1987, when, covering an undeclared "tanker war" in the Persian Gulf, a *New York Times* correspondent wrote, "British correspondents even credited Iran with an 'own goal'—an allusion to the soccer player who scores one for the other side—when an Iranian gunboat reportedly shot up a Japanese tanker carrying Iranian oil somewhere in the dark the other night."

The term's growth in the United States may have been spurred by a 2010 article in *Harper's* that got a lot of attention: "Own Goal: How Homeless Soccer Explains the World." However, it wasn't until seven years later that the *Times* published a use that was not in reference to sports or a quote from a British person. The columnist Ross Douthat, referring to how George H. W. Bush's Supreme Court pick David Souter turned out to be a reliable liberal vote, wrote, "For Republicans and conservatives, it was the most extraordinary of own goals— as if Obama had been persuaded . . . to appoint a jurist who turned out to vote like [archconservative] Samuel Alito."

It's been fairly frequently seen in the paper since then, for example in a 2021 piece by another columnist, Jamelle Bouie:

"For conservative Democrats, handing Biden a major legislative defeat . . . is the very definition of an own goal."

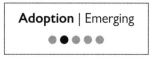

Adoption | Emerging

Plural Verb for Collective Noun

What I call "collective nouns," H. W. Fowler in *A Dictionary of Modern English Usage* (1926) referred to as "nouns of multitude." He gave as examples *army, Government, company,* and *party.* Fowler allowed that they could be treated as singular or plural, and that the decision of which to choose was not always easy:

> "The Cabinet is divided" is better, because in the order of thought a whole must precede division; & "The Cabinet are agreed" is better, because it takes two or more to agree. . . .
> In general it may be said that while there is always a better & worse in the matter there is seldom a right & a wrong, & any attempt to elaborate rules would be waste of labour. [Fowler was fond of ampersands.]

In keeping with Fowler, the British have continued to use both plural and singular, depending on logic, whim, or even politics. A reader of my blog commented, "The Tories (the Conservative Party) tend to use 'the Government are' whereas Labour uses 'the Government is.' This was certainly the case in my day during the Thatcher and Heath eras."

But Americans, perhaps having more of a need for consistency, universally use the singular. In her book *The Prodigal Tongue,* Lynne Murphy writes, "One study showed that Americans use plural verbs after 'army,' 'association,' and 'public' less than 1% of the time in written and spoken English. The respective numbers for written British English were 21%, 10%, and 38%, and for spoken British they were 21%, 50%, and 72%."

Watching ESPN's coverage of an England-Croatia European Cup match in 2012, I was jarred by this on-screen graphic: "If results hold, England advance." But it was not a one-off. In short order, I found an American newspaper writing, "The team are composed of two types of people who usually don't mingle." From another, "As for the Midwest bias, I imagine it's because the team are Big 10 fans." And my hometown *Philadelphia Inquirer*, referring to Manchester City, wrote, "City are undefeated in eight home games."

Also in 2012, the public radio show *On the Media* had a conversation between host Bob Garfield and Tom Scocca, the editor of the online sports magazine *Deadspin*, that brought up another thing Americans sometimes pluralize this way, and showed the surprising passion this issue can provoke. Scocca began by noting the British convention, with the example "Arsenal are the superior side in this match." (Note: The *OED* defines *poncy* as "affected, pretentious, self-consciously refined or superior; overly fancy or elaborate; effeminate, homosexual." It's a Britishism that has not penetrated to the U.S.)

GARFIELD: But the problem is, as you observed, if you use the British convention, you sound like a poncy—

SCOCCA: Rock critic, yeah. That's a longstanding problem in writing or talking about rock music, because so many bands have these names that are singular to describe this collective unit that's the band. And, you know, there's a lot of Anglophilia in rock writing, and so there are people who will say things like, "Pavement are the most important band since Wire."

GARFIELD: [*Laughs.*] And how does that make you feel, when you run across—"Pavement are the greatest band since Wire"?

SCOCCA: Despite the fact that I might agree with the sentiment, the skin crawls on the back of my neck.

GARFIELD: And you basically want to find the critic and just kind of slap him around, come on—

SCOCCA: Yeah, give him a wedgie or something.

Adoption | Emerging

"Soccer"

Americans are sometimes mocked or derided for using this word to denote the game the British (and more or less the rest of the world) know as "football." So it might be surprising to learn that it is a NOOB. The term originated in Britain as a reference to the Football Association, and to differentiate it from other forms of football, notably rugby, or "rugger." (How and why *association* was abbreviated as *soccer* I do not know.) The first *OED* citation is from 1885: "This was pre-eminently the most important 'Socker' game played in Oxford this term." In 1894, the *Westminster Gazette* referred to "the rival attractions of 'rugger' and 'socker.'" The familiar spelling (and the abandonment of quotation marks) shows up in 1902 in some verse published in a different periodical with a similar name, the *Westminster Hospital Gazette*:

> When we've won the Rugger Cup, boys,
> And the Soccer Mug as well
> When our fame throughout the world is being rung,

Shall we miss the filthy lucre as our hearts with pride will
swell?
There's no one that will regret that it was done.

Sarah Lyall of the *New York Times* has noted that in Britain, *soccer* continued to be used "happily—right alongside
'football'—until at least the 1970s, when a surge of bad temper and anti-Americanism made it virtually radioactive." She
mentions the autobiography of Matt Busby, the manager of
Manchester United in the 1950s and 1960s, *Soccer at the Top*,
and another book of the period, *George Best: The Inside Story
of Soccer's Super-star*.

Back to the early days, *soccer* got picked up quickly in
America, seemingly first by headline writers as a conveniently
short word, as in the *New York Times* in 1906: "Penn Beat Harvard's Soccer Team." (Headlines are customarily in the present
tense, meaning that "Penn," is, or are, treated as a plural. See
previous entry.) The article, in its entirety, reads, "The University of Pennsylvania's Association football team defeated the
team representing Harvard to-day by a score of 8 to 1."

The year before, Francis H. Tabor of New York had written
a letter to the editor of the *Times* to protest the appellation:

> It seems a thousand pities that in reporting Association foot-
> ball matches *The New York Times*, in company with all the
> other newspapers, should persistently call the game "socker."
> In the first place, there is no such word, and in the second
> place, it is an exceedingly ugly and undignified one. . . .
>
> It is to be hoped that this heresy will not spread, and
> that *The New York Times* will henceforth head its articles
> "Association Football."

As we all know, Tabor's hopes were in vain and in short
order *soccer* became the U.S. term of choice. There was an

obvious reason for this. America was developing both a game of its own—the one with the quarterback and field goals—and a name for it. That name was used as early as 1881, when the *New York Herald* reported, "A splendid game of football was played yesterday at the Polo Grounds between . . . Harvard and Princeton."

Compared with all the other British soccer terminology that's been adopted here, *football*, indicating the game with the round ball, is only a modest NOOB. That's because 99.9 percent of Americans understand *football* to mean what the Giants and Cowboys play on Sundays. The one exception I'm aware of is the uber-pretentious Lisa, of TV's *The Simpsons*, who refers to the homegrown sport as "American football."

Adoption | Outpaced

"Sport"

Between 2012 and 2020, I addressed *sport*—as opposed to the American *sports*—on the blog five times. My first go was prompted by a quote on the *New York Times* website that year by a writer who is actually a friend of mine, Michael Sokolove. Mike had written an article about the runner Oscar Pistorius, and in a Q and A he said, "One of the great things about sport is that it is in some ways primitive, or we want to imagine it is." *Times* columnist David Brooks wrote at about the same time, "The moral ethos of sport is in tension with the moral ethos of faith, whether Jewish, Christian or Muslim. The moral universe of modern sport is oriented around victory and supremacy." And *Slate* ran the headline, "Politics and Sport: A Dangerous Mix."

To clarify: Americans have generally used *sport* to refer to a singular pursuit: baseball is a sport, as is football. But the general field of endeavor is *sports*, and in traditional American usage, that word would have been used in all three quotes.

I wasn't the only one who took note of the American move into the collective singular. Later in 2012, Republican presidential candidate Mitt Romney said of the Daytona 500 auto race, "This combines a couple of things I like best—cars and sport." Jon Stewart ran a clip of the quote on *The Daily Show* and remarked, "Here in the human world, we call things like NASCAR 'sportsss.'" (I have no comment on Stewart's equation of "the human world" with America.)

An English reader of the blog, LBS, commented, "I first heard someone talk about 'playing sport' in Australia in 1967, and then thought, What a silly expression! Now you hear it in England. Except for 'sports day' (athletics) we never spoke of sport or sports at school, only of games. Otherwise sports were what people did with guns or fishing rods or hounds."

LBS apparently traveled in superannuated circles in his youth. The *OED* confirms that in "the 18th and 19th centuries the term [*sport*] was often used with reference to hunting, shooting, and fishing." But the dictionary has this 1863 citation: "If recreation is found, or pastime is sought in activity or change, . . . it is called diversion; and if we set ourselves to take part in the amusement, . . . it constitutes sport." And this from 1884: "All other branches of athletic sport . . . have their ruling bodies, and so has cycling."

I glimpsed some of the intricacies in British use from another commenter on the blog, Kevin Flynn, who gave as an example the sentence, "BT Sport is a sports channel." Kevin went on to say,

In BrE the mass noun "sport" (e.g. "sport is a business") becomes "sports" when used adjectivally—thus: "I used to play a lot of sport," but "We train at the sports centre." One of the longest-running BBC radio programmes is "Sports Report," which has been broadcast every Saturday afternoon since 3 January 1948, and there were other programmes with titles like "Weekly Sports Review" as early as 1924—but also "Sport and Sportsmen." That contrast between "sports" (in compounds) and plain "sport" elsewhere is also shown by the fact that items within "Sports Report" have included the likes of "Talking Sport," "Sports Round-up," "Sport in the Midlands," "Sports Quiz," etc.

Using his terminology, in the U.S., *sports* was established long ago as the mass noun. How long? At least by 1909, when the *New York Times* ran the headline "Notable Achievements in the World of Sports." Seven years later, this appeared in the *Iowa City Citizen*: "Cole was well known to sports fans." By that time the *Times* and other papers were calling the section in which athletic pursuits were covered "Sports"—and newspapers' use of this form no doubt encouraged the widespread U.S. adoption.

Then there is the term for what the *OED* defines as "a jacket, typically resembling a suit jacket and now usually worn by a man, for informal wear." It presents a rather confusing reversal of the two countries' pluralizing habits. Ngram Viewer shows that in 2010, the most frequently used terms for this item in British English, in decreasing order of popularity, were *sports jacket, sport coat, sports coat,* and *sport jacket.* In America, they were *sport coat, sports jacket, sports coat,* and *sport jacket.* ("And there was old Dick. . . . Sitting at a table in blue jeans and a gruesome sports jacket."—J. D. Salinger, "Franny," 1955.) What is one to make of this? I got nothing.

I mentioned that the most recent time I covered U.S. *sport* on the blog was in 2020. The post was occasioned by this tweet from Nike:

Sport has the power to change your life.

Sport has the power to change the world.

#SportChangesEverything

In other words, game over.

"Support"; "supporter"

The traditional American equivalents for these terms are *root for* and *fan*. The latter (which derives from *fanatic*) seems to have preceded *supporter*. The *OED* has an 1890 quote from the *Omaha (Nebraska) Sunday Bee*—"There has not been much enthusiasm shown among the baseball fans of the city"—and a definition of *fan* from a 1901 edition of *Dialect Notes*: "a base ball enthusiast; common among reporters."

By contrast, the first reference to *supporters* (of the Chelsea Football Club) in the *OED* is from 1958. A use of the verb form appears four years later: "When you think of all that, what other football club is there worth supporting?" The British equivalent of American *fan club* was used in a typically witty line from Tom Stoppard's 1972 play *Jumpers*: "That he [God] should have been taken up by a glorified supporters' club is only a matter of psychological interest."

As far as American use goes, the noun and the verb present slightly different cases. *Supporter* means precisely the same thing as *fan* and sometimes is applied merely for elegant variation—that is, using a synonym in order to avoid word repetition. That would appear to be the case in this 2021 tweet from the celebrity-news outfit TMZ: "A Blue Jays fan gave a young Yankees supporter an Aaron Judge home run ball during Tuesday's game in Toronto . . . and the kid's reaction was priceless."

But *support*, which implies a permanent state, is arguably an improvement over *root for*, which can be momentary. ("I rooted for Podunk U to beat Alabama because they were the underdog.") That may be why it's creeping in. A New York City news site reported in 2021,

> NY1 also found that there are some households that are split over which team they support. While some cited season statistics as the reason they support either the Yankees or Mets, there were others who choose to be at odds with their family members because they like to be different.
>
> That's the case for Isabella D'Introno and her brother, Nicholas. "I like to go against him," said Isabella of why she supports the Yankees while her brother roots for the Mets.
>
> NY1 found fans who said that they would never support a different team, even if family or friends encouraged them to.

It still sounds a bit jarring to my ears, as does this quote from a baseball website: "[Jerry] Seinfeld, in the first *Seinfeld Chronicles* episode, supported the Mets, but in subsequent episodes, he supports the Yankees." The writer is identified as "a proud supporter of his local team, the Toronto Blue Jays," so it may be a Canadian thing.

In any case, I have some anecdotal evidence that American *supporter* at least existed as long ago as 1969. Harry Allison, who taught seventh graders at my prep school, used to ask new kids which teams they rooted for, just so he could reply, "I'm an Athletic supporter."

That would never fly today.

Adoption | Emerging
●●●●●

CHAPTER SIX

Food and Drink(s)

Peckish for a boozy brunch with a coffee and some nice veg? You've come to the right place.

"Book a table"

When I first spent significant time in London, in the mid-1990s, one of the first words that struck me as unusual was *book*, used as an all-purpose verb to indicate, well, as the *OED* puts it, "to engage for oneself by payment (a seat or place in a travelling conveyance or in a theatre or other place of entertainment)." The dictionary cites a first use in Benjamin Disraeli's 1826 novel *Vivian Grey*—"I'll give orders for them to book an inside place for the poodle"—and then an 1887 theatrical advert: "Seats can be booked one month in advance."

And when I was in London a hundred-plus years later, people were always talking about booking theater—excuse me, theatre—tickets, hotel rooms, and tables at restaurants.

The usage was not unheard of in the U.S., but *reserve* was much more common in reference to eating and sleeping. For plays and ballet and opera, I guess our best word has been *get*, which isn't very good. In all three cases, *book*—with its strong consonants and one-syllable oomph—is the better word, and hence it's not surprising that it has gotten traction here.

An early use came from *New York Times* tech columnist Peter Lewis in 1994. (His charming use of quotation marks and capitalization shows that this was the internet's very early days.) "With the proper 'Web browsing' software—available free on the Internet—the traveler can see photographs of a hotel's lobby and of a typical room, check maps of its neighborhood, and even book a room and get a confirmation via the PC."

Just about a decade later, according to Ngram Viewer, *book a room* overtook *reserve a room* in American English. The transition was helped, no doubt, by the hotel-reservation website Booking.com, founded in the Netherlands in 1996 and now worldwide.

Book a table isn't quite there, but it's gaining. *Book tickets* hasn't caught even to that extent. I give it another decade.

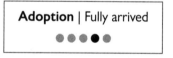

Adoption | Fully arrived

"Boozy"

In 2022, a row (this term for argument is not quite yet a NOOB) erupted in the U.K. regarding some greater-than-one number of drinks (see "Plural Collective Nouns" in chapter 7) parties Prime Minister Boris Johnson gave at 10 Downing Street, in defiance of COVID-19 regulations. The repeated use of the adjective *boozy* to describe them made me wonder if the term (also recently popular in the U.S.) was a NOOB. The answer is yes.

Before getting to that, I'll point out something else I found: a lot of dictionaries have some catching up to do with regard to *boozy*. The *OED*, *Merriam-Webster*, Lexico, and Dictionary.com all define it as a quality of a person: as Dictionary.com puts it, "drunken; intoxicated; addicted to liquor." But even some of the citations provided by Dictionary.com use a newer meaning:

- "That's likely to be truly historic, a cause in some parts for the kind of boozy 'carousals' that horrified that Union reporter back in 1887."—Voice of San Diego
- "Anything slightly tart, bitter, spicy, or on the boozier side is what I gravitate toward."—*Washington Post*
- "When we don't have to be concerned with consuming drinks while wearing masks, boozy park picnics or a dinner party supplied with professional cocktails will be all the more enjoyable."—*Eater*

There are two new meanings, really: first, an alcohol-driven event or experience (like Johnson's parties) and, second, as a 2007 Urban Dictionary definition puts it, "referring to any item, substance, or food that has had booze added or applied to it, thereby greatly enhancing its appeal and/or taste. 'Damn Gina! That's some kickass boozy Pecan pie you done whipped up for me.'"

By the way, my daughter Maria, a food writer and editor, informs me that this second *boozy* has become such a cliché that no one at any publication she writes for would deign to use it.

The first example of nonpersonal *boozy* I've found is from the House of Lords in 1976, when the Earl of Selkirk said, "I am asking for something which is quite small: that people should be given a little notice before a boozy festival takes place: I am not against boozy festivals from time to time; but the neighbours are entitled to a measure of protection." (Tellingly, Lord Kirkhill responded, "My Lords, I do not want to prolong this matter but I do not know what the noble Earl means by 'boozy festival.'")

As for NOOB-ness, looking at Google Books data from roughly 1975 on, *boozy* has consistently been roughly twice as commonly used in the U.K. as in the U.S., and it has increased four- or fivefold in both countries.

But the Americans might catch up, as not all of our journalists are as scrupulous as my daughter and her colleagues. The *New York Times*, for example, used *boozy* six times over the course of the last month of 2021, referring to, among other things, a revel, chats, a retirement, and two different cakes, including a Romanian one served at a Brooklyn bakery that I am determined to try: "Spongy, creamy, fruity, boozy, the tiny savarin covers most all of the dessert food groups."

> **Adoption** | Fully arrived
> ● ● ● ● ●

"A coffee"

The first *OED* citation for *a coffee* is a 1920 quote from the New Zealand–born writer Katherine Mansfield, and there's this from the British magazine *Woman's Own* in 1959: "If you're not in a hurry will you let me buy you a coffee?" The somewhat subtle distinction is that Americans would traditionally tend to say "a cup of coffee" or "some coffee" to indicate a serving of this beverage.

All three expressions rose significantly in America starting in the 1980s (mirroring the growing fascination with the drink). *A coffee* was used more and more in the 2000s, as in this quote from *Time* magazine: "Jeff Israely's journey was a little shorter—just round the corner from his apartment in Rome to have a coffee and a chat with his local barista, Vincenzo." Ngram Viewer shows it finally passing *some coffee* in 2015 (figure 22).

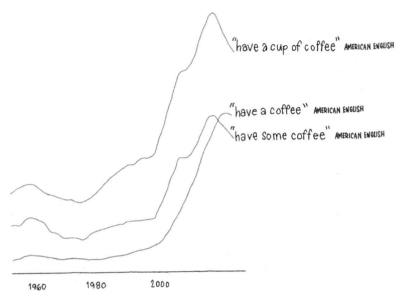

"have a cup of coffee" AMERICAN ENGLISH

"have a coffee" AMERICAN ENGLISH

"have some coffee" AMERICAN ENGLISH

1960   1980   2000

Figure 22

At this point *a coffee* is completely normalized, especially among coastal types, and it would almost have been surprising to hear Julia Roberts use any other term in this description she recently gave the *New York Times* of what she and her husband do for fun after the kids go off to school: "We'll take a bike ride or have a coffee or a meal somewhere, and then I'll have time to myself and now it's almost 3 o'clock."

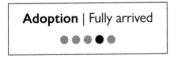

Adoption | Fully arrived

"Cuppa"

Continuing in the hot beverage department, a few years back, a colleague from the University of Delaware, McKay Jenkins, emailed me, "What's with the newly trendy use of the word *cuppa*, to imply a coffee- or tea-drinking experience? My lovely wife tells me that this is a '400-year-old' British expression. Is she right?"

Well, McKay, four hundred years, ninety years, what's the diff? The *OED* says the term is used "elliptically" and colloquially to mean cup o' tea and offers a first citation from New Zealand–born mystery writer Ngaio Marsh's *A Man Lay Dead* (1934): "Taking a strong cuppa at six-thirty in their shirt sleeves." All subsequent citations are from New Zealand or Australian sources until the first British one in 1949.

By the time McKay contacted me, it had indeed reached these shores. I looked around after I got his email and found a *Tampa Bay Times* article referring to local establishment that serves "lunch and an old-fashioned cuppa," and a *Palm Beach Post* one that said of a tea house in that city, "The experience isn't complete without a girl to chatter with and a good, strong cuppa." (Must be something about Florida.) An early use came in a 1982 *New York Times* article that remarked, "For some people, 'a cuppa' has replaced the early evening cocktail."

Note this 1968 *OED* citation: "'Good morning,' Joyce said. 'Coffee?' 'If it's no trouble I'd prefer a cuppa.'" That is to say, a cuppa tea, which remains the only meaning in the U.K. But as McKay's question suggested, an America cuppa can indeed contain something else, especially coffee. An Associated Press dispatch about rare coffee grown in Thailand says, "For now, only the wealthy or well-traveled have access to the cuppa, which is called Black Ivory Coffee." And the *Philadelphia Daily News* noted, "One trick is to stir chopped chocolate into a little of the milk to make a paste, then add that to the rest of the steamed milk, for a smoother, richer cuppa." That's right, a hot chocolate cuppa. The idea.

Adoption | On the radar

● ● ● ● ●

"Main"; "starter"

These two words designate the part of a meal Americans traditionally have called "main course" (or, more fancily, "entrée") and "appetizer."

To start with *starter*, the *OED*'s first few citations (starting in 1908) are actually from American sources. But I believe they were outliers. (It's hard to get hard data on *starter* as a culinary term, because it's used in reference to so many things—baseball pitchers, sourdough, horse racing, houses, marriages—not to mention the NOOB *non-starter* [see chapter 3].) The word had shown up in Britain by 1968, when an article in *New Society* sniffed, "The first course of a meal is sometimes called a 'starter,' which is perhaps not so much non-U as jargon." (In an essay published in 1954, Alan S. C. Ross coined the terms *U*, for upper class, and *non-U*, for everything else.) Writing in 1979, Victor Canning was more derisive: "There was avocado pear for what some people disgustingly called 'starters.'"

The first American use I've found is in an unsigned restaurant review in *Texas Monthly* magazine in 1982. But I don't think it really started to penetrate till the 1990s, as in a *New York Times* review from 1991: "Several salads on the menu proved to be better appetite arousers than some of our starter choices." Even then the writer doesn't seem to be quite comfortable with the word, possibly reaching for it to avoid the awkward repetition of "appetite"/"appetizer." But in the course of the next thirty years, *starter* became established in the U.S., and a 2020 use in the *Times* roundup of Thanksgiving ideas is but one among dozens in recent years: "My husband will make his great-grandmother's antipasto for a starter."

It's not surprising that *main* should be a not one-off Australianism, because it's a shortening of "main course" and Aussies love their abbreviations. The *OED*'s first citation is from the Brisbane *Sunday Sun* in 1987: "The best news is the prices—entrees \$4 mains \$6.50–\$7.50." (The rest of the world, other than the U.S., uses *entrée* to indicate appetizer or starter.) The word was still unfamiliar enough in the U.S. in 1994 to warrant quotation marks in this *New York Times* piece about Queensland: "The standard 'mains' are an eclectic selection, from a vegetable couscous to Thai-style green chicken curry and beer-battered fish and chips."

But it was being used in Canada by 1991 (an *OED* citation shows) and the U.K. by 1996, when this appeared in the *New Statesman*: "The set-price menu offers three starters, three mains, and three desserts." The *New York Times* started using it (to describe a San Francisco restaurant) in 2008, and five years later it was common enough that the editors of *Cooking Light* magazine could reasonably expect readers to understand this teaser on the magazine's cover: "Skillet Mains."

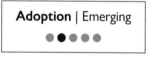

Adoption | Emerging

"Peckish"

As is the case with many words, I distinctly recall the first time I heard *peckish*. The student group I was leading on a British trip in the mid-1990s was on a touring bus (which I was learning to call a "coach"), and the tour guide said there would be cafés in the next town we'd stop in, "in case you're feeling peckish." From the context I inferred that it meant a little hungry—that is, less than "starving" or "famished"—and so it does.

The *OED* reveals that the term popped up in Britain as early as 1714. All the pre-1988 *OED* citations are British, including my favorite, from P. G. Wodehouse in 1936: "Not since the distant days of my first private school had I been conscious of such a devastating hunger. Peckish is not the word. I felt like a homeless tapeworm." A notable use came in Monty Python's "Cheese Shop" sketch from 1972:

OWNER: What can I do for you, sir?

CUSTOMER: Well, I was, uh, sitting in the public library on Thurmon Street just now, skimming through *Rogue Herries* by Hugh Walpole, and I suddenly came over all peckish.

OWNER: Peckish, sir?

CUSTOMER: Esurient.

OWNER: Eh?

CUSTOMER: 'Ee I were all 'ungry-like!

A *NOOBs* commenter wrote in to describe "some famous graffiti some years ago in Peckham, south London. Someone had written on a wall 'Ireland for the Irish' and underneath somebody had added 'Peckham for the peckish.'"

As befitting its prerevolutionary origin, *peckish* migrated to the U.S. more than two centuries ago; however, like *reckon* (see chapter 3), for a long time it was found mainly in western or rural settings. The *Dictionary of American Regional English* quotes a line from *The Clockmaker* (1838) by the Nova Scotia author Thomas Haliburton: "I don't care if I stop and breakfast with you, for I feel considerable peckish this morning." Its first appearance in the *New York Times* came in an 1872 Western tale, where a character says, "All hands got to be pretty peckish." And the word shows up in an 1899 dictionary of Virginia "Folk-Speech," defined as "inclined to eat, somewhat hungry."

The Coen brothers may or may not have been aware of this when they wrote the script for *O Brother, Where Art Thou?*, their 2000 backwoods Depression-era version of *The Odyssey*.

Big Dan Teague, the character played by John Goodman, says, "Thank you boys for throwin' in that fricassee. I'm a man of large appetite, and even with lunch under my belt, I was feelin' a mite peckish."

In America, meanwhile, *peckish* developed another meaning, kind of befitting the way it sounds. The *OED* defines this as "irritable, peevish; touchy," and has an 1857 quote from *Putnam's Monthly* magazine: "I have observed that mothers are apt to be oversweet on their daughters-in-law at first, and terribly peckish on them afterwards."

Both senses of the word fell out of use in the U.S. until the age of NOOBs. That 1988 *OED* citation is from the American novelist Laurie Colwin's book *Home Cooking*: "At four in the afternoon, everyone feels a little peckish, but only the British have institutionalized this feeling. Every year one English magazine or another carries an article about the decline of the tearoom, but teatime still exists and many tea shops serve it."

That was a bit of an outlier, and notably dealt with a British topic. The word really didn't start taking off in the U.S. until a decade or so later. I saw *O Brother* but didn't notice the word, and the first time I recall encountering it here was in 2015, when one of the producers of the TV show *Crazy Ex-Girlfriend* said in a radio interview that she'd chosen a California town as the setting in part because the local mall had pretzel shops at both entrances, "just in case you got peckish for a pretzel." (When I posted that quote on the blog, several commenters objected to the *peckish for* something construction as a vulgar Americanism.)

From 1995 through 2022, the word appeared in the *New York Times* 110 times, including in a review of a bar on the Lower East Side: "If peckish, try the matzo-meal fried chicken with pastrami-spiced gravy ($23)." And it was in the first sentence of a fitness article: "Why are we so peckish after some workouts but uninterested in eating after others?"

Why, indeed?

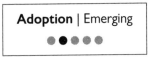

Adoption | Emerging

"Schooner"

Wandering around in Brooklyn one day not long ago, I came upon a bar with a sign reading, "$3 Bud Schooner." I knew that "Bud" meant Budweiser beer, but "Schooner"?

The *OED* tells an interesting, somewhat complicated story about the word. It gives a U.S. origin for *schooner* as a beer vessel, citing a definition in an 1879 edition of *Webster's* dictionary: "a tall glass, used for lager-beer and ale, and containing about double the quantity of an ordinary tumbler." An 1896 quote from a Scottish newspaper shows the term had crossed the Atlantic, and specifies its size: "'The schooner' [contains] 14 fluid ounces, or 2 4-5ths imperial gills . . . [and is] found in everyday use, under various names, in London, Glasgow, Aberdeen, and elsewhere."

But then, the term seems to have receded in both Britain and the U.S., only to reappear, by the 1930s, in Australia and New Zealand. A recent article called "How to Order a Beer in Australia" reports that in most of the country, *schooner* currently signifies a glass containing 425 milliliters, or three-quarters of a pint. An exception is the state of South Australia, where that size is called a pint and a schooner is a glass of ten ounces. Go figure.

Meanwhile, in Britain, by the 1960s the meaning of *schooner* had changed to, as the *OED* puts it, "a tall, waisted sherry glass" holding 3.5 ounces. The writer of a 1973 article in *The Times* (of

London) wasn't happy with this development, referring to "the abominably proportioned waisted Elgin glass, sometimes used for sherry, or its vulgar outsize version, the schooner."

And what of North America? Not surprisingly, we have supersized the schooner. Wikipedia reports,

> In Canada, a "schooner" refers to a large capacity beer glass. Unlike the Australian schooner, which is smaller than a pint, a Canadian schooner is always larger. Although not standardized, the most common size of schooner served in Canadian bars is 946 ml (32 US fl oz); the volume of two US pints. It is usually a tankard (mug) shaped glass, rather than a pint-shaped glass. . . .
>
> In the United States, "schooner" refers to the shape of the glass (rounded with a short stem), rather than the capacity. It can range from 18 to 32 US fl oz (532 to 946 ml). In the Pacific Northwest, "schooner" refers to a smaller size pour, usually 8 to 12 ounces. It's often available off-menu.

I found an article from a Lawrence, Kansas, newspaper about a bar in that college town that serves thirty-two-ounce schooners in the rounded shape—though "if the bar runs out of clean glasses on a busy night, you'll get your 32 ounces of beer in a giant plastic cup."

In my preliminary research on the topic, I posted on Facebook the Brooklyn sign and a query as to the meaning of *schooner*. Someone replied that in New England, it's ten ounces—perhaps an example of a British usage that has been retained in that region, like *rubbish*. But my favorite comment came from my friend Jan Ambrose, who is discriminating in her beer tastes: "There is no amount of Bud I would pay $3 for."

Adoption | Emerging

● ● ● ● ●

"Veg"

If you've watched Jamie Oliver cook on TV for more than ten minutes, you've heard him say something like, "Now we'll prepare a lovely veg" (pronounced "vedge"). In the U.K., this three-letter word is commonly used in the expression *fruit and veg* and can mean "a vegetable," "some vegetables" or "vegetables in general," "a vegetable or produce stand or market," or "vegetarian food" or "a vegetarian," as in this exchange someone posted to Urban Dictionary:

"Do you want to go to Steak Hut?"
"No, I'm veg."

(My British correspondents inform me that the most common slang term for "vegetarian" there is *veggie*, which, confusingly, is the traditional American slang for "vegetable.")

The *OED*'s first citation for *veg* is a menu listing or advertisement from 1844: "Meat Pudding with Veg." A line from Graham Greene's *A Gun for Hire* (1936) shows it being used in the plural: "He could have a slap-up meal . . . cut off the joint and any number of veg." A period tended to be used as late as 1940, when this appeared in a P. G. Wodehouse novel: "Have a custard apple? It's on the house. The fruit and veg. department has just given of its plenty."

The verb *veg* or *veg out*, to (often facetiously) indicate hanging out in a more or less vegetative state, seems to have originated in North America. *Green's Dictionary of Slang* locates it in a 1967–1968 compendium of American college slang, and the *OED* in a 1979 line from the Toronto *Globe and Mail*: "There's not the same flavor there used to be to travelling. . . . People just go to veg out, not to find out." It quickly spread to the U.K.

As for U.S. *veg*-for-*vegetable*, Ngram Viewer shows it starting to make an appearance in the 2000s, though it's still used considerably less frequently than in Britain.

Some U.S. examples:

- "Haeg, who lives in a geodesic dome in the easterly neighborhood of Mt. Washington, was talking about his ongoing project Edible Estates, which encourages people to tear out their lawns and plant fruit and veg instead."—*New Yorker*, 2008
- "Courtney Ring decided to poke a couple of skewers through the famed Klement's Racing Sausages (dog, brat, chorizo, Polish, and Italian) and grill them with some veg."—*Philadelphia Inquirer*, 2011
- "It comes together in about an hour—even less, if you roast the veg ahead of time—and it's made with store-bought puff pastry, so it's very little fuss."—*New York Times* recipe, 2023

Adoption | Emerging
● ● ● ● ●

CHAPTER SEVEN

Under the Hood

GRAMMAR AND SYNTAX, SPELLING, AND PRONUNCIATION

British people don't just use a lot of terms that are unfamiliar to Americans. They also spell differently, pronounce differently, punctuate differently, and put sentences together differently. Some of those differences have been traveling west.

GRAMMAR AND SYNTAX

Plural Attributive Nouns

It's challenging to generalize about transatlantic difference in plural nouns. The British engage in "sport" (see chapter 5), eat "scrambled egg," pay "tax," and play with "Lego," while for Americans, it's "sports," "eggs," "taxes," and "Legos." On the other hand, Brander Mathews observed back in 1891, "In America *coal* is put on the grate in the singular, while in England *coals* are put in the grate in the plural." Currently,

Lynne Murphy writes, "in the U.K., if you can't get your *flies* closed, you might need to step on the bathroom *scales*. In the U.S., if you can't get your *fly* closed, you might need to step on the bathroom *scale*." Then there's the British *maths* for "mathematics" (as opposed to American *math*), which isn't really a plural but a contraction: the British would say, "Maths is [not "are"] my favorite subject" (not "subjects").

One difference that shows up frequently, though not always, is in the use of plural or singular in attributive nouns—that is, a noun modifying another noun, where the first element is a count noun. In some cases, the two countries are in step. They both say "shoe store" and "glove factory," and on the other hand "parks commissioner" and "weapons analyst." However, generally, the British have a penchant for plural attributives. It's hard to back the contention up with numbers, but expert opinion supports it. In his 1980 monograph *Plural Attributive Nouns in Present-Day English*, Stig Johansson endorsed the idea that plurals are "more characteristic" of British English. In a blog post, the noted language writer David Crystal concurred and offered the example *trades union* (American *trade union*) and the British headline "Strikes Issues Back on the Table" (American: "Strike"). And in an academic paper, the eminent linguists Geoffrey Pullum and Barbara Scholz also endorsed the idea and gave another example: "Where National Public Radio in the USA will use the term a *drug* problem, the BBC is likely to use a *drugs* problem."

That is actually a good lead-in to the NOOBs angle on this. In his review of the English nature writer Robert Macfarlane's book *Underland*, *New York Times* book critic Dwight Garner wrote, "There's the prickling sense, reading Macfarlane like [Geoff] Dyer, that a library door or a manhole cover or a bosky path might lead you not just to the end of a chapter but to a drugs party or a rave."

I hope "drugs party" jumped out at you. It is British phrasing. The first example I have been able to find is in a 1985 book called *Smack: The Criminal Drugs* [not *Drug*] *Market in Ireland.* Garner, an enthusiastic user of Britishisms, could be considered a bit of an outlier. (And in addition, his use of *drugs party* in the Macfarlane review might be an example of what I call "ventriloquism": the conscious or unconscious adoption of British terminology when writing about British people or topics.)

A more robust NOOB refers to another stimulant, alcohol. The British talk of "drinks cabinets," "drinks menu," or "drinks party," where Americans would traditionally use "liquor" in the first example and "cocktail" in the second two. But the winds of change are afoot. The *New York Times* commented in 2004, "At the height of summer, nothing makes a splash like a drinks party at your weekend house." And Troy Patterson wrote in *Slate* in 2011,

> The other day, at loose ends in Midtown at the tenebrous end of happy hour, I larked into an averagely bad, decently fun Tex-Mex restaurant in the Theater District. The barman presented the drinks menu. The drinks menu presented an assault, its plastic cover a window onto a plane of existence where 29 distinct margarita flavors live, or at least refuse to die.

(Patterson was getting his NOOBs on in the passage, using *barman* instead of *bartender* and [mis]using *lark*, which is usually followed by "about" and rarely if ever "into.")

Another example is how to refer to the document the government issues (or issue) giving figures and trends on employment. As the Ngram Viewer chart of American usage (figure 23) shows, *jobs report* basically didn't exist in the U.S. in 1950, but now it's used more than three times as often as *job report.*

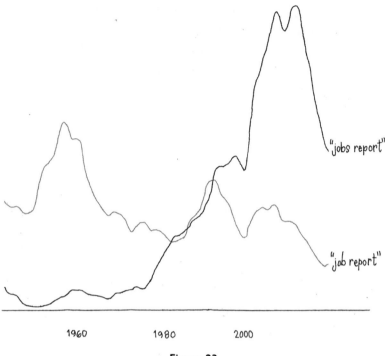

Figure 23

One more: in an NPR promotional spot for Amazon Business, the plummy-sounding speaker touts the way it "helps simplify the supplies-buying process with a one-stop shopping experience." I acknowledge I can't prove that the typical American term would be "supply-buying process"; both variations of the phrase are uncommon enough that Ngram Viewer and other tools aren't able to shed much light. However, I can report that "supply buying" has been used nine times in the history of the *New York Times* and "supplies buying," as of this writing, has never appeared in the paper.

In 2015, the *New Yorker* published a poem called "Covers Band in a Small Bar," by John Koethe. I enjoyed the poem a lot but, almost needless to say, what mainly interested me was the decision by the American Koethe to use *covers band*, which I didn't recall ever encountering, instead of the familiar *cover band* to mean a musical combo whose repertoire consists of songs popularized by other performers—that is, covers. *Covers band*, you'll now recognize, fits with the British pluralizing thing. Ngram Viewer shows that in Britain, the two terms were used roughly equally from their coining in the 1980s until about 2002, when *cover band* shot ahead, presumably as a not one-off Americanism.

Indeed, the U.S. has for decades been the land of the cover band. The phrase was first used in the *New York Times* in 1982, by a writer who felt the need to explain it: "New Jersey may eventually shake its reputation as 'Cover Band Heaven,' namely a state filled with bar bands playing only the tunes of such groups as The Doors or The Grateful Dead." The paper has used *cover band* 529 times since then, and *covers band* only 3, all between 2012 and 2019.

One advantage of the age in which we're living is that you can email people and ask them questions; surprisingly frequently, they reply. And so I asked John Koethe what the deal was with *covers band*. And he graciously responded, reporting that he was born in San Diego and, far from engaging in a Britishism, had only ever heard the *covers* version. So I'll label that an interesting regional variation and put it on my someday-research list.

Email isn't the only way one can communicate with unexpected people these days. A few years ago, I was watching a *Simpsons* episode in which an unsuspecting Marge had taken a job at "a high-end cannabis boutique." On figuring out what was going on, she exclaimed, "I'm a drugs dealer!"

The last two words in Marge's quote were jarring because the alternative, *drug dealer*, is so common here. The *New York Times* used that phrase 4,503 times from its founding in 1851 through 2022, but *drugs dealer* only twice, and one of those was in a quote from an English tabloid editor. (I suspect the other one, in 1972, was a typo.)

Truth to tell, *drugs dealer* is quite rare even in the U.K. The News on the Web Corpus, encompassing more than sixteen billion words published between 2010 and the present, shows a mere forty-three hits in Britain, *drug dealer* being about one hundred times more common there. (Ireland is the place where *drugs dealer* is used the most frequently.) In the U.S., News on the Web doesn't show any examples of Americans using it.

Back to the *Simpsons*, the episode's writer was Carolyn Omine, an American. When my wife, Gigi, and I talked about the *drugs dealer* line, I (naturally) claimed it was a NOOB. But she disagreed, saying that Omine wrote it in an awkward way to suggest Marge's discomfort. I polled *NOOBs* readers on the question, and about 96 percent agreed with Gigi.

I tweeted the results, and Omine herself responded: "That was supposed to [be] a mom-like mistake. It was to show Marge is so far removed from the drug world she doesn't pronounce drug dealer correctly."

The moment was so delicious, I didn't even mind that I was wrong.

Pro-predicate "do" . . . in Utah

On her blog, Lynne Murphy gave an example that I believe will explain this bit of usage.

She wrote that British people might answer the question, "Have you sent Lynne any chocolate yet?" in the following ways:

- I have done.
- I haven't done.
- I will do.
- I might have done.

- I could do.
- I could have done.
- I should do.
- I should have done.

Americans, by contrast, would say, "Yes, I have," "No, I haven't," "No, but I will," "I might have" . . . you get the idea. We omit the *do* or *done*, which in the British examples stands in for "sent Lynne any chocolate." Grammatically, the *do* is referred to as a "pro-predicate," sometimes shortened to "pro-*do*," similar to the way a word that stands in for a noun is called a pronoun.

The custom, or fashion, didn't arrive in Britain until the late nineteenth or early twentieth century, according to research by the linguist Ronald Butters. The detective novelist Raymond Chandler was born in Chicago in 1888 and lived in England from 1900 to 1912, at which point he returned to America for good. He wrote in a letter in 1956, "I didn't see as much of the boys and girls this time as I should like to have (done, as the British say, a disgusting locution to me)."

The moment at which the usage appeared in Britain is significant. In a 1993 article in the journal *American Speech*, Marianna Di Paolo writes,

> Pro-*do* occurs in at least one dialect of American English, that of the Mormon Dominance area of the Intermountain West. . . . Its current geographic and ethno-religious distribution is probably a result of the relatively large-scale migration to Utah by members of the Church of Jesus Christ of Latter-day Saints (the LDS or Mormons) from England in the late nineteenth and early twentieth centuries.

Di Paolo gives examples from her field research:

- "I don't know if Martha saw it. She may have done." [Middle-aged West side Salt Lake Valley man on phone with me. Summer 1986]

- "Even 'Dad' did not interrupt or converse that much, but he did do more than most of the other males, probably because of his own solidarity in the family conversation." [Middle-aged female, March 1990, term paper, undergraduate course]
- "I have sent Express Mail to foreign countries and have done for several years." [Middle-aged woman on phone to KSL Sound-Off, radio talk show, Winter 1990.]
- DW: "We should get these phones ringing." BL: "We should do, Doug." [Bob Lee, middle-aged male talk show host. KSL radio during a radiothon. 10:10 a.m. 2/6/90]
- "How will the Clinton people deal with this, or can they do?" [Doug Wright, KSL radio talk show host (middle-aged, Mormon, native of East side of Salt Lake Valley) speaking to another newsman in regard to Ross Perot's announcement that he would not run for President. 7/16/92]

Di Paolo's principal explanation stems from the large migration of Mormons from England to Utah in the late nineteenth and early twentieth centuries. She writes that of the pro-*do* users "whose affiliation I know, all were active Mormons or descendants of Mormon families. Half of the . . . speakers had an English ancestor." She goes on to note that some 56 percent of Utahns have exclusively English ancestry, almost three times as many as the country as a whole.

Now, a broader swath of Americans *do* say, "I might could," but that is a subject for another book.

Adoption | On the radar

● ● ● ● ●

PRONUNCIATION

"Aunt"

In the United States, there are three main ways to say the word
for your parent's sister. One is like the insect, "ant." Centuries
ago, it was pronounced that way throughout the British Isles,
but then much of southern England switched to "ahnt." And
that is the second U.S. pronunciation. The third, quite close to
the second, is "awnt," similar to the vowel sound in *caught*. In a
nationwide dialect survey conducted by Bert Vaux of Harvard
around the turn of the twenty-first century, 75 percent of the
respondents reported saying "ant" compared with 9.6 percent
for "ahnt" and 2.5 percent for "awnt." The map accompany-
ing the survey made it clear that "ahnt" and "awnt" were con-
centrated in New England. In addition, something close to
that is the "typical" pronunciation among African Americans,
according to John Algeo and Carmen Acevedo Butcher's *The
Origins and Development of the English Language* and my
own experience.

   I have a sense that the British pronunciation has grown in
popularity over the past couple of decades. Vaux, now at Cambridge University, has continued his investigations under the
project title Cambridge Online Survey of World Englishes, and
the results for *aunt* would seem to confirm that a change is
afoot: A mere 60 percent of American respondents now report
saying "ant," and 25 percent (more than twice the number in
the earlier survey) either "ahnt" or "awnt." Hot spots for the
latter two include (besides New England) Virginia and the
Upper Midwest.

   I conducted my own semiscientific test and listened to
the twenty most recent times Americans have said the word
on NPR's air. Eleven said "ant," including Tom Hanks, Joe

Biden, Gene Wilder's nephew, and the hosts Rachel Martin and Terry Gross (the last was overdetermined, since Gross is a Brooklyn native then in her sixties whom one would invite to a "cawfee tawk"). Of the nine who said "ahnt," five were from the traditional African American group. But there was also an eighteen-year-old New Yorker whose parents were born in Ecuador, a white drug counselor from Minneapolis, the reporter Hansi Lo Wang (a native of Philadelphia and a fairly recent college graduate), and *Weekend Edition* host Scott Simon, a Chicagoan who at the time was sixty-four years old. (I didn't detect any "awnts.")

That was the biggest surprise to me since the other examples, and my own experience, suggest the pronunciation is most popular among young people. Perhaps in his next survey Vaux can ask for respondents' ages and we can find out for sure.

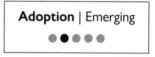

Adoption | Emerging

"Organ-eye-zation," "eye-ther," etc.

I have in my repertoire one parlor trick. I do it when chatting with someone whose speech is generally unremarkable but who employs a pronunciation like "global-eye-zation" (the typical American schwa in the third syllable would render it something like "global-ih-zation"). I say, "I bet you're from Canada, aren't you?" And they invariably say, "Yes!"

Or at least they used to. Don't misunderstand. Canadians still say such words this way. It's one of the things people in the country have retained from Britain, along with the long *o* in *process* and pronouncing the first *a* in *pasta* as in *cat* or *hat*. You can hear this long *i* when Canadian hockey players and fans refer to teams as "organ-eye-zations" and when, in the opening monologue of *Star Trek*, the Canadian-born William Shatner says that one of the missions of the starship *Enterprise* is "to seek out new life and new civi-lie-zations."

But my little trick is not long for this world. That's because Americans have started to adopt the long *i* vowel in such words. The data I have to support this assertion is admittedly preliminary, but it is suggestive. Over the course of a week on NPR, I heard a reporter say "author-eye-zation," a newsreader say "denuclear-eye-zation" and an interviewee say "organ-eye-zation." I searched the YouGlish pronunciation website for Americans uttering the word *globalization*, and of the first ten video clips to pop up, the speakers in four said the third syllable to rhyme with *eye*.

The same long *i* sound is also a British import in the words *either* and *neither*. As late as 1777, when the *Royal Standard Dictionary* was published, "ee-ther" and "nee-ther" were the predominant pronunciations in England. But that gradually changed. A 1932 article on the subject in the journal *American Speech* observed, "The *eyether* pronunciation undoubtedly made great headway in the nineteenth century, although the *Oxford Dictionary*, in its volume of 1907, still gives it second place, remarking that, though it is not in accordance with the analogues of Standard English, it is in London somewhat more prevalent in educated speech than is *eether*." H. W. Fowler predicted in *A Dictionary of Modern English Usage* that "eye-ther" would "probably prevail," and by 1965, when Sir Ernest Gowers revised Fowler's book, it had "almost wholly displaced" the long *e* pronunciation.

For a long time, the United States stuck with "ee-ther," for the most part. In 1873, the American philologist W. D. Whitney harrumphed that "eye-ther" had "spread . . . by a kind of reasonless and senseless infection, which can only be condemned and ought to be stoutly opposed and put down."

A 1928 satirical sketch called "The Lady Buyer" noted of that personage,

> Always, standing her in good stead, and ready at the tip of her tongue is her crystal-clear, British pronunciation of "either." She says the staunch word with such hauteur as to make one forget other mistakes and even feel apologetic for having noticed them. Nothing on earth could make her whisper "ether" in the darkest corner of a stock-room. She knows it would ruin her socially.

Memorably, "eye-ther" was one of the British pronunciation choices (along with "to-mah-to") in Ira Gershwin's 1937 lyric to "Let's Call the Whole Thing Off." In 1961, Hans Kurath and Raven McDavid called "eye-ther" "a sporadic feature of the cultivated speech of Metropolitan New York and Philadelphia. . . . It is in all probability a recent adoption from British English."

My ears tell me that "eye-ther" and "neye-ther" are currently on the rise in America, especially—as with all the pronunciations in this section discussed up till now—among young people. My own millennial-generation daughter, despite having two parents who say "ee-ther," says "eye-ther."

Finally, there is another, similar set of words, such as *missile, agile, futile, mobile,* and *hostile.* Brits pronounce the two syllables with roughly equal stress and use the long *i,* while Americans put the accent on the first syllable and use a schwa—for example, "miss-uhl." An informant reports that in the corporate world, rhyming *agile* with *badge-mile* is all the rage, and I've noticed more than a few Americans very Britishly refer to their phone as "my moe-bile."

In conclusion, let's call the whole thing off.

Adoption | Taking hold
● ● ● ● ●

"Scenahrio"

MSNBC host Rachel Maddow is American, but she received a Rhodes Scholarship to study at Oxford in 1995 and later earned a doctorate at the university. The experience clearly was formative for her, at least in terms of language. At least five times, she has referred on the air to someone being "in hospital" (instead of the American *in the hospital*). She repeatedly used an even less familiar Britishism in this quote:

> Standing for re-election as president in 1972, Richard Nixon was due to make history. He was going to match FDR's record for being on the national ticket for his party in five different elections. FDR had stood for vice president once. Of course, he stood for president four times.

Every other American would say "run for" rather than "stand for."

Those are outliers, but a British pronunciation favored by Maddow is a legit NOOB: the word *scenario*. She and British people say "sce-nah-rio," while the traditional American pronunciation is "sce-nare-io." An early example of an American saying it British style came in Jay-Z's 2001 "Big Pimpin'," in which the rapper Bun B rhymes (language warning) "sorry ho" with "my sce-nah-rio." Then he raps, "Oops, my bad, that's 'my scenario,'" and rhymes the last word with (another warning) "scary ho." That is, he mispronounces the word for the sake of the rhyme—and then apologizes for doing so and makes another rhyme with the "right" pronunciation. In the canon of witty song lyrics about pronunciation, it stands right up there with Ira Gershwin's "You say 'to-may-toe,' I say 'to-mah-toe'" (referred to in the previous entry).

I hear a fair amount of American "sce-nah-rio" these days but, admittedly, mostly from Maddow and on NPR. I've heard it said by NPR hosts, correspondents, and guests, but most often—probably a hundred times—in a sponsorship message, where a posh American voice says, "Workday: an enterprise management cloud focused on providing organizations with a system to continuously plan for all what-if sce-*nahr*-ios."

Adoption | Emerging

●●●●●

SPELLING: "GREY"

The color that combines black and white has for centuries been spelled two ways, *grey* and *gray*. James Murray, the man behind the *OED*, was intrigued by the variation. The dictionary reports in an etymological note that in 1893, Murray sent out a query that

> elicited a large number of replies. . . . Many correspondents said that they used the two forms with a difference of meaning or application: the distinction most generally recognized being that *grey* denotes a more delicate or a lighter tint than *gray*. Others considered the difference to be that *gray* is a "warmer" colour, or that it has a mixture of red or brown.

The note cites two sources with more or less opposite assertions. An 1867 text on art criticism says,

> Professional, if not primitive English usage has made a distinction between *gray* and *grey*. The spelling *gray* may with propriety be employed to designate admixtures in which simple black and white are employed. The form *grey* may indicate those admixtures which have the same general

hue, but into which blue and its compounds more or less slightly enter.

But according to a 1925 book, *Popular Superstitions*, "An attempt has been made to differentiate between 'grey' and 'gray'—many artists claiming that the old spelling should only be used for mixtures of white and black; the other form being reserved for those tones where some other colour has been introduced."

In any case, *grey* has always been the favored spelling in Britain. In a 1948 supplement to *The American Language*, H. L. Mencken wrote that it is one of the orthographic "rocks upon which the Englishman founds his pride, patriotism and faith." Others, he asserted, were "'storey' (for a house), 'waggon,' 'for ever' (two words), 'nought,' 'cheque,' and 'pyjamas.'"

Mencken was overstating the case, a little. *Gray* has been used in the U.K. for centuries. ("The night is chill, the cloud is gray."—Samuel Taylor Coleridge, "Christabel.") It's just that *grey* has always been more common. In the mid-twentieth century, *grey* was used as much as ten times more frequently than *gray*, while since 2000, *gray* has had a sharp upswing, no doubt due to American influence.

And *gray* is definitely American. An Ngram Viewer chart of U.S. uses of the two forms tells the story (figure 24).

The remarkable thing about the chart is that *gray* begins its triumphant ascent in 1828. What's so special about that? It's the year in which Noah Webster published *An American Dictionary of the English Language*, which defiantly put forth such spellings as *center*, *color*, and *wagon* (instead of *centre*, *colour*, and *waggon*). In a previous dictionary, published in 1807, Webster had the entry "Gray or Grey, a hoary, white mixed with black." But twenty-one years later, in his magnum

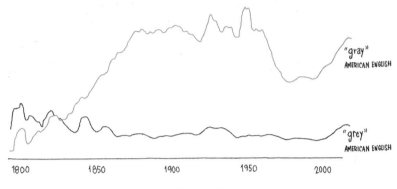

Figure 24

opus, he showed no such equanimity. There, if you looked up *grey*, you would read the words, "*See Gray.*"

As you can see in the graph, *grey* is on the upswing in the American twenty-first century. I taught college students in the period and can report that they strongly preferred that version. U.S. style guides still call for the *gray* spelling, but the other one occasionally makes its way into print. In 1995 *Time* reported that President Bill Clinton visited the Tomb of the Unknown Soldier "on a grey and misty morning." In 2011, according to a California newspaper, "The hills [were] shedding their summer gold for their fall grey." A 2013 *Vox* article said, "Much of the world seems to think that [Nate Silver] is pure grey matter." And in a 2022 headline, the *New York Times* referred to Edinburgh's "pearl-grey skies."

I ascribe the U.S. boomlet in equal parts to the NOOBs phenomenon and to a veritable barrage of *grey*s in popular and commercial culture: products like Grey Goose vodka and Grey Poupon mustard, the film and musical *Grey Gardens*, the cultural phenomenon that kicked off with the 2011 novel *Fifty Shades of Grey*, and the long-running TV series *Grey's Anat-*

omy, which is a play on words about a British book written by a guy whose name was spelled—wait for it—"Gray."

Adoption | Taking hold

LOGICAL PUNCTUATION

Consider two sentences:

> Anna said updating the guide was "a difficult and time-consuming task."
>
> Anna said updating the guide was "a difficult and time-consuming task".

Their meaning is obviously the same. The subtle difference is in the punctuation at the end. The first, in which the period or full stop (see chapter 3) comes before the closing quotation marks, is American style. The second, in which the period comes at the end, is British and is sometimes referred to as "logical punctuation." In fact, the example comes from *The Guardian*'s style guide, which states, "Place full points and commas inside the quotes for a complete quoted sentence; otherwise the point comes outside."

Here's another example of the British way, from Evelyn Waugh's novel *Put Out More Flags* (1942):

> They began singing 'Roll out the Barrel', 'We'll hang out the Washing on the Siegfried Line', and 'The Quartermaster's Store'.

(British style also tends to use inverted commas for quotation marks, like 'this,' while Americans "double" the marks, but that subject is well beyond the scope of this entry.)

Before the end of the nineteenth century, the conventions on both sides of the Atlantic were a bit fast and loose. Writing in 1859, Henry Beadnell, an English printer and typographer, endorsed the placement of the first comma in this passage:

> . . . to a man of what Plato calls "universal sympathies," and even more to the plain, ordinary citizens of this world . . .

Beadnell averred that, "for the sake of neatness . . . commas and periods should always precede quotation marks."

Indeed, this style is sometimes known as "printers' quotation" or "typesetters' quotation" and was apparently initially promoted by those artisans for aesthetic reasons. As Rosemary Feal, then the executive director of the Modern Language Association, commented to me in an email, it was instituted "to improve the appearance of the text. A comma or period that follows a closing quotation mark appears to hang off by itself and creates a gap in the line (since the space over the mark combines with the following word space)." In America, the style was close to universally adopted by the turn of the twentieth century.

But across the Atlantic it was still the Wild West, as it were. The Fowler brothers devote five and a half pages to the matter in *The King's English* (1906), noting that "general usage, besides being illogical, is so inconsistent, different writers improving upon it in special details that appeal to them." Their recommendation, for the most part, amounted to the current British system—though "we must warn the reader that it is not the system now in fashion." They mock Beadnell and others for holding that "neatness is the sole consideration" and conclude, "Argument on the subject is impossible; it is only a question whether the printer's love for the old ways that seem to him so neat, or the writer's and reader's desire to be understood and to understand fully, is to prevail."

This had not prevailed by 1926 when one of the brothers, H. W., wrote in *A Dictionary of Modern English Usage* that while the outside-quotation-marks style was "right," the inside-quote-marks style was still "usual." As late as 1947, Eric Partridge could (disapprovingly) note in *Usage and Abusage* "a tendency among printers to put the period . . . and comma inside the 'quotes'"—though "careful printers are beginning to follow the more logical rule." Not too long after that, the "logical rule" prevailed in Britain once and for all.

In America, meanwhile, only rarely was the consensus challenged. The only early example I've found is the *American Bar Association Journal*, whose use of the British style so infuriated a reader named Sidney Alderman (who had been a member of the prosecution team at the Nuremberg war crimes trial) that, in 1950, he wrote and submitted a letter of some 1,100 words to protest it. "I can hardly enjoy the excellent articles," he maintained, "because the periods and commas dangling outside the quotes scratch my eyes like grains of sand or hot cinders, and I spend my time proofreading them back inside the quotes, losing the substance of the articles." (A perusal of the journal's archives shows that it was still using the style in 1970 but had dropped it by 1980. I hope Sidney Alderman was alive to see the change.)

Lawyers being famously literal and logical, it's not surprising that the editors of the *ABA Journal* should have gone this punctuational route. Those traits are also associated with people who work with computers, and this cohort is probably mainly responsible for the rise of the British style in America. In 1991, Eric Raymond wrote in *The New Hacker's Dictionary*,

Hackers tend to use quotes as balanced delimiters like parentheses, much to the dismay of American editors. Thus, if "Jim is going" is a phrase, and so are "Bill runs" and

"Spock groks", then hackers generally prefer to write: "Jim is going", "Bill runs", and "Spock groks". This is incorrect according to standard American usage (which would put the continuation commas and the final period inside the string quotes); however, it is counter-intuitive to hackers to mutilate literal strings with characters that don't belong in them. Given the sorts of examples that can come up in discussions of programming, American-style quoting can even be grossly misleading. When communicating command lines or small pieces of code, extra characters can be a real pain in the neck.

Consider, for example, a sentence in a *vi* tutorial that looks like this:

> Then delete a line from the file by typing "dd".

Standard usage would make this

> Then delete a line from the file by typing "dd."

But that would be very bad—because the reader would be prone to type the string d-d-dot, and it happens that in vi(1), dot repeats the last command accepted. The net result would be to delete *two* lines!

The horror.

Continuing on the logical/literal theme, *Language*, the journal of the Linguistic Society of North America, has adopted the British way. The first item under "Punctuation" in its style sheet says,

> The second member of a pair of quotation marks should precede any other adjacent mark of punctuation, unless the other mark is part of the quoted matter: The word means 'cart', not 'horse'.

The other notable American user is *Pitchfork*, the online music magazine. A review there notes,

> Covers on the LP [from Iggy Pop] include the Beatles'
> "Michelle", Fred Neil's "Everybody's Talkin'", and tracks
> from Serge Gainsbourg and Henri Salvador.

I emailed then-managing editor Mark Richardson to ask
why *Pitchfork* did it that way, and he responded that it was
"partly because it makes sense when the quoted titles don't
contain punctuation (which I guess is why it's called 'logical') and partly because it was absorbed from reading the UK
music press."

But the biggest current user of logical punctuation is
Wikipedia, which was founded in America but whose single
English-language version is of course read all over the world.
The site's style guide requires that periods and commas be kept
"inside the quotation marks if they apply only to the quoted
material and outside if they apply to the whole sentence."

Thus the Wikipedia entry on Frank Sinatra reports that in
1946 he

> released "Oh! What it Seemed to Be", "Day by Day", "They
> Say It's Wonderful", "Five Minutes More", and "The Coffee
> Song" as singles.

Despite all this, there are no signs of the American style diminishing in professionally edited prose: what you'll find in the
New York Times, the *Washington Post*, or any place adhering
to *Chicago Manual of Style*, MLA, or Associated Press guide-
lines. But in copyeditor-free zones—the web and emails and
texts—with increasing frequency, commas and periods find
themselves on the outside of quotation marks, looking in.

To take a couple of examples out of millions, or maybe bil-
lions, Conan O'Brien once tweeted,

> Conan's staffers' kids say the darndest things. Unfortu-
> nately, in this case "darndest" means "incriminating".

And a commenter to the online magazine *Slate* wrote,

> Ironically, given the anecdote about "Tales of the City", PBS
> is the ONLY widely available channel that has any serious
> LGBT content; e.g. documentaries such as "Ask Not" and
> "Out in the Silence".

I can say from personal experience that, since the early 2000s,
the college students I've taught have overwhelmingly favored
logical punctuation. When first presented with this, I would
make "humorous" remarks to the effect that we were in Delaware, not Liverpool. When that didn't make a difference, I
instituted a one-point penalty on every assignment for infrac-
tions. For the most part, that hasn't helped either.

The reason the students and others are so drawn to the
style isn't that they're aping *Pitchfork* or Wikipedia, much less
imitating the British. Rather, they use it because, as the name
says, it's logical. These writers follow the logic because they
don't know the American rules, which is in turn because they
don't read very much edited prose. Instead, they read plenty
of tweets and texts and Instagram comments that put periods
and commas outside.

I predict an even more pronounced separation between
official and unofficial practice. That is, for the foreseeable
future, prose published by established entities will follow the
traditional rules, while everyone else will follow logic.

Adoption | Emerging

CHAPTER EIGHT

Faux NOOBs and Alterations

Not too surprisingly, when Americans attempt to speak British, they sometimes get it wrong. Herewith, some cases in point.

"Advisor"

Quick quiz: What do you call a person whose job is to offer advice? Or, rather, how do you spell that job?

If you answered *advisor*, you would be in accordance with 100 percent of my students at the University of Delaware; with the practice of that university and I believe most others in this country; with the popular website TripAdvisor; with Merrill Lynch, which sends to its customers a publication called *Merrill Lynch Advisor*; and, in fact, with the English-speaking world generally.

If you answered *adviser*, you would be right. Or, to be more precise, right from the perspective of the *New York Times*, the Associated Press, and history. *Adviser* first appeared at least as early as 1575, according to the *OED*. It was formed by appending the suffix *-er* (in this case, merely the letter *r*) to the verb *advise*, along the lines of such similar constructions as *baker, candlestick-maker*, and, well, not *butcher*, which comes from the Old French *bouchier*, but *teacher, seeker*, and *beekeeper*.

The *advisor* spelling shows up now and again through the nineteenth century, including in an 1839 letter from Charlotte Brontë: "I trust sincerely that your medical advisor is mistaken in supposing you have any tendency to pulmonary affection." But it really took hold in the United States, so much so that *American Speech*, the journal of the American Dialect Society, mocked it in 1931: "Following the advent and acceptance in this country of *advisors*, newspapers now occasionally mention *debators*." (There are, of course, many *-or* nouns for occupations and identifications, including *doctor, debtor, proctor, author, executor*, and *donor* but, as the examples suggest, they are usually not formed from verbs. *Curator* and *editor* might appear to be exceptions, but they preceded the back-formation verbs *curate* and *edit*.)

Ngram Viewer sheds some light on the issue in general and transatlantic differences in particular (figure 25).

In other words, *advisor* is an American phenomenon, dating (as the *OED* citation suggests) from around 1900 and passing *adviser* around 2010. In Britain, it arrived later and still lags behind the traditional spelling. But its U.S. popularity, I submit, stems largely from the fact that it *sounds* British. And fancy. That is an unbeatable combination.

That popularity is even greater than what's suggested by Ngram Viewer, whose database consists only of books and some periodicals. A Google search—including worldwide blogs, websites, Reddit discussions, and what have you—yields

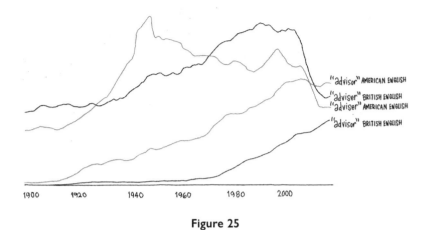

Figure 25

196 million hits for *adviser* and 839 million for *advisor*, more than four times as many.

"Bollix up"

Bollocks, which means "testicles" and apparently derives from *balls* (a onetime common spelling was *ballocks*), has been in wide currency in Britain since the late fifteenth century. And I mean wide. Some of the expressions derived from the word and included in *Green's Dictionary of Slang* are *the dog's bollocks, ballocks workers, ballocks in brackets, big ballocks, do one's ballocks, have his brains in his ballocks, have one's ballocks in the right place, have someone/something by the ballocks/bollocks, in one's ballock, knock the ballocks out of, not give a ballock*, and *my bollocks!*

Bollocks was considered quite offensive at least until 1977. That year, a Virgin Records store in Nottingham that displayed in its window a poster advertising the album *Never Mind the Bollocks, Here's the Sex Pistols* was brought to court on obscenity charges. According to a recent article on the case by Michelle Dhillon, the defense brought in as a witness Professor James Kinsley, head of English at Nottingham University and an Anglican priest.

> He said that during the word's history, it had meant a small ball, a type of orchid and a nickname for a clergyman. According to Kinsley: "Clergymen are known to talk a good deal of rubbish and so the word later developed the meaning of nonsense." Kinsley ended by stating that the understanding of the word today (in 1977) was to mean "nonsense."

The record store won.

Presumably due in part to the ruling, the use of the word in Britain shot up, increasing more than 1,000 percent between 1980 and the mid-2010s. American use did not follow suit. In fact, the only example I could find after a reasonable amount of searching was a quote from a 2018 *New York Times* opinion piece about Democratic politicians saying they shouldn't squabble among themselves: "To which I feel moved to reply: Bollocks." So it's an outlier.

I am nevertheless talking about it here because of one more apparent variation. During the 2020 American election, MSNBC commentator Joy Reid said about a Donald Trump rally (helpfully defining the term after using it), "They completely bollixed it. They completely messed it up." *New York Times* reporter Tariq Panja, a British native, posted a video clip of Reid's comment on Twitter and commented, "Not heard the phrase 'bollocksed it' [more on the spelling issue in a minute] used on the news before, and certainly not in the US. But, it has to be said, she's used it correctly here!"

Well, the fact is *bollix* is a common American verb of long standing, admittedly usually followed by *up*. *Green's Diction-*

ary of Slang's first citation is from a Purdue University publication in 1902; then from Jerome Weidman's 1938 novel *I Can Get It for You Wholesale*, "You're getting your cues all bollixed up"; then another "bollixed up" from Arthur Kober's *Parm Me!* (1945). Interestingly, both Weidman and Kober strongly identified as Jewish American writers, but there doesn't seem to be any Yiddish antecedent for *bollixed*.

The first British use cited by Jonathon Green doesn't come till a 1973 book called *Billy Rags*: "All that had happened was that someone had ballocksed up the hook." The *x* spelling shows up in an Irish book published six years later: "For one wild moment I came near to bollixing it all." And from then on, Irish and British uses are common, with various spellings.

But why would *bollix up* have been established in America first, when all other forms of *ballocks* were much more widespread in Britain? I believe I know the answer, or at least part of it, and it has been suggested (though even there not accepted) only once before as far as I know, in a short article in 1949 in the academic journal *Modern Language Notes*. It's this: American *bollix up* does not derive from *ballocks = testicles*, but rather from an older verb phrase with a different etymology, *ball up*. The *OED*'s first definition: "Of a shoe (esp. a horseshoe), hoof, etc.: to become clogged with balls of mud, snow, or the like. Also with the horse as subject." The dictionary has citations, all but one American, dating from 1760. This is from George Washington's 1787 diary: "Apprehension of the Horses balling with the snow."

And that verb led to this broader, exclusively American definition of *ball*: "To clog or tangle; to bring into a state of entanglement, confusion, or difficulty. Frequently as past participle, esp. in balled up." An 1885 citation is from a Mark Twain letter: "It will 'ball up' the binderies again."

It seems evident to me that that expression led to *bollix up* within a couple of decades—pace the *OED*, which gives a *ballocks* etymology. (*Green's* is silent on the question.) The one thing I don't know is *why* it took on the extra syllable. It may indeed have been a conscious or unconscious nod to *ballocks* (which was commonly used in the U.S. to refer to testicles, though mostly in a farming context). Or it may have been merely to add emphasis. Either way, I'm convinced that American *bollix up* doesn't *principally* derive from *ballocks*.

By contrast, the author of that 1949 article in *Modern Language Notes*, Thomas Pyle, concluded that it did. Otherwise, he wrote, "the similarity in form and the identity in meaning taken together must be accounted a truly remarkable coincidence." I'm going with truly remarkable coincidence.

A couple of more wrinkes before I move on. The expression *balls-up*, a noun meaning "a blunder or error," shows up in an 1889 British dictionary of jargon and cant, and definitely derives from *balls = testicles*. Robert Graves used it in his 1929 World War I memoir, *Goodbye to All That*: "Tomorrow's going to be a glorious balls-up." Then it became a verb with the same meaning as *ball up*, no later than 1947, when Dan Devin used it in *For the Rest of Our Lives*, his novel about the New Zealand Expeditionary Force in World War II: "If only they haven't ballsed up the bomb-line we gave them." From then on it appears frequently in British and Australian texts.

I haven't found *balls-up* in any U.S. sources, but a more or less synonymous noun, *cock-up*, has had some recent American popularity. The first citation in the *OED* is from a 1946 letter by Kingsley Amis: "The postal service between the two countries is a cock-up." The dictionary comments, "Rare in North American usage," but that might be changing. In a 2021 interview about gene-editing technology, biographer Walter Isaacson remarked that if "we go step by step, preferably hand in hand, we can avoid doing a massive cock-up." I can't resist pointing out that "massive" is a fairly massive NOOB.

"Bumbershoot"

Shortly after I started monitoring the phenomenon that provides the subject of this book, I wrote an article about it for the online magazine *Slate*. In it I wondered aloud, "Why have we adopted *laddish* while we didn't adopt *telly* or *bumbershoot*?" More than one British person responded to my query with their own: "*Bumbershoot*? What do you mean, *bumbershoot*?"

I told them I had always thought of this funny term for "umbrella" as one of those words, like *cheerio* and *old bean*, that the stage Englishman is required to say. I asked my wife and a few (American) friends, and they all had the same impression. But when I looked into the matter, I learned that we were woefully mistaken. The *OED* identifies the word as "originally and chiefly U.S. slang." And the digital archives of *The Times* (of London), comprising more than twelve million articles commencing in 1780, have zero mentions of the word until 2001, when there was a reference to the Bumbershoot music and arts festival in Seattle, Washington. (The festival adopted the name in 1973.)

The British connection hadn't been made as late as 1933, when the *New York Times* ran a short editorial praising *bumbershoot* as "a term that drips with poetry and magic" and referring to it as "the mystical name, the children's name, for an umbrella." Some days later, R. A. McGlasson wrote a letter to the editor saying that the word was commonly used during his childhood in Dutchess County, New York, fifty years earlier; another correspondent, Louis Margolis, reported he first heard it while "spending a summer on a Connecticut farm in New London County at the tender age of ten or eleven years."

But things had changed two decades later. In 1953, *Time* magazine ran a review of *The Little Emperors*, Alfred Duggan's historical novel about Roman Britain, with these two sentences:

> As an extra dividend, the book is clearly intended for reading as an oblique comment on the British character, and especially on the modern British bureaucracy. Author Duggan seems to suggest that, given a bowler and bumbershoot to go with his tidy, official face, Felix might patter along Downing Street without winning a second glance.

Five years later, the same magazine noted, "British Mystery Writer Agatha Christie, 66, chugged up the sheer Acropolis, posed—looking not unlike her own fictional Miss Marple with bumbershoot and catchall."

In 1968, the (American) songwriting Sherman brothers wrote this couplet for the film *Chitty Chitty Bang Bang*, where it was sung by the English character played by Dick Van Dyke:

> You can have me hat or me bumbershoot
> But you'd better never bother with me ol' bam-boo.

And in the early 1990s, the writers of *Frasier* used the notion of *bumbershoot*-as-Britishism to underpin this exchange between the Anglophile Niles and his English crush, Daphne:

> NILES: Take my bumbershoot.
> DAPHNE: Oh, isn't that nice, well at least someone appreciates my mother tongue.
> NILES: Yes, I've always had an ear for your tongue.
> FRASIER: Niles!

My research has actually led me to propose the year when *bumbershoot* changed from U.S. regional slang to presumed

Britishism. In 1938, at the Munich Conference, British prime minister Neville Chamberlain was typically and frequently depicted holding a (furled) umbrella, similar to the way St. Peter is always shown in Renaissance paintings holding a key, or St. Jerome with a lion. In Chamberlain's case, the imagery suggested a weaponlike thing that was not and would not be used as a weapon, hence its aptness and its stickiness. The following year, the prime minister traveled to Rome to try, unsuccessfully, to apply some diplomatic pressure to Benito Mussolini. And the *New York Times* ran a feature that reproduced several editorial cartoons about Chamberlain's mission. Every one showed him with an umbrella. The overall caption was, "Mr. Chamberlain's 'bumbershoot' provides inspiration for British and American cartoonists." So it would appear that in 1939, an anonymous caption writer started it all.

I hypothesize that *bumbershoot* succeeded as a fake Britishism because of a confluence of factors. First, the intense association of Chamberlain with umbrellas. Second, the well-documented fondness of the English *for* umbrellas, in part due to the fact that it rains a lot in their country. Third, the fact that *bumbershoot* sort of *sounds* British. And fourth, the presence of an actual British slang term for "umbrella," *brolly*.

In any case, by 1940, this misapprehension was in place. A book published that year, *War Propaganda and U.S.*, noted, "To many upper-class Americans there was nothing so thrilling as having an Englishman around the house, complete with Oxford accent, school tie, and bumbershoot."

All this research made me recall when I first encountered the term, or at the least first associated it with the British. It was in the rip-roaring Marvel comic book series Sgt. Fury and His Howling Commandos, about a World War II squad that included Isadore "Izzy" Cohen, Robert "Reb" Ralston, Dino Manelli, Gabe Jones (a bugle-blowing African American), and the Englishman Percival "Pinky" Pinkerton. According to a Marvel fan site,

> Pinky's chief tool is his umbrella (bumbershoot). He has used this device as a club, fenced with it as a sword, used it to aid him in climbing, to slow his descent while falling, and to shield himself from sunlight. Does it serve any particular function in a rainstorm? The world may never know.

"Can't be asked"

Online comments sections have a bad reputation, but sometimes you can learn a lot there. After I wrote a piece about Britishisms for the *Chronicle of Higher Education*, a commenter who goes by the handle "englishwlu" noted,

> Imagine my surprise when my kid (Virginia born and bred) started saying "I can't be asked . . ." and "go on about" and "sweet f. a."—all with the right intonation! It turns out that for many years some of the kids he hangs out with inside games like Minecraft on X-Box Live are British. Evidently their idioms of teenaged ennui have transferred and stuck.

englishwlu mentioned three expressions. *Go on about* is more commonly heard without the "going"—as in "What's he on about?" meaning "What is he talking at length (and, by implication, tediously) about?" I'd call it an on-the-radar NOOB. *Sweet f.a.* is an abbreviated form of *sweet fuck all*, meaning "nothing at all," which has not to my knowledge crossed the Atlantic to any significant degree.

As for *can't be asked*, NOOB friend Nancy Friedman commented on the comment, "I believe you or your child misheard *can't be arsed*." To elucidate: the *OED* defines *arsed* as "to be willing to make the required effort; to be bothered. Usually in negative constructions, such as can't be arsed (*to do something*)." The first citation is from Hunter Davies's 1968 book *The Beatles*, in which Paul McCartney is quoted as saying, "If they can't be arsed waiting for me, I can't be arsed going after them." In the same book, John Lennon says, "I like 'A Day in the Life,' but it's still not half as nice as I thought it was when we were doing it. I suppose we could have worked harder on it. But I couldn't be arsed doing any more."

The only quibble I have with Nancy is the word "misheard." In fact, Americans started using *can't be asked* to mean *can't be arsed* as early as 1979, when the pianist Keith Jarrett was quoted as saying, "There are things now that I can't be asked to do that maybe five years ago I would." Now, that raises the question of whether Jarrett actually said "can't be asked" or whether he said the British "can't be arsed" and the interviewer mistakenly rendered it in print. By a stroke of fortune, that 1979 interviewer, Mikal Gilmore, is a Facebook friend of mine, and I asked him if he remembered what Jarrett said. In a kind of *Annie Hall*–Marshall McLuhan moment, he responded quickly and definitively: "He said 'asked.'"

I can understand why Jarrett and others would have made the change. First, most British people pronounce *arse* and *arsed* without voicing the *r*, so it *sounds* like they could be saying *asked*. Second, *can't be asked* actually would appear to make more sense than *can't be arsed*—suggesting the idea that I won't do something even if someone asks me to.

Perhaps for those reasons, *can't be asked* had spread to the U.K. by 2007, when someone posted a definition of the phrase on Urban Dictionary: "Used by some Southern UK speakers in place of 'can't be arsed' because they misheard it, or want to be more polite."

Helpfully dispelling any *arsed/asked* confusion is the version that has apparently become popular among young people in their texting and commenting: the initialism *CBA*.

"Divissive"

The first example I know of an American pronouncing the word *divisive* to rhyme with *permissive* or *dismissive* is George H. W. Bush, who said it that way in his inaugural address in 1988. Twelve years later, Charles Harrington Elster, in *The Big Book of Beastly Mispronunciations*, rhetorically asked, "Was this just a venial bit of Ivy League snobbery, or was the president letting fly with a beastly mispronunciation?" Elster charged snobbery because "divissive" *sounds* fancy and British, along the lines of the way people there say "vittamin" and "dinnasty." But that's a misapprehension, as British *divisive* rhymes with *incisive*.

In any case, U.S. "divissive"-saying grew to the point that, in 2001, the *American Heritage Dictionary* polled its Usage Panel on the question. The traditional pronunciation was overwhelmingly preferred, but 16 percent considered "divissive" to be "acceptable." That number ballooned to 65 percent in a 2013 survey, and I can give the reason for the jump in two words: Barack Obama. Indeed, the first time I was aware of anyone pronouncing *divisive* with a short *i* was Obama's March 2008 speech on race, when he did it at least twice. He kept saying it that way as president, and in fact, if you key *divisive* into the YouGlish pronunciation site, choosing American speakers, two of the first half dozen "divissive" hits are Obama himself.

As the *American Heritage* votes suggest, "divissive" is edging toward respectability, with both that dictionary and *Merriam-Webster* listing it as an acceptable alternate pronunciation. I have to confess I'm not happy about that, as the pronunciation is nails-on-chalkboard for me. What is even more alarming is something a British commenter wrote on my blog: "*Divissive* has come in recently in Britain, usually in the mouths of those business types who deploy Managementspeak."

"Good on [someone]"

Like *no worries* (see chapter 3) and a few other entries, this expression—roughly equivalent to the American *good for you/ him/etc.*—is a not one-off Australianism. Or at least it became one. Although the *OED* says it was chiefly found in Australia and New Zealand before the 1970s, the dictionary's first citation (from 1881) is from a poem by the English author Edwin Coller. I dug up a *good on you*, apparently meant as Norfolk dialect, in an 1892 book by the American-born, English-bred author Peter Emerson. The *OED*'s second citation is from a 1905 book called *The Bush Boys of New Zealand: or Dinkums and Mac*: "First one and then another came up and congratulated in true British boys' style. 'Good on you, Dinkums, old man. Put it there, old feller.'" So perhaps the expression, like rabbits, was introduced to the antipodean countries and went forth and multiplied.

And there are any number of American examples in recent years, including these relatively early ones:

- "The Elton John party, held in Taj Mahal-size tents outside Pacific Design Center off Melrose. . . . It's the 16th year Sir Elton has done this, and good on him." —*Washington Post*, 2008
- "We all contain multitudes, so if Mr. [Anderson] Cooper—who likes to work all the time and has another job on the side doing occasional stories for

'60 Minutes'—wanted to take on another assignment, good on him."—*New York Times*, 2011

Back to the *OED* entry, another odd thing about it is this note: "With the stress on *good*, unlike 'good for you' where the stress is on *you*." That gave me pause because my experience is that in the Australian original, the stress is on the middle word, *on*. I asked if any *NOOBs* readers from Down Under could shed light on the matter and one, from Tasmania, gave a helpful reply:

> "Good on you" is usually pronounced "goodonya" (no real stress), "g'donya," or if you're really pressed for time, "onya (mate)." If one were to say it as if it weren't a single word, the stress usually falls on the "on" unless you want to stress the last syllable in case the him/her/it/they actually earned the compliment.
>
> It might be worth mentioning that as in a lot of Australian sayings, the meaning can have a positive or negative connotation—"good on ya" can also be used to highlight that someone has actually done something not commendable. Australia must be a confusing place to the uninitiated.

I put this entry in the "Faux Noobs and Alterations" chapter based on my sense that, in speech, U.S. users (unlike Australians) almost always put the stress on the pronoun, as if they were merely using a variation on *good for you*. That was indeed the case with a 2015 address by former U.S. intelligence officer Michael Hayden, who said Turkish president Recep Tayyip Erdogan had given "voice to a voiceless part of the Turkish population—good on *him* for that." (I know the way he pronounced it because I heard it on YouTube.)

An amusing confirmation of the Australian emphasis—and of how foreign it sounded to American ears, at least in 2008— can be seen in a correction that appeared in the *Los Angeles*

Times that year. I present it without comment: "In Monday's Morning Briefing column in Sports, Australian swimmer Leisel Jones was quoted as saying 'Good honor,' referring to former swimmer Amanda Beard's appearing in a Playboy pictorial. In fact, Jones said 'Good on her.'"

"Off-ten"

I was listening one day to *Reply All*, a late, lamented podcast about the internet, and P. J. Vogt, the reporter/host, had occasion to say the word *often*. I was pretty confident that I knew how he was going to pronounce it. After all, Vogt at the time was young (I would judge in his early thirties), and I'd noted that he spoke with vocal fry, uptalk, and, generally, a pronounced Ira Glass–esque lack of slickness.

In other words, I knew he would say "off-ten," pronouncing the *t*.

And he did.

A good deal of history was embedded in his choice. The *OED* notes that *often* became commonly used (supplanting *oft*) only in the fifteenth century, and that in the sixteenth and seventeenth, it was sometimes said with the *t* voiced, sometimes not. Queen Elizabeth I said "offen" (the dictionary doesn't disclose how it knows this), and that pronunciation became the accepted one. In the blog *Daily Writing Tips*, Maeve Maddox quotes *John Walker's Critical Pronouncing Dictionary*, published in 1791: "In *often* and *soften* the t is silent."

John Keats rhymes just those two words, presumably *t*-less, in a draft of "Endymion" (1818):

. . . O foolish rhyme!
What mighty power is in thee that so often
Thou strivest rugged syllables to soften . . .

Gilbert and Sullivan's *The Pirates of Penzance* (which premiered on December 31, 1879) contained an inspired "Who's on first"–style exchange that, in poking fun at upper-class pronunciation, showed that, in at least that world, the *t* was still silent:

> GENERAL. Have you ever known what it is to be an orphan?
>
> KING. Often!
>
> GENERAL. Yes, orphan. Have you ever known what it is to be one?
>
> KING. I say, often. . . .
>
> GENERAL. When you said "orphan," did you mean "orphan"—a person who has lost his parents, or "often," frequently?
>
> KING. Ah! I beg pardon—I see what you mean— frequently.
>
> GENERAL. Ah! You said "often," frequently.
>
> KING. No, only once.

But the *t* version would soon revive. According to the *American Heritage Dictionary*, "With the rise of public education and literacy and, consequently, people's awareness of spelling in the 19th century, sounds that had become silent sometimes were restored, as is the case with the *t* in *often*."

The dictionary is noncommittal about the shift, but in the twentieth century, usage commentators often got exercised about "off-ten." H. W. Fowler wrote in his 1926 *Modern English Usage* that the *t*-voiced version was "practised by two oddly consorted classes—the academic speakers who affect a more precise enunciation than their neighbours' . . . & the uneasy half-literates who like to prove that they can spell." Alan S. C. Ross's 1954 essay that coined the terms *U* and *non-U* put "off-ten" decidedly in the non-U camp. Eric Partridge's *Usage and Abusage* (1957 edition) approvingly quotes a contemporary edition of *The Concise Oxford Dictionary* as calling the *t* pronunciation "vulgar." He adds, "It is certainly unnecessary and is usually due to an affectation of refinement."

In the United States, there is a regional as well as a class element to the matter. *The Dictionary of American Regional English* quotes a 1928 issue of *American Speech*: "The Ozarker nearly always pronounces the *t* in *often*." And *DARE* also cites *The Linguistic Atlas of the Gulf States* (1989) as reporting 453 informants who said the *t* as opposed to 290 who did not.

Data on pronunciation, as opposed to writing, is hard to come by, but I did my best. I listened on YouTube to twelve versions of the opening line of "On the Street Where You Live"—"I have often walked on this street before." It was "offen" in both the *My Fair Lady* original cast album and the movie soundtrack, and in the renditions by Vic Damone, Etta Jones, Bobby Darin, Nat King Cole, Harry Connick Jr., Dean Martin, and Willie Nelson (whose version is my favorite). Only Tom Jones (a Welshman), Nancy Wilson (African American, born in Ohio), and Smokey Robinson (African American, born in Detroit) sang "off-ten."

As I suggested at the outset, it's my sense that in recent years, young people have become partial to "off-ten." The former *Boston Globe* language columnist Jan Freeman agrees and offers anecdotal support:

> I've been interested in this one since my daughter, brought up as an OFF-en speaker, went to college at the University of Michigan and came back saying OFF-ten. I don't think it's a regional thing—I grew up two hours south of Ann Arbor, and I don't remember OFF-ten even as a variant. It must have been something she picked up from friends.

To at least pseudoscientifically test this proposition, I met individually with the undergraduates in the class I was teaching and asked them to read aloud the sentence, "Experience has shown that first impressions are often lasting ones." Eight said "off-ten" and five said "offen." (Obviously, their pronunciation may have been affected by seeing the *t* on the piece of paper in front of them, or by self-consciousness.)

In any case, in keeping with these trends, the question of how to pronounce *often* may soon cease to matter. Just as it replaced *oft* back in the day, it is being supplanted—if my students' example can be trusted—by an antique word. That's right, I'm talking *oftentimes*, with neither *t* silent.

"Snooker" (verb)

A reader named Colum Aikman wrote in:

> I was wondering if you could perhaps find out how frequently the word "snookered" now features in contemporary American discourse. It literally means "to confound" or "to place in an impossible situation," and is a word that I've always considered quintessentially British, for it derives from the game of snooker (which, if you're unaware, is a form of billiards popular in the UK; it gets its name from the tactic of "snookering," whereby a player obstructs the path between cue ball and object ball in order to force his/ her opponent to commit a foul). Few Americans seem to have ever encountered snooker, so imagine my surprise last week when watching an episode of *Judge Judy* and hearing the eponymous courthouse diva using "snookered" several times whilst berating a particularly egregious example of modern youth. In fact, she must be quite fond of the term, as she deployed it again on the *Queen Latifah Show* in 2013.

I remember the first time I became aware of the word. It was on July 31, 1987, when I was watching the U.S. Congress's

Iran-Contra hearings. Former White House chief of staff Donald Regan testified about his frustration that Iran had not freed American hostages, despite the U.S. sending arms to the country. He said he told President Ronald Reagan, "We'd been snookered again, and how many times do we put up with this rug merchant kind of stuff?" (Incidentally, after the testimony, rug merchants lodged a protest.)

I particularly remember the way Regan, a Massachusetts native, pronounced *snookered* nonrhotically—that is, without sounding the *r*. And speaking of pronunciation, Americans pronounce the first syllable of the word to rhyme with *book*, and British people to rhyme with *kook*.

The *OED* dates both the noun (the game of snooker) and the verb to 1889. The verb's first citations are in line with the snooker strategy described by Aikman, and the first figurative use—meaning "to place in an impossible position; to balk, 'stymie'"—is in 1915. A line from a 1925 novel is, "'I can't see any solution,' he said. 'I'm snookered.'"

(The etymology of *snooker* itself is, the *OED*, says "obscure." The dictionary observes, with palpable skepticism, "It is commonly held that the word represents an allusive use of snooker [meaning] a newly joined cadet, first applied to the game by Col. Sir Neville Chamberlain [1856–1944], a subaltern in the Devonshire Regiment stationed at Jabalpur in central India in 1875, with reference to the rawness of the play of a fellow officer. The story is often repeated.")

Ngram Viewer confirms British origin of the verb but indicates American use rising in the 1960s and surpassing the Brits in about 1979.

Americans generally use the word in a different way from what is suggested by the *OED* definition. Lexico, a lexicographic website operated by the Oxford University Press, gives this distinct U.S. meaning: "trick, entice, or trap." That's in keeping with the Regan testimony; more recently, a right-wing figure named Allen West claimed George W. Bush "got snookered" when he referred to Islam as a religion of peace. And what Judge Judy told Queen Latifah was, "If you choose a bad boy, you're going to get snookered." She actually might have meant "put in an impossible position," but her affect and tone of voice suggest something more devious.

CHAPTER NINE

Bits and Bobs

Not one-off Britishisms don't always fit into neat categories. Here are some noteworthy trends and some words and phrases with interesting backstories.

European Date Format

As of this writing, "European Date Format" has been viewed more than 190,000 times on *NOOBs*, more than twice as many as the post in second place, "Mewling quim." (That phrase is uttered in the 2012 film *The Avengers* and is very much a one-off, hence is not covered in this book. But feel free to read my short post and the many comments on the blog.)

I have a hunch why the entry has been so popular: the American way of writing dates makes the rest of the world very, very angry. You can get a sense of the rage from the head-line and subhead of a 2018 Australian news article:

Why Do Americans Put the Date the Wrong Way Around?

Wrong, wrong, wrong. We have all encountered the stupid way Americans write their dates, putting the months first. Now we answer the eternal question.

Just to be clear, Americans render the date when their country declared its independence as 7/4/1776. Not only in the United Kingdom, not only in Europe, but in most of the rest of the world, it would be 4/7/1776 (or 4.7.1776). According to Wikipedia, the only countries that exclusively do it the American way are the Marshall Islands and the Federated States of Micronesia. (Practice varies in Canada, the Cayman Islands, Panama, and the Philippines.)

Not too many historians have devoted themselves to this topic, so it's difficult to sort out origins, but it appears the current American way was actually first on the scene. According to a stamp-collecting website, the "Bishop's mark," a London postmark first used in 1661, originally consisted of "a bisected circle with a two-letter abbreviation for the month in the top half and the day of the month in the bottom half. . . . In 1713, the day and month switched positions so that the month was on the bottom."

Month-first appears to have had some staying power in Britain. In the transcription of a letter to Lord Chesterfield from Samuel Johnson, the date was rendered as "February 7, 1755." The British eventually switched over, but the American colonies apparently stuck, for some reason, with the original style. The Declaration of Independence itself begins, "In Congress, July 4, 1776." Joseph Manning Hull's American primer *English Grammar by Lectures* (1830) reproduces the Johnson letter and advises readers to "observe the exact position of . . . the *month*; *day* of the *month*; and *year*."

The convention of rendering dates strictly in numbers (with the months ranging from 1 to 12) arrived in the twentieth century, and at that point the American way really began to stick out. Not only the news article quoted earlier but countless comments on my blog post have blasted it as illogical and really dumb. The style has been dubbed "Middle-endian," the terminology deriving from a passage in *Gulliver's Travels* in which Lilliputians who break the shell of a boiled egg at the large end are called "Big-Endians." For dates, the "Big-Endians" would be the Japanese, Chinese, and Koreans, who go year/month/day. The day/month/year supermajority are "Little-endian." The problem with both Little-endian and Middle-endian systems coexisting arises on dates that occur in the first twelve days of a month. That is, 8/10/2023 could be August 10. Or it could be 8 October.

The United States seems to be slowly falling in line with the rest of the globe. The U.S. military has adopted the International Standardization Organization style, in which 2023-08-10 would signify August 10, 2023. (*The Chicago Manual of Style* calls for it to be written as 10 August 2023, which has the value of not requiring a comma.) When filling in customs declaration cards upon entering the U.S., passengers are required to write dates in the numeric "dd mm yyyy" format (e.g., "22 02 1954"). Visas and passports issued by the U.S. State Department also now use the day/month/year order.

President Barack Obama used Little-endian format when he visited Westminster Abbey and, after signing his name in the guest book, wrote "24 May 2008." Unfortunately, the actual year was 2011, possibly signifying that Obama's when-in-Rome gesture made him so nervous he forgot the date.

Glottal Stops and Aspirating

Consider the words *water*, *butter*, and *later*. There are three main ways of pronouncing the *t* or *ts* in the middle. One is characteristically American, and two are characteristically British. The American thing is called flapping and basically renders the *t* as if it were a *d*: "wadder," "budder," "layder." British people, especially those who engage in so-called Received Pronunciation, much more frequently say the *t* like a proper *t*: "wah-ter," "buh-ter," "lay-ter." This is known as aspirating.

I believe Americans used to aspirate more than they do now, especially in situations where they were performing, addressing an audience, or emphasizing a word. Think of Ed Sullivan saying in 1964, "Ladies and gentlemen, the Beat-els." Three years before that, in the film version of *West Side Story*, (American) Marni Nixon sang, "I feel pret-ty and wit-ty." And in *The Wizard of Oz* (1939), the Wicked Witch of the West said, "I'll get you, my pret-ty." (Of course, she followed it up with "and your liddle dog, too.")

Performative American aspirating is still a thing. It's part of the way Karina Longworth puts over the script on her podcast, *You Must Remember This*. Reading the credits, she says the program is "wrih-ten, edih-ted, and narray-ted" by her. During the actual program, she goes back and forth. In one episode I listened to recently, she flapped *Satan, threaten, duty*, and *unwritten*, and aspirated *duty, city, twenty*, and *immortal*. On the sitcom *Parks and Recreation*, an aspirated *literally*— "LITT-trally"—became a catchphrase, or catchword, for the character played by Rob Lowe. Americans will sometimes aspirate words they have to say a lot. When NPR correspondent Martin Kaste signs off, he quite pointedly gives his first name as "Mar-tin."

The third way of dealing with that *t* is known as glottal stop or glottalization and involves more or less swallowing the letter: "wah-er," "buh-er," and so on. Glottalization has traditionally been associated with working-class Cockney, Liverpudlian, and Glaswegian dialects. You can hear it in your mind's ear if you think of Stanley Holloway singing "With a lih-ill bi' o' luck" in *My Fair Lady* or one of the Beatles saying, well, "Bee-ulls."

There has historically been some regional glottalization in the United States. It has been found in Utah, and residents of New Britain, Connecticut, are famous for referring to their city as "New Breh-en." A New Yorker born in 1954 commented on my blog, "Things like 'bah-uhl' (for bottle) were commonplace among older people in NYC when I was a child, and equally so among my peers; so much so that my mother was constantly correcting me, because she considered it low-class."

But there has in recent years been an upsurge in American glottal stops. Indeed, it arrived like a wave in the early 2000s among the college students I taught, especially the female ones, for some reason, and especially in syllables that ended with *n*: "im-por-uhn," "Man-hah-en" (for the New York City borough), "buh-en" (for the thing you push). It seems to have only grown since then, and I often hear it on radio and TV, with the users skewing young and female. (Sorry to complicate things, but there is a fourth common option for these words, in both Britain and the U.S., known as "syllabic *n*." In it, the final syllable is voiced as a sort of vowelless *n*, breathed out through the nose and with the tongue remaining on the roof of the mouth: as in "butt-n," or, to give two names often in the news, "Clint-n" and "Pute-n.")

My students were mostly Caucasian, but the origin of this glottalization appears to be African American vernacular

English, specifically the New York version. Think of the catch-phrase "Oh no she dih-ent" (or "you dih-ent"), which was out there as early as 1993, the date of a Usenet rap forum on which the indefatigable language writer Ben Zimmer found it. It subsequently gained fame as a ritualized audience response on *The Maury Povich Show* and spread as a catchphrase. This sort of glottalization is all over hip-hop, especially by New York-bred artists. In "Big Pimpin'" (2001), Jay Z—born in Brooklyn in 1969—raps "Y'all be fruh-in" ("fronting") and "I hate way-in" ("waiting").

I believe that young white female Americans got it from the African American style starting sometime around the turn of the twenty-first century. As to exactly how and why, I do not have a clue.

Lexical Anatopism

I coined this phrase out of necessity: something kept coming up in the novels I was reading, and I didn't have a term to describe it.

I first became aware of the phenomenon while reading the excellent *Room*, by Emma Donoghue, a native of Ireland who is now based in Canada. The book is narrated by a five-year-old named Jack, whose entire life has taken place in an eleven-by-eleven-foot room, where he is confined with his mother. (That situation becomes apparent in the first few pages of the book, so this is not a spoiler.)

At first the location is unspecified, but we eventually learn that Room is in the United States. I was surprised to learn this because Jack and Ma sure don't talk like Americans. Consider:

- At one point, Jack says, "*Now I'm* 5, I have to choose."
  An American kid (or adult) would say, "Now *that* I'm 5."

- He observes, "Ma's *washing up* real slow." American English: *washing the dishes* or *doing the dishes*.
- Ma tells Jack, "And I also had—I have—a big brother *called* Paul." An American would say *named Paul*.
- Jack says *poo* instead of *poop* (see chapter 4).
- He uses the very British *proper* (see chapter 3) as in "if I put on my proper shoes" and "I'm not doing proper pictures, just splotches and stripes and spirals."

Probably the most common Britishism is *bits*, used to mean "pieces" or "parts" (see chapter 3). The word appears sixty-two times in *Room* (having a book on Kindle is great for this kind of investigation), and most are pure British, including, "She doesn't have many soft bits but they're super soft"; "She's putting the hem back up on her brown dress with pink bits"; and "For dessert we have a tub of mandarins between us, I get the big bits because she prefers the little ones."

I decided to call this phenomenon "lexical anatopism." *Lexical*: having to do with words. *Anatopism*: the equivalent of *anachronism*, except referring to something that is located in the wrong place, instead of happening at the wrong time.

And now (that) I had a name for it, it kept rearing its head. A somewhat similar case to *Room* is *Klara and the Sun*, by Kazuo Ishiguro, the Nobel Prize–winning author who was born in Japan but moved to England at the age of five and is strongly identified as a British writer. *Klara* is a science fiction novel taking place in a dystopian United States and narrated by an American. That narrator and other American characters utter a veritable catalog of Britishisms, some of them NOOBs but others unfamiliar here.

- "It's not enough just being *clever*" (see chapter 3)
- "*smart*-looking" (as opposed to "cool-looking" or "good-looking")

- "The animal *carried on* making its noise" (as opposed to "continued" or "went on")
- "Josie always visited her *en suite* before retiring to bed" (as opposed to "bathroom"—I'm not sure about "retiring")
- "These were slightly *different to* the ones outside our store" (as opposed to "different from" or "different than")
- "There it was, throwing out Pollution from three funnels the way it *had always done*" (see chapter 7)
- "For a while she was *keen on* a German car" (see chapter 3)
- "*If I'm honest*"
- "Chrissie will come and *collect you* in half an hour" (as opposed to "pick you up")
- "*on the day*" (see chapter 3)

Room and *Klara* are unusual books, and the anatopism could be argued (not by me) to be in service of the unsettling atmosphere. But that doesn't explain the fact that in recent years, virtually every time I read a British novel with American characters, I found lexical. In *Trio*, William Boyd puts two Britishisms in one sentence in the mouth of an American actress describing her role in her current project: "I'm meant to be a famous film star who's making a film in Brighton." *Meant to* for this particular connotation of *supposed to* is pure British. And an American would say "movie star" instead of "film star."

Anthony Horowitz's mystery *Moonflower Murders* contains a novel-within-the-novel called *Atticus Pünd Takes the Case*, Pünd being the detective main character. The embedded novel has a character named Charles Pargeter, who we're told "had the look of a Harvard professor" and "spoke with an American accent." He does have a home in Knightsbridge as well as New York. Yet I don't think that can explain the number of Britishisms Pargeter uses. He says, "The combination was sent to me *by post*"; "We were actually *at college* together" (Americans would phrase it as either "in college" or "went to college"); "There was *no joy* there" (see chapter 2); and "That horse *has bolted*, as the saying goes." (The American version of that British saying is "the horse has left the barn.")

I have read no book with more lexical anatopism than David Mitchell's *Utopia Avenue*, which is about a (fictional) late 1960s British rock band who, at various points, encounter (real-life) American rock and roll figures. Guess what? They talk like Britishers. Janis Joplin cuts short an impromptu performance because, she says, "*I've* a session tomorrow." (Americans would say "I have a session" or "I've got a session.") Using the same locution found in *Room*, Gene Clark says, about quitting the Byrds: "*Now it's gone*, I want it back." Paul Kantner of Jefferson Airplane comments, "Chalk and cheese," a very British expression indicating two things very different in quality or value. And Frank Zappa says, "Accidents are often art's best *bits*."

It's not only rock stars who talk this way. Other American characters in the book haul out not only NOOBs like *spot on* and *reckon* (see chapter 3 for both) but rather obscure British expressions like *hey presto* (all of a sudden), *the chop* (getting fired), and *till* (cash register).

There's also a recent book by an American novelist, with American characters, where Britishisms abound: *The Plot*, by Jean Hanff Korelitz. I reckon that some of the examples merely prove the point of the book you are currently reading: they're British words and expressions that have become popular in the U.S., and hence an American character might use them. Others are flat-out Britishisms that I've rarely or ever heard here. I'll list them in order, from the most common NOOBs to the least likely.

- "*in the fullness of time*"
- "She *straightaway* found a job" (see chapter 3).
- "'Would it kill you to *do* an avocado toast?'" (That's *do* in the sense of a restaurant offering a dish.)
- "'Who knows what else this Dianna Parker *got up to*?'" (Americans would say "was up to" or "was involved with.")
- "The guy . . . *supported* the Red Sox" (*support* meaning "root for" or "be a fan of").
- "Maybe the *punters* [customers] out there believed novels followed a visit from the muse."
- "Jake opted not to correct this remarkable statement in any of the ways he *might have done*" (see chapter 7).

Jean Korelitz studied at the University of Cambridge in the 1980s and since 1987 has been married to the Irish poet Paul Muldoon. So she might come by these British words and phrases naturally. But that doesn't mean that her editor shouldn't have flagged them.

And the blame for these miscues, such as it is, belongs with editors. Not that they have an easy task. There are so many big and small differences in the dialects: How can we possibly be aware of every case where our friends across the pond say it differently? For British copyeditors, lexical anatopism is a potential blind spot, a Donald Rumsfeldesque "unknown-unknown" situation. That is, they are aware that Americans would say *elevator* instead of *lift*, or would never say *telly*, but there are thousands of other expressions they probably don't even realize are exclusively British. They just sound normal. Hence they don't flag or query them when they come out of the mouth of an American character.

American editors could presumably spot them, but when a British book is published in the U.S., it gets only an editorial once-over: the inverted commas are changed to proper quotation marks, logical punctuation (see chapter 7) is dismantled, and *honour* is respelled *honor*. But editors generally do not scrutinize the text on the level of word usage. Since anatopism can be discordant enough to break the spell of an otherwise compelling novel, I humbly propose that they start.

"The long game"

At a certain point in 2012, it became impossible to pick up the paper or listen to the news and escape "the long game." I'm not talking about coverage of golf or other actual games, but this sort of thing:

- The example of guitarist Doc Watson should "serve as inspiration to any musician interested in the long game, in making music that endures not because of its shock value or its keen marketplace vision but because within its measured tones lies universal truth."—*Los Angeles Times*
- "I mean, [Queen Elizabeth] has played the long game better than anyone one can think of. I mean, she has understood from the beginning, for instance, even not to become too celebrated and popular."—Tina Brown, speaking on NPR's *Morning Edition*
- "[Lawrence] Summers's talent was for influencing a particular decision at a particular moment. He was not someone with a flair for the long game—for the week-in, week-out slog of bringing colleagues around to his views."—Noam Scheiber, *The Escape Artists: How Obama's Team Fumbled the Recovery*

246 BITS AND BOBS

That led me to look into the *New York Times'* nonsporting *long game* uses. I found the first in 1964, in a letter from Arthur Upham Pope crediting the Persian statesman Hussein Ala with "for over fifty years playing the long game of democratic ideals and reform as the only permanent solution for his country." The next appearance was in a recorded 1973 Oval Office meeting in which President Richard Nixon's adviser H. R. Haldeman, referring to the *Washington Post*'s Watergate coverage, said, "They are playing the long game."

The long game appeared in the *Times* four subsequent times through 2005, thirty-one times between 2006 and 2012 (including quoting Barack Obama at a 2010 news conference on his tax plan: "To my Democratic friends, what I'd suggest is, let's make sure that we understand this is a long game. This is not a short game"), and 211 times between 2013 and 2020. That included the headlines "Golf's Long Game in Turkey," "More Colleges Are Playing the Long Game," "Playing the Long Game for the Supreme Court," and "How the Radical Right Played the Long Game and Won."

Where did this expression come from? Why is it so popular? The second question is relatively easy to answer. It is a vivid metaphor for an idea that frequently comes up in consideration of politics, business, and other human endeavors: to wit, the possession and use of a long-term strategy. (The very phrase *long-term*, so flat and overplayed, suggests the need for a replacement.) It sounds British, always a good thing. And catchphrases, no less than videos or memes, have the capacity to go viral: to attain uncanny popularity at the drop of a dime.

But where did *the long game* come from? There's no entry in the *OED*, but the phrase clearly seems to be of British origin. Certainly there are plentiful uses in such sources as *The Economist*, *The Times* (of London), and the *Times Literary*

Supplement. The most common contexts have been diplomacy, espionage, and statecraft, as in a 1944 comment in *The Times* that "so well and successfully have conspirators played the long game." But it's been used in all sorts of ways. In 1917 an anonymous author in the *Times Literary Supplement* intriguingly commented, "We are reminded of a pregnant saying of Hart's that the long game is the Church's game." A 2005 episode of the BBC series *Dr. Who* was titled "The Long Game," as was a posthumous collection by the Australian poet Bruce Beaver published the same year.

Using Google Books as my Wayback Machine, I came upon an 1860 quote from an opera review in the journal *The Athenaeum*: "To continue speculations, in the soundness or unsoundness of all who play 'the long game' are interested, others besides ourselves, while hearing 'Robin Hood,' were recalled to a former opera, produced more than thirty-five years ago, a certain 'Maid Marian.'"

And the *Hansard* corpus of parliamentary speeches yielded this from John O'Connell in 1847: "Irish Members had no means of resistance in their power, nor had they any opportunity of redress. . . . They could not hope to succeed even in playing what was vulgarly called 'the long game,' such was the temper of the House."

The use of quotation marks in both examples suggests recent coinage. And indeed, the oldest example I'm aware of, found by a *NOOBs* reader, dates only to 1840: "The aristocracy can afford to play the long game, for they have the bank at their back."

Bohn's New Hand-book of Games, published in 1856, provided a clue to the origin of the figure of speech. In the section on whist, the book notes, "In playing the long game, when both sides mark five, they are precisely in the same position with those parties who are beginning the short game." And indeed, as I discovered, "the long game" and "the short game" are whist variants. *Chamber's Encyclopedia* explains, "About 1785 the experiment of dividing the game into half was tried, and short whist was the result. The short game soon came into favour; and in 1864 the supremacy of short whist was acknowledged."

Apparently, just as the long game was losing its popularity as a game, it came into its own as a metaphor. It took the Yanks a century and a half to catch up. And while we may have been slow about adopting it, we definitely made up for lost time in using it.

Adoption | Fully arrived

The *New Yorker*'s Got

Mary Norris is a former copy chief at the *New Yorker* and the author of the book *Between You & Me: Confessions of a Comma Queen*. A couple of years ago, she tweeted that the "rule" at the magazine (to which she still contributes) "is to double the consonant whenever the dictionary permits (*focussed, traveller*), with a few exceptions (*bused*), for the same reason that words ending in -er are spelled with -re (*theatre*): the early style editors were Anglophiles." She could have added *marvellous*, which is a word I would apply to her book.

She is on the money there. The thing I would add is that a part of the magazine's DNA is, whenever possible, to do things the way they have always been done. Thus, as I write, ninety-eight years after Harold Ross started the *New Yorker*, the magazine *still* spells the words *focussed, traveller*, and *marvellous*, never mind that literally no one else in the United States does so. (*Theatre* admittedly has some American adherents.)

But of all the quirks of the *New Yorker*'s house style, maybe the quirkiest is the insistence on *got* as the participle form of *get*—that is, to write *had got* instead of *had gotten* to mean "become" or "obtained" or "arrived" or any of the numerous other senses of *get*. I hasten to say that Americans use *got* in lots of ways: "Got milk?" "You got this." "I got to stop smoking." "I got plenty of nuthin'." But we say, "You've gotten so tall!" and "I'd gotten there two hours before Bill."

Gotten has a long pedigree in the English language. The 1535 Coverdale translation of the Bible has the line, "Treasures that are wickedly gotten, profit nothinge." But the word started falling out of favor in Britain in the seventeenth century and was moribund by the twentieth, having been supplanted by *got*. When Henry Higgins in *My Fair Lady* sings, "I think she's got it," he means "I think she's gotten it," not "I think she has it."

For some reason, *gotten* reemerged in America in the late 1800s, and it was quickly noticed by British commentators, not favorably. *Garner's Modern American Usage* quotes Charles Whibley, who in 1908 wrote that adding the extra syllable to *got* "suggests either willful archaism or useless slang, adds nothing of sense or sound to the word. It is like a piece of dead wood in a tree, and is better lopped off." In *The American Language*, Mencken counts *gotten* (along with *druggist* and *fall*, for the season) as one of those archaic English terms "that have been denounced by English purists as abominable Americanisms." I was once interviewed on an Irish radio station about my blog and was asked for an example of a British usage that had popped up in the United States. I mentioned the *New Yorker*'s preference for *got* over *gotten*. The host was outraged. "*GOT-ten?*" he bellowed. "*GOT-ten?* Do you expect me to believe people over there actually say *GOT-ten?*"

They do indeed—but when I investigated, I was surprised to learn it hasn't been the predominant form in the U.S. for very

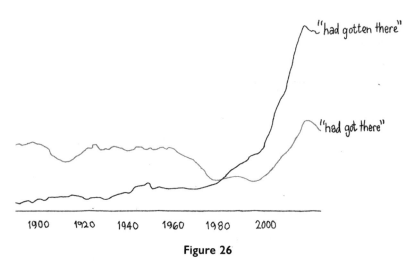

Figure 26

long. An Ngram Viewer graph of American usage (figure 26) suggests that *had gotten* didn't surpass *had got* until about 1980.

As late as 1994, *Merriam-Webster's Dictionary of English Usage* could write of U.S. practice, "We find both *got* and *gotten* in use as past participle." Of course, of the six examples given of past-participle *got*, five were from *New Yorker* writers.

And indeed, the magazine has leaned in to *got*. In the late 1990s, when I was researching my history of the *New Yorker* (published in 2000 as *About Town*), a friendly member of the staff (not Norris) gifted me with a copy of the then-current style guide. And there it is on page 82: "'Alright'; 'transpire,' meaning 'happen'; and 'gotten,' unless dialogue or country style, are banned." That's right, "banned." And before you ask, I have no idea what "country style" means.

Things have not changed since then, although once in a while a nondialogue, noncountry *gotten* slips into the magazine, as in a line in an essay by Tobias Wolff: "If it hadn't been for a black sergeant I served with in Vietnam, I doubt that my sorry ass would've gotten shipped home in one piece." I imagine that an editor changed Wolff's original *gotten* to *got*, the writer saw it on a galley and said "absolutely not" or words to that effect, and that he is eminent enough to have, well, gotten his way.

But *got* predominates, by far. Here are some examples of recent uses of the word in the magazine, in chronological order:

1. "When she was a young child, her stepfather had got the family involved with Scientology."—Lawrence Wright, 2011

2. "I had got poison ivy on my hands."—Reed Krakoff, an American and the CEO of Coach Leather, quoted in a 2011 profile

3. "Kennedy got about seventy per cent of the African-American vote, much more than Stevenson had got." —Louis Menand, 2014

4. "I had got such satisfaction out of the systems she introduced, the sharp pencils and crisp manila folders."—Lena Dunham, 2014

5. "There was something that was going on that would've been stopped if they had got the same scrutiny as JPMorgan Chase."—Former congressman Barney Frank, in a 2023 interview

Numbers 1 and 3 aren't surprising, being examples of long-time staff writers for the magazine using *got*. (The notable thing about the Menand is that his first use of the word—"Kennedy got"—is standard American usage.) Lena Dunham is an infrequent contributor, and young to boot, and I would bet dollars to donuts she originally wrote *gotten*; I imagine she didn't care enough about the issue to protest, à la Wolff. Numbers 2 and 5 raise my eyebrow, or both of them, in being quotes from Americans who would almost surely have said *gotten*. According to the magazine's own rules, the word could have been allowed since it occurred in quotations, which would presumably fall under the "dialogue" exception. But it was changed anyway.

At one point, the whole thing annoyed me so much that I started a Facebook group called "Get *The New Yorker* to Start Using 'Gotten.'" It attracted more than one hundred members, including two *New Yorker* staff writers, whose names I will not divulge. But it did not get the *New Yorker* to stop using *got*.

"Po-faced"

The following quotations all appeared in print over the course of a year recently:

- "And it is satisfying to be allowed to hoot publicly at a man who is likely to remind you of every po-faced schoolteacher who told you to stop giggling."—*New York Times* theater review
- "To me, the scurrilousness has the pasty complexion of po-faced error. The worry, the criticism, feels tacky and fatuous."—Darin Strauss, *New York Times*, on the supposed death of literary fiction
- "Rather than coming off all po-faced and 'I told you so,' . . . *Muse* is instead busy smirking, raiding the mini-bar and slurring 'I told you so.'"—*Buffalo News*
- "A crop of foreign-language films in which po-faced pedantry has taken a back seat to dynamic storytelling." —*Variety*
- "A yearning Irish busker and a po-faced Czech pianist." —*New York Post*, review of the musical play *One*

If you don't know what *po-faced* means (as I did not the first couple of times I came across it), the examples won't be very helpful in instructing you. The *OED*'s definition is, "Characterized by or assuming an expressionless or impassive face; poker-faced; (hence) humourless, disapproving." The first citation is from *Music Ho!*, a 1934 book by the British composer and critic Constant Lambert, and suggests an origin not long before that: "I do not wish, when faced with exoticism, to adopt an attitude which can best be described by the admirable expression 'po-faced.'"

Searching through Google Books, I found a quotation in *Who's There Within?*, a 1942 novel by the British author Louis Golding (1895–1958), that suggests an earlier origin: "But how could she act like that, like an outraged Victorian matron, how *could* she? How could she be so *po-faced!* (She was using the favourite word of the Bohemians in the London of the early twenties, the Cave of Harmony, and Harold Scott, of Elsa Lanchester, and all that.)"

That the *OED* is far from certain on the expression's origin can be gleaned from the fact that, in a two-line etymological note, it uses the word "perhaps" four times. Perhaps it derives from the interjection *poh* (or *pooh*), or perhaps from the noun *po*, meaning "chamber pot." Or perhaps it's a shortening of *poker-faced*. A comparison to *pie-faced* could be useful as well. Perhaps.

The American Heritage Dictionary is a bit more definitive than the *OED*, stating that the term comes from *pot* (pronounced "po") *de chambre*, French for "chamber pot," "a po-faced expression being likened to that of a person observing the contents of a chamber pot with disgust." Maybe because it's so colorful, this is the hypothesis I'm inclined to accept.

All Americans to whom I've mentioned *po-faced* initially thought that the first word was a Southern rendition of *poor* (as in the New Orleans po' boy sandwich) and that the term was related to the familiar American verb *poor-mouth*, meaning (the *OED* says) "the action of claiming to be poor, or of belittling or understating resources, abilities, etc." And I believe recent American adopters have somewhere in the front or back of their minds a *po-faced/poor-mouth* relationship. That is, to them, *po-faced* is an attitude characterized by some sort of combination of impassiveness, disapproval, and feigning of poverty or humility.

Clearly, further research is called for. For the time being, I'll merely note that the second use by a *New York Times* staff member (the first was in 1984 by the columnist Anthony Lewis, a well-known Anglophile) came in a 1988 piece datelined London. Howell Raines—a Southerner who would later become the *Times*' executive editor—wrote about a British performer who adopted the identity of an American named Hank Wangford, a "self-described 'po-faced' country singer." Can anyone doubt that in his mind Raines connected *po* and *po*?

I'll close with the observation that no matter how popular *po-faced* becomes on these shores, no one can use it like a Brit. A case in point is the Conservative leader Quintin Hogg (1907–2001), otherwise known as Baron Hailsham of St. Marylebone, KG, CH, PC, QC, FRS. In 1966 *The Times* (of London) reported,

> Mr. Hogg said at Watford that he had been given five new walking sticks since he broke his at Chiswick on Mr. Wilson's portrait. [Apparently a Labour supporter had waved a Harold Wilson placard in Hogg's face, whereupon he struck it with one of the two canes he employed, owing to the many times his ankles had been injured while he was engaged in his favorite pastime, mountain climbing.] "Politics should be fun," he said. "Politicians have no right to be pompous or po-faced."

"Streets ahead"

I was unaware of this expression until a *NOOBs* reader named Gareth commented, "Is *streets ahead* well-established in American sources? Earliest *OED* reference is 1885 in Ireland. Recently a character in NBC's *Community* tried to 'coin the phrase,' without realising it already existed."

First of all, in answer to Gareth's initial question, no. The *OED* defines the expression as "far ahead of something or someone, far superior," and has British and Irish sources from that first one in 1885 through this from *The Telegraph* in 2005: "The company [Toyota] is streets ahead of GM on profitability." By my reckoning, the phrase—as uttered or written by an American—has appeared in the *New York Times* exactly once, from 1851 to the present. (That came in 2013, when, in an interview, the poet Cynthia Zarin said that she and her daughter were both learning Italian and "she is streets ahead of me.")

Yet it somehow has the *reputation* of being a catchphrase. A *New Yorker* blog post from January 2010 revived the venerable character created by Frank Sullivan for the magazine in days of yore, Mr. Arbuthnot, the Cliché Expert, and had him say this about the then-brand-new Apple iPad: "It reflects the company's commitment to cutting-edge design and elegant technology solutions. They're the eight-hundred-pound gorilla in the room. They're streets ahead of their competition and they have both the ground game and air attack to take on anyone." Just a couple of months later, the *Community* connection began. It all started during an online competition for best TV show in which fans of *Community* were vying with those of a couple of other series. A supporter of the other shows tweeted, "Both *Modern Family* and *Glee* are streets ahead of your meta bullshit." The creator of *Community*, Dan Harmon, got wind of this and, apparently unaware that *streets ahead* was an actual British expression, spent the next couple of months mocking it online, such as in these tweets:

- "Streets ahead! [trumpet] Get your lingo out of the bed! [tambourine] You don't have to say miles, you can use the word streets instead!"
- "Streets ahead! [twang] Light years and leagues are dead! [trumpet] use a word that makes your measurements sweeter than cinnamon bread!"
- "They call me Streets, last name Ahead, and I'm the longest distance you ever said!" #StreetsAhead

Art started imitating life, or maybe it's the other way around, with this Twitter exchange between Harmon and a fan:

@TIM_STOLTZ: Your hatred of "Glee" has made its way into "Community;" how long till your new favorite phrase makes it?

@DANHARMON: I'm putting it in the current script, so it'll be a few weeks. But I have to get the world understanding it by then!

And sure enough, in the April 22, 2010, episode, Pierce Hawthorne, the character played by Chevy Chase, made a star-crossed attempt to push *streets ahead* as a catchphrase.

PIERCE: Abed, your social skills aren't exactly "streets ahead." Know what I mean?

ABED: [*Thinks*] I don't.

JEFF: You're not alone in this case. Pierce, stop trying to coin the phrase "streets ahead."

PIERCE: Trying? [*Laughs.*] Coined and minted! Been there, coined that! "Streets ahead" is verbal . . . wildfire!

ANNIE: Does it just mean "cool," or is it supposed to be
    like, "miles ahead"?

PIERCE: [*Scoffs.*] If you have to ask, you're streets behind.

In fall 2011, NBC announced it was putting *Community* on hiatus. Dan Harmon posted, "Streets ahold."

"Yoicks"

In the course of a couple of weeks in 2020, this line appeared in the *LA Review of Books*: "Yoiks! Dostoyevsky at his weirdest is for me the most-Gogol-like of the Russians." And this in the *Pittsburgh Current*: "Yoiks! Are we totally sure Lincoln didn't commit suicide?"

I am familiar with this *yoiks*. My dear departed mother-in-law Marge Simeone used to say it. I always thought it was a jokey, mock–New York rendition of the word *yikes*. But it isn't. Or, more precisely, it isn't only that.

A look at the *OED* showed me how unaware I was. The main definition for *yoicks* is, "Chiefly Fox-hunting. A call or cry used to urge on hounds. Sometimes also used more generally as an exclamation indicating excitement or encouragement." The first citation is from 1774, and here's one from 1838: "The wood begins to resound with shouts of 'Yoicks True-bo-y, yoicks True-bo-y, yoicks push him up, yoicks wind him!'"

Evidence of American awareness of the term can be found in the 1958 Warner Brothers cartoon short "Robin Hood Daffy." Daffy Duck is the legendary outlaw, and every time he attempts an acrobatic feat, he shouts, "Yoicks! And awa-aaay!!!"

As early as the 1880s, according to the *OED*, the word began to be used in a slightly different way, as "an exclamation expressing surprise, astonishment, or fright." It popped up on both sides of the Atlantic, including in a 1942 article in the

American magazine *Boys' Life*: "Yoicks! What a day for the game!" This jibes with the use of it by my mother-in-law (born 1914). And the 1942 date is interesting, because it suggests that *yoicks* begat *yikes*, rather than the other way around.

You see, it was precisely in the early 1940s that the now-familiar American interjection *yikes* was born. The *OED*'s first citation is 1971, but a crowd-sourced etymological investigation on Twitter was able to move that up by more than three decades. Joshua Friedman found this November 1941 quote from an Iowa college newspaper: "And if you can't think of anything else to be grateful for, just be thankful you're not a turkey. It can't be too bad, though; they get the axe and we get the bird. Yikes!"

So I hypothesize that *yikes* is an Americanized version of *yoicks*. And I speculate that the folks who started to use *yikes* in the early 1940s may even have (mistakenly) thought that it was the original term, of which *yoicks* was a Cockney rendition. (Such a process, which you might call hypercorrective back-formation, happened with *hoity-toity*, which originated as such in the seventeenth century and was sometimes subsequently rendered as *highty-tighty*.)

I almost hate to complicate the story further by bringing this up, but another variant also arose in the 1940s. Here's a line of dialogue from a story in a 1941 issue of the American magazine *Good Housekeeping*: "Eddie had lots to say, but 'Yipes!' was all that came out." And *Green's Dictionary of Slang* quotes a 1943 *Washington Post* article: "Indicating that the hallowed 'Three B's' may play almost as vital a role as the 'Four Freedoms' in the restoration of world harmony (yipes!) is the announcement of the launching of a British chapter of the society." The *OED* suggests that *yipes*—sometimes rendered *yipe*—may have derived from *yikes*, *cripes* (a euphemism for *Christ* that arose circa 1910), or both.

Getting back to the *yoicks-yikes* timeline: there's a significant chronological gap between the 1942 *Boys' Life* quote and my came-of-age-in-the-1920s mother-in-law's *yoicks*, on the one hand, and the 2020 quotes cited in the opening of this entry. And so the question presents itself, why did Americans come back to *yoiks*?

The example of another word suggests an answer. In 1999, the Beastie Boys—white rappers from New York—put out a song called "Three MC's and One DJ," which followed a line ending with "golden voice" with, "Cause when it's time to rhyme, you know I get noice."

I tried to send Mike D (Mike Diamond) a message asking what was going through his mind when he decided to pronounce the final word this way, but the Beastie Boys are hard to get in touch with. So I'm going with the idea that he was doing a version of a New York accent.

Even that is complicated. Without a doubt, the *oi* sound—/ɔɪ/ in the International Phonetic Alphabet—is associated with New York, and in particular New York Jewish, talk. The Jewish association stems from the very word *oy*, and the more general one from both the unmistakable dipthongy way New Yorkers pronounce /ɔɪ/ (listen to Terry Gross of NPR's *Fresh Air* say *boy* if you want to know what I mean) and the "I met a goil on toity-toid street" idea, a caricature of what was once a prevalent feature of New York speech but that has mainly faded away.

The definition of *noice* on the website Know Your Meme says, "It is often associated with the Australian or English [to my ears Cockney] accents." *Noice* even *has* a definition on Know Your Meme because it is, well, a meme. The site says it "is an accented version of the word *nice*, used online as enthusiastic, exclamatory internet slang to declare approval or sarcastic approval of a topic or achievement." By 2013, *noice* had moved from hip to a trying-too-hard cliché. I specify that year because it's when the comedy team Key and Peele broadcast a skit in which they both play rap "hype men" who clash over possession of the word *noice*.

Also in 2013, the TV comedy *Brooklyn Nine-Nine* premiered. The main character, Jake Peralta (Andy Samberg), tries too hard to be hip. Naturally, his personal catchphrase is *noice*. He even tries too hard to expand it, saying "toight" for "tight."

So what I think happened is that the popularity of *noice* as a jokey version of *nice* led to the reemergence of *yoiks* as a jokey version of *yikes*. The theory isn't possible to prove, but it's supported by the fact that the more common spelling is now *yoiks*, not the fox-hunting-derived *yoicks*. And *yoiks* even *looks* like *yikes*.

If I ever hear back from Mike D, I'll post his answer on the *NOOBs* blog. I hope to see you there.

CHAPTER TEN

What Will Happen
in (the) Future?

I TRUST THAT by now readers will agree that, for some time, words and expressions have been crossing the Atlantic, with increased frequency, in an eastward as well as westward direction. In closing, I'd like to take a moment to acknowledge that, in the grand scheme of things, the traffic both ways has been modest. That is, American English and British English remain distinct dialects, with little danger of being homogenized into a boring sameness.

Consider this book's section on lexical anatopism (chapter 9), where I discuss how such British or Irish novelists as William Boyd, Emma Donoghue, Anthony Horowitz, Kazuo Ishiguro, and David Mitchell make the error of having American characters use Britishisms like *washing up* instead of *doing the dishes* or *different to* instead of *different from* or *different than*. These authors are smart people, and furthermore, words are their stock in trade. Yet they are so immersed in their own country's lexicon that they don't seem to realize the country across the ocean has a somewhat different one.

Or consider the title of this chapter. Just as Americans say "in *the* hospital," they refer to something happening "in *the* future." But in Britain, there are two slightly different expressions. *In the future* refers to a general or specific time that has yet to occur, and *in future* is used to mean "from now on." (The recent business jargon, on both sides of the Atlantic, is *going forward*.) This is just one of thousands of small differences, the majority of which stay put.

A few years ago, I read a book called *Idiot Brain: A Neuroscientist Explains What Your Head Is Really Up To*, by Dean Burnett, a neuroscientist at Cardiff University, in Wales. If you think there aren't many differences between British and American English anymore, the book will quickly disabuse you of that notion. On the very first page, Burnett does these distinctively British things:

- spells the words *apologise* (American: *apologize*) and *behaviours* (*behaviors*)
- refers to a little boy "dribbling" (the more common American word is *drooling*)
- uses logical punctuation (see chapter 7) and single quotation marks when he refers to 'something people say'

Page 1 is not an aberration. From beginning to end, the book is packed with Britishisms. Most apparent are the different spellings, including *sceptical* (U.S.: *skeptical*), *aeons* (*eons*), *travelling* (*traveling*), *tyre*, *pyjamas*, *foetal* (*fetal*), *centre* (*center*), and *hippy*.

As far as vocabulary goes, in this 302-page book, I counted forty distinctively British terms, including *dribbling*. Here are the others, in order, with American equivalents in parentheses:

- without any bother (without any trouble)
- petrol (gas)

- worrying (troubling; see chapter 3)
- mum (mom; see chapter 3)
- crisps (chips or potato chips)
- she used to live in the street next to us (on the street)
- well done (good job)
- "Not now, mate" ("Not now, buddy")
- here's the clever bit (smart part; see chapter 3)
- massive (not exclusively British but used massively more often there than here)
- turning up drunk (showing up)
- at university (in college; see chapter 3)
- row (argument)
- chap (guy)
- knock-on consequences (secondary or indirect effects)
- queue (line; see chapter 3)
- maths (math)
- have a look (take a look)
- "you were crap" ("you stunk"; see chapter 4)
- boffin (expert; see chapter 2)
- sport (sports; see chapter 5)
- daft (crazy)
- games consoles (game; see chapter 7)
- trainers (sneakers)
- estate agent (real-estate agent)
- check your emails (email)
- goal-orientated (oriented)
- different to (from)
- a bit of fun (some fun)
- cut you up (cut you off, in the motoring sense)
- down to you (up to you)
- waiting staff (waitstaff)
- I went to the shops (I went shopping)
- forecourts (flat area in front of a building)

- noughts and crosses (tic-tac-toe)
- heard it from some bloke down the pub (heard it from some guy at the bar)
- carry on (continue, go on)
- messes about (messes around)
- lift (elevator)

Some of the forty words, expressions, and usages are common enough in American English to be discussed in this book. But about 80 percent are not. That strikes me as a decent approximation of the proportion of Britishisms that have stayed in Britain.

How often, by the way, does Burnett use American lingo? I'm at a bit of a disadvantage here, since I wouldn't necessarily recognize an Americanism as such; it might just seem normal to me. So bear that in mind when I say I counted only four terms that appear to be Yank imports: "up for grabs," "fans" (in a sports context—the more common British word is *supporters*; see chapter 5), "smart" (Burnett alternates it with "clever"), and the cowboy-movie "pronto." (There were a few others that initially struck me as Americanisms but turn out not to be: *hubbub* came from Ireland as early as 1555; *a big ask*, meaning "a large or important request," is an Australianism, according to the *OED*; and the dictionary's first cite for *the middle man*, meaning "an intermediary," is from Edmund Burke in 1797.)

The foregoing evidence is anecdotal. For scholarly support, I turn to Paul Baker, a professor of English language at Lancaster University in England. He crunched numbers and massaged corpora for his academic study *British English: Divided by a Common Language* (2018). He concluded that despite borrowings in both directions, "for the most part, the two nations [have been] maintaining their differences."

In discussing this topic a few years ago, Lane Greene, *The Economist*'s "Johnson," observed that despite (and to some extent because of) American imports, British English was "in rude health." I would say the same is true of American English. And note that *rude*—as an adjective meaning "robust" or "sturdy"—is a somewhat archaic Britishism that I haven't yet encountered in America but that is very much on my radar.

APPENDIX

U.K.-to-U.S. Words of the Year, as Chosen by Lynne Murphy

EACH YEAR ON HER BLOG *Separated by a Common Language*, Lynne Murphy chooses two words of the year, one that traveled from the U.S. to the U.K. and one that traveled from the U.K. to the U.S. Here are her choices in the latter category. I've covered all of them on the blog; for the ones discussed in this book, the chapter reference is in parentheses.

2023: *If I'm honest*
2022: *fit* (sexually attractive)
2021: *university* (chapter 3)
2020: *jab* (getting the COVID-19 vaccine by hypodermic needle)
2019: *knock-on* (a secondary or indirect consequence of another action, occurrence, or event, most commonly found in the phrase *knock-on effect*)

2018: *whilst* (chapter 3)

2017: *shitgibbon* (chapter 4)

2016: *gutted* (chapter 3)

2015: *backbencher* (a legislative member who doesn't have a senior or leadership role)

2014: *dodgy* (chapter 3) and *gap year*

2013: *bum* (chapter 4)

2012: *bollocks* (chapter 8)

2011: *kettling* (the police practice of herding demonstrators into a restricted, exitless area)

2010: *ginger* (chapter 3)

2009: *go missing* (chapter 3)

2008: *vet* (chapter 3)

2007: *baby bump* (cute way of referring to a visible sign of pregnancy)

2006: *wanker* (chapter 4)

Acknowledgments

MY BIGGEST THANKS go to the readers of my blog *Not One-Off Britishisms*, who took to it with enthusiasm, kept on reading, and inspired me to keep it going lo these fourteen years. And a special thank you to the commenters, who (almost) unfailingly have clever and interesting things to say, who gently correct me when I make a misstep, and who have provided many ideas for posts. The most prolific voice belongs to Paul Dormer, who has commented 363 times as of this writing; shout-outs also to Anthony, David Ballard, cameron, David Griggs, Hal Hall, Arthur Jack, popegrutch, Catherine Rose, and Nick L. Tipper.

The three people thanked in the dedication have contributed massively to the blog and to the book. Nancy Friedman continually sends me good ideas, not only in her specialty of commerce but from a variety of sources, a lot of them quite obscure, that have caught her extremely sharp eye. Jonathon Green—in what I view as one of the greatest acts of civic scholarship of our time—has made available, free of charge, the fruits of his lifelong study of slang at the website *Green's Dictionary of Slang* (greensdictionaryofslang.com). Lynne Murphy, an American-born professor of linguistics at the University of Sussex, paved the way for my project with the blog she started in 2006, *Separated by a Common Language* (separatedbyacommonlanguage.blogspot.com). She has also been a generous and dependable sounding board for my questions about, well, anything.

Language mavens Stan Carey, Jan Freeman, Lane Greene, and Ben Zimmer have provided good ideas and counsel. Jack Lynch's review of the manuscript was so sympathetic and smart. David Crystal's endorsement and fact-checking of the manuscript were brill, and much appreciated. Siobhan King valiantly tried to teach me the nuances of "a cheeky Nando's." My friends Wes Davis, Andy Feinberg, David Friedman (a West Ham supporter and connoisseur of footballisms), and Nanette Tobin have been enthusiastic about this endeavor from the jump and seem to be always on the prowl for NOOBs. (Nanette, I still am holding out hope that "leaving do" will make it over here.)

Thank you to Eric Hanson for the splendid illustrations, and to Linda Herman for her contribution to the book design.

Thanks to Rick Valelly for making the connection to Peter Dougherty, and to Peter for introducing me to Anne Savarese at Princeton University Press. Anne was immediately enthusiastic about this idea and suggested the brilliant title.

As always, this goes out with thanks and love to Gigi Simeone, Nathan Truman, Lizy Yagoda, and "fully" to Maria Yagoda.

INDEX

British (and Faux-British) Words and Phrases That Have Entered American English

Note: Page numbers for main entries and discussions appear in **bold**.